The Worm of Consciousness and Other Essays

Edited by Miriam Chiaromonte

Preface by Mary McCarthy

Harcourt Brace Jovanovich

New York and London

Copyright © 1976 by Miriam Chiaromonte

"The Jesuit," copyright February, 1948, by *Partisan Review;* "Paris 1951," published as "Paris Letter," copyright January–February, 1951, by *Partisan Review;* "The Political Theater," from *The Rarer Action: Essays in Honor of Francis Fergusson,* edited by Alan Cheuse and Richard Koffler, copyright © 1970 by Rutgers, the State University, and reprinted by permission of the author, translator, and the Rutgers University Press; "The Worm of Consciousness," published as "Moravia and the Worm of Consciousness," copyright © 1961, by *Partisan Review*

The quotations from the letters of Antonin Artaud appear in *The Theatre and Its Double,* by Antonin Artaud, copyright © 1958 by Grove Press, Inc., and are reprinted by permission of Grove Press, Inc.

Printed in the United States of America

Library of Congress Cataloging in Publication Data
Chiaromonte, Nicola.
The worm of consciousness and other essays.
Includes index.
CONTENTS: The Jesuit.—Spain: the war.—Lost
Italians. [etc.]
I. Title.
AC45.C525   081   75-31868
ISBN 0-15-199440-4
0-15-698370-2 (pbk.)

A B C D E F G H I J

To Pina and Franco Chiaromonte

You pronounce a name, but it is not known to anyone.

Either because that man has died, or because
He was famous on the banks of another river.

Chiaromonte
Miomandre
Petöfi
Mickiewicz

Young generations are not interested in what was
at some other time, in some other place.

And what about your teachers, who repeated:
Ars longa, vita brevis?

Their laurel-crowned deception soon will be over.

Do you still say to yourself: *non omnis moriar?*

Oh, yes, not all of me shall die; there will remain
An entry in the fourteenth volume of the encyclopedia
Next to a hundred Millers and Mickey Mouse

CZESLAW MILOSZ
"Whence the Sun Rises to Where It Sets"
vi. The Accuser

Acknowledgments

The editor wishes to thank all those who kindly granted their permission to reprint the articles that appear in this book: *Atlantic Monthly, Commonweal, Dissent, Encounter, Il Mondo, Partisan Review, politics,* and *Tempo Presente;* as well as Richard Koffler, the translator and co-editor, and Rutgers University Press for their permission to reprint the essay from the book *The Rarer Action.* The editor is especially grateful to Czeslaw Milosz for permission to quote from his poem.

Contents

SPECULATION

Preface

Nicola Chiaromonte died in January 1972 of a heart attack. He had been taking part in a radio discussion program on J. F. Revel's *Without Marx or Jesus* and was stricken just afterward in the elevator. The program, recorded, went on the air the afternoon of his funeral. I heard it with his former colleagues in the offices of *L'Espresso*. In his apartment, a few blocks off, in the Via Po section of Rome, telegrams, telephone calls from abroad, letters were pouring in. It was a kind of mass outburst of emotion. Messages of grief came from Italy, naturally, but also from England, France, America, and from people of the most varying kinds—the old woman we had always considered cross who sold postcards and newspapers in the village on the Ligurian coast where he used to spend his summers, a nun in an American convent, the head of state. One of the most moving was from a young member of Lotta Continua (an extreme leftist group), which read something like this: "He has been a model for all of us of intellectual and moral lucidity."

When he died, Chiaromonte was in his late sixties and far in his thinking from the extreme left. The memorial tributes in the press that followed during the next weeks were, again, from the most varying sources, ranging from the centrist *Corriere della Sera* and *La Stampa* to the Communist-inclined *Paese Sera*. And, beyond sheer quantity, there was the additional interest that in all those words written and wired scarcely a one had an official or conventional ring, even those sent by official "personalities." It was as though Chiaromonte's ghost had imposed his own severity and truthfulness on the writers.

Yet Chiaromonte would hardly have guessed that he had "stood for something" to so many and might even have tried to refute the evidence as it piled up in stacks on tables in the rooms he had lived and worked in. He had left Italy as a young man to become an anti-Fascist exile in Paris, where he was close to non-violent anarchist groups and to an unusual figure called Andrea Caffi, whose writings he later collected in a volume called *A Critique of Violence.* Despite these principles, he enlisted in André Malraux's air squadron during the Spanish Civil War; he is the character in *Man's Hope* who is always reading Plato. When the Nazis came, he fled with his first wife, a painter, to the unoccupied south; his wife died in Toulouse, and he eventually continued on, reaching the United States via North Africa. I heard a characteristic story about him from the organizer of a group of American Unitarians who was in Toulouse helping anti-Fascist escapees to get away, trying to secure them visas from the consulate, providing them with bogus papers: on being stopped one day by a Vichy policeman ("Let's see your papers!"), Chiaromonte was obliging: "Do you want the false ones or the real ones?" Nicola later insisted that it had not been like that at all, but I think the story must be basically true.

In North Africa, he met Camus, who became his close friend. Arrived in America, he wrote for *The New Republic, Atlantic Monthly, Commonweal, Partisan Review,* and Dwight Macdonald's *politics.* He married Miriam, then a high-school teacher of English in the New York public school system, and his friends were Macdonald, Meyer Schapiro, James T. Farrell, Lionel Abel, Niccolò Tucci, Constantino Nivola, Saul Steinberg, and—less close then—me.

In the late forties, he went back to Europe. He found a job first at UNESCO in Paris, but bureaucratic life did not suit him, and he finally returned to Rome, where he became—surprisingly to some—a theater critic. From 1953 to 1968 he did a regular theater column for the old *Il Mondo*, a liberal (in the American sense) weekly. In the fifties, with Ignazio Silone, he founded the monthly *Tempo Presente*. When he died, both *Tempo Presente* and *Il Mondo* had themselves died, and he was doing theater reviews for *L'Espresso* and writing political and philosophical reflections about once a month for *La Stampa*. His ideas did not fit into any established category; he was neither on the left nor on the right. Nor did it follow that he was in the middle; he was alone. Though his thought remained faithful, in its way, to philosophical anarchism, he had long lost the belief in political "effectiveness." After what he had seen in the Spanish Civil War, he had no taste for applying force to the realm of ethics and ideals; on the other hand, he was skeptical of the power of persuasion as represented in the mass political parties.

In America, after the forties, he was not well known. He sent occasional "Letters" from Europe to *Partisan Review* and wrote occasionally for *Dissent*. In 1966 he gave the Christian Gauss lectures at Princeton, on the novel and the ideas of history developed in it. These lectures, revised and amplified, were published, as a volume, in London, under the title of *The Paradox of History*, and in Italy as *Credere e non credere*. In America, though hopes were raised, no publisher was found for them. The same had happened with his volume of theater essays, *La situazione drammatica*, which had won an important Italian prize.

Since his death, his widow has had a grant from the Agnelli Foundation to prepare several volumes of his uncollected writings for publication. The first, consisting of political texts, has just appeared, and the second, theater reviews and essays not including those in *La situazione drammatica,* will be coming out soon. It is characteristic, probably, of our period that his death should have prompted what might almost be called his "discovery." Consciousness of a loss has awakened curiosity as to what exactly was in the vacated space. For young people, I hope, finding him will be a revelation. What he says and said all along can speak directly to them, over the heads of his own positivistic generation. Young Americans, in particular, most of whom have surely never heard his name, will benefit from our loss now that an American publisher is at last making a varied selection of his writing available.

MARY MC CARTHY

EXPERIENCE

The Jesuit

We had been at school together, at the Collegio
Massimo, the time-honored Jesuit college where the
sons of the Roman middle class sit in the same class-
room, but do not mingle, with the scions of the "black"
aristocracy.* We had been together responsible for a
collective act that consisted in greeting the teacher of
French with the word *Scythian* whispered by thirty
mouths, and also for the editing of a mimeographed
school magazine, an initiative which was strictly for-
bidden by the Fathers. We had played soccer and ex-
ploded homemade land mines in the same vacant lot.
We had both been in love with Pearl White and had
done many irregular and dishonest things for her sake,
like selling textbooks and stealing from our fathers'
wallets in order not to miss the next episode of *The
Mysteries of New York*. But when we were fifteen our
roads began to part: Martelli went into the Catholic
Youth and embraced the ideology of the Partito Popo-
lare (the pre-Fascist version of the Christian Democrats), while I was for D'Annunzio and (because of
D'Annunzio) also for Mussolini. In the meantime, I
had also begun to disbelieve in God, and more especially in the necessity of submitting to the torture of
weekly confession, while Martelli remained a devout
boy and went into retreat every year to perform Saint
Ignatius's Spiritual Exercises under the direction of a
very old Father, famous all over Catholic Rome as an
outstanding specialist in that kind of devotion. As a
consequence, Martelli and I could not be intimate any

* A Roman aristocracy created by popes and not by kings. —Ed.

longer, and in fact we started having different friends. But our ideological quarrels remained a strong bond between us, especially since from politics we had both rushed into theology. It was Saint Thomas against Nietzsche (or, rather, Zarathustra), and Nietzsche suffered many logical defeats; at the same time Martelli consistently beat me at chess. By then, we were not friends any longer, and if I saw him from time to time, it was mainly to test some newly discovered idea or argument against his skillful adherence to tradition. Sometimes, he would suddenly interrupt the argument and, looking me straight in the eye, announce that he was praying for me. To which, what could I answer except "Thank you"? Then, at seventeen, Martelli told me that he was going to become a Jesuit. A year later, he entered the Novitiate.

I did not see him for three years, and when he emerged from his seclusion he had undergone a weird mutation. There was simply nothing spontaneous about him any more; behind every one of his acts and gestures there was premeditation. It was as if his innermost being had been submitted to an uncannily thorough process of plastic surgery. "Like a dead body, like a cane in the hand of a blind man": the aim starkly set by Ignatius in the chapter *"De Oboedientia"* had been attained in him, too. The adolescent, the young man, the defective human being, had been corrected, straightened, stamped into a fixed shape, made into a dependable spiritual tool. Of Martelli as I had known him only the outer shell was left, and not even that, since his countenance and gestures had also changed. No other organization, I thought, could get that much from a man, simply because no other organization would care to work on an individual so exhaustively. Certainly not a political party, and certainly not the state, either, however totalitarian. The conditioning of youth by the Fascist regime looked silly indeed when compared with this sort of achievement.

I found myself without any means of communicating with my old playmate, and I was able to talk to him only in distant and vague terms or else by treating him as the emissary of an evil power, the Church, and getting angry. The rare times we saw each other, I did not know what to do except to be polemical on the subject of the Church prostituting herself to Fascism. He answered that it was a mistake to judge the Church on such trivial grounds and that, anyway, if he was sorry for some of the things I said, he couldn't help feeling glad that I could get so passionate about Church politics: that was not a sign of indifference, was it? As for Fascism, he didn't like it either, but if the Church could advance her aims a bit because of Mussolini's megalomania, that consoled him for many a sad aspect of the situation. The point was that, being a Jesuit, he couldn't become excited about current events any longer; the real battle, the only one about which he could feel passionate, was being fought on a different level. Then Martelli would start talking about modern man drifting away from the Church, and the doctrines that were responsible for it. At that moment I would feel utterly bored and incapable of arguing; the line was too musty, and too preposterous.

Once, I tried to cut my opponent short by reminding him of Flaubert's saying, in 1850, that "our soul is a sealed book to the clergy." That, I said, had been true for some time before 1850 and was an irreparable fact, even if we had to admit that we didn't know what consequences would result from it.

"That is what I call drifting," retorted Father Martelli. "You call it freedom, I suppose. To me, this kind of freedom, as Plato will tell you, evokes its opposite, tyranny. If you don't have spiritual order, you are bound to get a police state of some sort, because society *has* to be kept together. The individual might imagine that to follow one's whims and mean well is a sufficient rule of conduct. But society is dogmatic by its very nature. Moreover, to take the only people I know, the Italians—I don't see that their souls are such a sealed book to us priests. It might appear to be so in the cities, because nobody knows what is going on in the cities, anyway. But, I assure you, in the cities and elsewhere, people keep coming to us, and not just to hear Mass, but to tell us something about their souls and bodies. Not as many as one could desire, I grant, but quite a number.

"We may be wretched soul readers, but we look after things in the life of the people that nobody else seems to care about. There is no substitute for the parish priest. All is not well with religion today. But the fact is that hardly anyone refuses to have his children baptized, and hardly anyone refuses a religious funeral, either. For us that is not enough, but at least it indicates that the Italians are still Catholic. We reject the distinction according to which ritual observance indicates only some kind of vague attachment to tradition, and the idea that, since people do not always follow the Church in politics, they have necessarily parted from her. As long as people will come to us to be married and to have their children baptized and their dead commended to God's mercy, it seems to me that it is your belief that is put in question, and not our faith.

"In other countries, Catholicism may be bolder or intellectually more refined, but it is in Italy that it is most concrete, that it is deepest in social life. It is in Italy that 'Christian' is synonymous with 'man.' The Church is very much like the family or the native village for us Italians: not an idea, but an attachment that cannot be broken, because nobody can get away from his memory. You intellectuals have gotten into the habit of damning your own people for that, saying that Italy is a wretched country because she didn't have a religious reformation, or a social revolution. As for me, I admire God's work in Italy: how lasting, successful, on the whole, Christian Catholicism has been in civilizing the Italians, that is, taming the beast in them. If, as you say so often, Fascism is bringing Italy to her ruin, then I am confident that in the hour of trial, between Italy and ruin, there the Church will stand."

I soon learned to listen to Father Martelli without arguing, simply to instruct myself in the Catholic mentality and logic, much as I would read *Civiltà Cattolica*, the Italian Jesuit monthly, or *L'Osservatore Romano*. Outside Italy, intellectuals are inclined to think that modern science, modern philosophy, modern civilization give them the right to be through once and for all with the Catholic question. In Italy, Catholic ambiguity is an ever-present fact. Neither sound logic nor stark political power seems quite to the point in combating it. One discovers Catholic casuistry just below the surface of Croce's neo-Hegelianism, while the space of the afterlife, even when no longer populated by angels and devils, is still an efficient cause of everyday conduct, accounting for much that is inert in Italian life but also for much that is gentle and humane. As for politics in Italy, the liberal state failed entirely to establish on anything like clear intellectual and juridical grounds the supposedly clear principle of the separation of Church and state. Fascism saw the point. But even more significant than Fascist appeasement of the Vatican was the fact that the atheist Mussolini was no sooner in power than he found himself flanked by a spiritual adviser in the person of Father Tacchi-Venturi, S.J., the "Black Eminence."

Confronted with such a state of affairs, a non-Catholic Italian is tempted to take a moderately skeptical, and moderately realistic, view of human affairs. But realistic skepticism, especially of the moderate kind, is an essential component of Italian Catholic mentality. Then, since moral and logical laxity seems to characterize Catholicism in Italy, moralistic rigor and sectarianism might seem more pertinent and more efficacious. But rigor and sectarianism require some sort of dogma, and how could a dogma be really anti-Catholic in Italy? When one has received a Catholic education, like me, one is made sensitive to such questions, and the difficulty of finding an answer to them becomes very fascinating. That is why I went to converse with Martelli, and submitted to such seemingly unrewarding exercises as reading Catholic literature and carefully scrutinizing papal Encyclicals. In a way, I was still looking for the politico-intellectual move that would end the intricate game between the Italians and Catholicism with an indisputable checkmate.

I left Italy in 1934 and did not go back until 1947. Meanwhile, I heard regularly from my Jesuit acquaintance at Christmas and Easter, when he would send me good wishes, prayers, and invitations to prayer. I couldn't, in turn, resist the temptation to send him a postcard from Madrid in August 1936. As for Martelli's personal history, I knew only that the Order had chosen him to be a parish priest, rather than a teacher, a scholar, or a publicist. That seemed to me a sign that certain personal qualities I had known and appreciated in him, and more especially a sincere evangelical spirit, the desire actually to serve and help people (if he had not decided to be a priest, I fancied, he would have become a Communist), had remained dominant in his character. During the war, I imagined Father Martelli ministering to the poor, organizing relief, giving one of those examples of self-denial that compel admiration and are really what keep the Church going, postponing time and again the retribution that would otherwise be coming to her, as it comes to other mundane outfits when they lay their bets on the wrong horse (and the Vatican surely had gambled on Fascism with some insistence).

Back in Rome, however, the first news I got about Father Martelli was that he had become an eminent exponent of the trend known as "neo-Fascism." A friend of mine had heard him preach one Sunday. The sermon was on the parable of the watchful servants and what follows—how Jesus came to bring fire and discord to earth, not peace (Luke 12:35–43). But the orator had spoken mainly on "authority," and my friend professed to have been truly scared by his ecstatic vehemence. The thesis was that authority is the supreme manifestation of God's will on earth; in inner life as well as in public affairs, Divine Truth reveals itself to man essentially in the form of imperious command; where there is no authority there is no truth; hence, the duty of Catholics in the present time is to pray and work for the restoration of authority, which had been reduced to rubble along with moral, economic, and national life.

Instead of being surprised by the news, I was struck by the fact that such an appeal was bound to sound solemn and inspiring in the Italy of March 1947. Even when they are patient with him, Italians are basically contemptuous of the priest who falls in with the powers-that-be: he looks superfluous and lackadaisical to them. But a priest who seems to go against the current, and to be free from temporal bondage, will sound apocalyptic and is sure to find an audience. (One limiting factor, in the case of Father Martelli, was the fact that his church was situated in

a middle-class section; Jesuits don't cater to the mob.)
And, as it happened, the Italians' newly recovered freedom, although enjoyed by everybody, including Fascists and Communists, was generally felt to be either precarious or provisional. Moreover, while the word *authority*, with its derivatives, was officially taboo, and the fact *authority* practically nonexistent so far as government prestige was concerned, the question of it hung over everybody's mind and found at best no definite answer.

The striking feature of post-Fascist Italy is how little Italy has changed. To be precise, the Italians have refused to be changed by events. They have refused to become bitter, somber, or niggardly. They have kept up appearances as prescribed by one of the basic unwritten laws of the national behavior, a law that is founded on the general disregard for any clear-cut distinction between appearances and reality. There is nothing stoical in the Italians' keeping up of appearances; quite the contrary. It means a certain naturalness, an unwillingness to curb normal human habits and incentives. There is no emergency that justifies losing sight of the values of everyday life. When such a thing happens, it is really bad. The Germans, the bombings, hunger, the battles were bad enough. But they were exceptions. The rule: normal life with its normal components, from money-making to day-dreaming, is never lost sight of, and couldn't be, since it appears to be one with nature itself. (In fact, to the Italian mind, war and the other man-made catastrophes come not from the human world so much as from the realm of nature; it is natural that, from time to time, man should lose control of events.)

Battles had hardly died down in central Italy when young and old men took over, picked up wrecked trucks, tires, screws, and nails, anything that could imaginably be put to use. During the last weeks of the siege of Rome, while the city was actually starving, in the poor sections people were feverishly busy repairing and improvising all kinds of contraptions for the expected black-market boom; only American supplies were needed to round off the job. One of the leaders of the resistance in the north tells, quite incidentally, in his memoirs that he took a few days off from the struggle to go to Trieste to pick up his family and take them back to Milan, where he had found an apartment—apartments were awfully scarce. And family life surely has a priority in Italy. In the same book, the reader is told that at one moment the commander in chief of the resistance, Parri himself, grimly announced to the assembled Committee of National Liberation that if his wife were arrested he would give himself up to the Germans. Hence, from then on, the fate of the resistance movement was dependent on, among other things, Parri's family. The decision, Parri had added, was the outcome of an agonizing moral struggle. Which was certainly true, but it also meant that in Italy not even the conditions created by the Nazis could persuade a man who otherwise accepted their challenge to make his commitment unconditional. Italy is no place for categorical imperatives.

While doing one thing, an Italian always keeps an eye on something else; sometimes it is a sentiment, sometimes a dream, often a strictly personal interest. This makes people say that Italians are realists. To be sure, Italians are a practical people, even if not exactly pragmatic or dedicated to efficiency. But they are realists also in another, more maddening, sense. Their view of things can be desperately trite, tied down not to facts so much as to details and details of details. They care infinitely about the tangible world. One should not forget the sense in which Leonardo and Galileo can be called realists, and which also is Italian. In any case, the most lonely Italian is certainly the "idealist," the man who is seized by one idea and carried away by it, heedless of consequences, because he wants a real "change."

Italy has not changed. The rich have become richer; the poor, poorer. The pitiless law according to which it is natural that those who are at the bottom should be miserable and good and those who are on top satisfied and wicked still dominates Italian life. In the collapse of Fascism, only Fascism has been refuted. Fascist authority and state structure are not there any longer. But, if the façade has crumbled, everything that was behind the façade before is still there, very much the same. Except that everything looks like the scattered fragments of a scattered society. Everything is in a state of suspension: conservatism together with the need for change; authoritarian habits along with libertarian impulses; nationalism and the natural cosmopolitanism of the Italians. Political freedom, as it exists today in Italy, *is* a state of suspension. But still it makes a difference. The simple fact of free speech has given the country an animation which looks like a new life. Misfortune has made the Italians feel united as they never felt before. The country is far from inert.

Yet the apparent immutability of Italian society weighs everybody down. On the large-scale level of politics, everything that has happened could have been predicted by the most commonplace imagination: the strength of the Communists, the dominating role of the Catholics, the practical inexistence of the "liberals." In fact, anybody who has tried to concoct something new in Italian politics has finally come to grief: the intellectuals of the Action Party, who thought they had to offer a new synthesis of liberalism and socialism; and the demagogues of the Common Man Front, who tried a peculiar mixture of the old-fashioned and the colloquial.

It is true that the war and foreign occupation left the Italians with a limited, and somewhat prearranged, number of choices. It is even truer that Italy, like all Europe, has been thrown on a rock bottom of hard facts. Against hard facts, as everybody knows, clever formulas are of no avail, though it is felt for some reason that traditional patterns (or vested interests) help. The new realistic school is triumphant. Except that in Italy realism is no news; it always meant cynicism. And a strong man at the top.

The point in today's political realism is that it turns political life into a question of mass inertia, not of change. *Realpolitik* necessarily feeds on mass habits and embedded traditions, not on new ideas and spontaneous surges. In fact, its efforts must be continually directed toward mobilizing the first and suppressing the second. It must consistently follow the logical pattern of the movie producer who maintains that bad movies are made by the public, not by him. To the *Realpolitiker,* the issue as it comes up or exists in social life is never primary; what is essential is what was there before: the vested interests, the reliable inertia of habits. The monarchy should be abolished, but to start with we must compromise with the monarchists; self-government is the goal, but bureaucratic tradition is a fact: we must let bureaucracy have its way until further notice; we want the Church curbed, but it is imperative that we don't alienate the churchgoers, hence let's give the Church what she wants *now*. In Italy, these arguments have all been employed by the Communists at one time or another.

But the kind of reasoning such arguments represent is by no means the monopoly of the Communists. When Togliatti arrived from Moscow, in 1944, to become a Minister of the King, it was not only a temporary deal he brought with him; he was bringing back to Italy the Golden Rule of Italian politics, which had been shaken by events. The fighting, Allied rule, and the cold war did the rest. Today, the Italian ruling class is thoroughly alive to the necessity of being "realistic." (Togliatti is universally regarded as a political genius. Until recently, conservatives were likely to tell you that he could become "a second Giolitti," an admirable liberal-conservative statesman, that is, if only he wanted to. It so happened that Togliatti wanted them to believe precisely that.)

The result is that, if one excludes the adventure of Communist conquest, the Italians, after a disaster that has completely changed the terms of their national problems, are being shown by their leaders only one clear path, the path that leads back to the traditional ways of their society. The most recent tradition is, of course, Fascism. It is not by chance that the Communists are diligently following the blueprint of Fascist conquest: armed squads, punitive expeditions, and so on. There are no two ways of doing the same thing, and why bother to invent new methods, anyway? Aside from that, there is the fact that nobody seems to know exactly how to avoid going back to the fundamental propositions of Fascism: state authority, state corporatism, and nationalism as a cement. Very few people are Fascists, of course, and everybody wants caution above all; the dangers are too many.

And what institution can, in Italy, give a better guarantee of caution than the Church, the locus of all tradition and of all prudence? If Italy goes authoritarian, the Church will palliate authoritarian harshness, as she did under Fascism. If democracy wins, she will see to it that it is accompanied by the right dose of authority. In Italy, the Church offers not heaven so much as protection from the sheer impact of history. And she has recently acted quite effectively as an intermediary between the defeated nation and the great of this world. Italians are, indeed, bound to feel protected by her.

In this respect, at least, Father Martelli had been right. I went to see him in his church. It is a horror of a church, built in a kind of streamlined Romanesque style which is the religious equivalent of the somber emptiness of Fascist official architecture: a parallelepiped of bricks laid flatly on the ground and flanked by another parallelepiped of the same material, but standing up, since it has to represent the church tower. The heart of the malicious infidel cannot help rejoicing at such a prodigy of structural insincerity. Martelli's office, however, was a plain whitewashed room, mostly empty, showing all the signs of exemplary Jesuit parsimony. There was the same implacable dreariness I had known in college. Martelli had by no means tried to make his bourgeois parishioners feel at ease in there.

Of the things I had imagined about him from afar, one proved to be right. Namely, he had clearly worn himself out with work. Outwardly he looked healthy and strong. But in walking he had to help himself with a cane, and he advanced at a slow and heavy pace, as if he were repressing a hidden pain or making a great effort at every step. There was effort in his speech, too. His shiny cassock was mended in more than one place. He wore thick-soled boots, battered but well polished. When I arrived he was counting small notes and ranging them in bundles in a basket. "The alms," he said. "They are meager."

One of the first things he told me was that he

wished he knew more about American democracy. The question was not quite clear to him. He had been told that for the Americans democracy finally rests on education. But what was the basis of education, then? How could there be education without a supreme truth binding together the teacher, the pupil, and the society in which they lived?

"I don't know about America," he went on. "But I do know about the kind of democracy we are supposed to have over here. It's an imposture: the lie you have to tell in order to succeed. The biggest lie of all is Christian Democracy, a contradiction in terms. At the opposite end, there are the Communists. The Communists are pursuing their own anti-Christian aim; but they do have a notion of authority. It is quite normal that they should exploit confusion in order to get Evil. You cannot say that they are lying. It is their faith itself which is imposture, the Error of our time. The other parties, however, are pitiful. For most of them, the lie they call 'democracy' is just a way of groping. Through confusion on to more confusion. In between lies this hapless country, 'a vessel without pilot in a mighty storm.'"

I told him that his bitterness was surprising to me. I should have thought that a Catholic would feel rather hopeful in Italy. The Church had never, for the last eighty years, been so politically and economically strong. And the Christian Democrats might prove a useful expedient, after all. Why object to them on the grounds of logic?

He had a tired smile.

"Diplomacy. I know, I know. The trouble is that it is not an adequate answer. Diplomacy might be necessary in high places, but you can't give diplomatic answers to people who come to you for advice and comfort. You have to take chances, and open your heart to them. The people are distressed. They find it more and more difficult to be Christians in a society that becomes less and less Christian every day. They are the prey of economic and political anxiety. They want to know what to do *now*. It is only by giving them straight answers that you can retain their confidence."

"And what is your answer?" I asked.

"They must have told you that I am a Fascist," he said with a boyish giggle. "Of course I am not. I am a Jesuit. Moreover, the only restoration I care for is the restoration of society to Christ. But, if we want to be serious and not just cry wolf after the wolf is dead, as people are doing today, we have to recognize that Fascism, insofar as it realized that the social problem is first of all a problem of authority and that there can be no authority without Catholicism, was a step in the right direction, and a most important one at that. The trouble was that, like so many Italians, Mussolini was an amateur. He thought it possible for a political leader of our time to be a Catholic only up to a certain point. In this he was no better than so many liberal politicians. Italy is now paying for his mistake. But the fact is that, if Fascism has been defeated, it has by no means been proved wrong. We knew that the moment we became a conquered people. If I were a cardinal I would be prudent. But I am a parish priest, and what can I, in all conscience, tell people who come to me for advice, except that the principle which was beginning to give the Italian nation a true Catholic shape must not be given up? What comforts me is that the younger generation seems to be aware of this duty."

All this was asserted with passion, as if it were an absolutely personal belief. But it wasn't. In fact, another Jesuit, Father Lombardi, the most popular orator in Italy after Togliatti, was saying very much the same thing, in public places as well as over the radio. He introduced himself on the radio with the words "Jesus is at the microphone. Jesus wants to speak to you. Listen to Jesus" (the cover of the volume in which his radio talks have been collected bears a reproduction of the head of Christ from Raphael's *Transfiguration*, with the addition of a neatly drawn microphone in the right corner). As for Father Lombardi's political message, it was quite straight. He tried to give heart to the distressed Italians by pointing out that "a newly reorganized life might be better than the one we have been *forced to renounce*." Italy, he said, still has the greatest possessions of all, Rome and the Pope. Italy's greatest glories have all been Christian and Catholic. The nation can be reborn in spite of the "shameful peace treaty" imposed on her by "the cowardice of the conquerors." Italy has a right to have her colonies back and also to have a new army, whose young soldiers "can again confidently sing the motherland's songs." If the Italians stick by their "two mothers, the motherland and the Church," there can be no doubt about "the final triumph." In his final talk, the speaker was troubled by the query whether "the devil will not unleash a battle in order to prevent Italy's rebirth in Christ . . . and spill new blood over our soil." "That blood," the Father reassuringly answered himself, "if it should be spilled, will spell doom for the men who have committed the crime. And from that blood Italy will be reborn, more beautiful than ever."

I told Martelli that his remarks reminded me of what Father Lombardi had been preaching. The general idea seemed to be National Catholicism, or was I wrong?

"I can see the logic of it," I said, "but I don't see

how your notion of authority can be made to work. If what you have in mind is straight theocracy, then allow me to say that in my opinion it hasn't got a chance. Granted that the Italians are by and large still Catholics, you must admit that their Catholicism is of such a kind that it excludes precisely the notion that the Church should become an absolute power. And you are not thinking of a new adventure in dictatorship, are you?"

"You have been away a long time," he answered. "Apparently you have remained more of an optimist than I have. You still think in terms of intellectual alternatives. But, my dear friend, there are no alternatives. Would to God that theocracy, as you call it, were today an actual choice. It would mean that society had remained essentially Christian. Harmony between religion and politics would then still be the generally accepted norm, and it could always be achieved through some kind of wise adjustment. Unfortunately, we don't live in the thirteenth century. We live in a time that is the negation of any harmony. If you were a priest, you would know to what a horrible extent the moral life of the individual is constantly yielding ground under the pressure of social disorder. Christian restoration today means Christian reconquest of society. The only question is 'Where should we start from?' If by dictatorship you mean emergency power, I can only answer that the present situation is, indeed, one of dire emergency. There is no other point from which to start except an act of authority."

I left, and found myself back in the Roman streets and squares: the Roman space, so generous, so free of compulsion, rejecting nothing, asking nothing of the individual, except that he pick up a disguise and play a role, forgetting himself in it. The cast is innumerable, the stage set once and for all. There is room for the Fanatic on it, and for the Cynic. Only the real person is excluded: the heretic. Or isn't he?

Partisan Review, February 1948

2

Spain: The War

I am sitting in a sort of funnel-shaped space, my knees doubled against my chest; I peer through the small opening from which the machine gun protrudes. We are reconnoitering. Below us in the distance puffs of thick white smoke burst unceasingly, thinning away only to be renewed. The slight pressure of my foot on the pedals turns the turret to right or left in a brief dizzy movement. Below, things change suddenly, but the sky is always the same. However, we are absorbed not by the sky but by the space between the sky and us, between the earth and us. That is where danger lurks. Danger is anything that moves. When you are in a plane, whatever moves can only be another plane; other things are still, or, if they do move, like the cars that roll over the ribbonlike roads, their motion seems directed, planned ahead of time—it isn't an *active* motion.

The Tajo, a sluggish, worn-out river, flows through the plain of Castile deep in its bed. But at Talavera de la Reina it comes back to the surface and seems to overflow the sand. At least, that is the impression one has of the Tajo near our "objective," Talavera, where the altimeter reads 1,200 meters above sea level. On September 3 the Moroccans captured Talavera and the fight for Madrid began. With

Chiaromonte served in André Malraux's squadron in Spain in 1936. He was the original of Scali in Malraux's *Man's Hope* (*L'Espoir*).

three bombers and five pursuit planes, outnumbered ten to one by the "others," we have to do what we can to give the demoralized militiamen and the anxious peasants of Castile the impression that a Republican air force exists. Now the railroad station and the airport at Talavera are being bombed. On the ground, sheafs of thick black smoke unfold here and there, yellowish flames shoot up from the buildings, a locomotive is torn open, a long red roof disappears. The bombs trace a perfect line splitting the airport in two—which gives us enormous satisfaction.

That's the end. Our planes have done their work. It seemed as though this flight back and forth over a motionless prey, spiraling, turning, darting, would never end. A kind of forced gaiety takes possession of the seven members of our crew; we communicate it to each other by glances.

Suddenly there comes a cry from the rear turret, piercing and inhuman in its attempt to be heard over the roar of the motors. That means but one thing; hands and eyes obey instantly, the one at the machine gun, the other sweeping the sky. I see three black spots directly behind us. The next instant I see only two, and lower. I choose the nearer and train my gun on it. But there is no longer anything there; it is maddening. Nevertheless, my comrade in the rear fires a few short, angry rounds. The "thing" is approaching from above. From my position I can see nothing. I wait interminably in the emptiness, with a frantic sensation of solitude. Suddenly something zooms close by; the world becomes alive again, lucid and precise. I see quite distinctly. My machine gun belches fire three times. Then, again, emptiness. We dive and bank. The rear machine gun fires again, in brief rhythm. And then my comrade turns around and shakes his fist, laughing. His mouth opens in strange fashion; he is singing. Far away against the sky a plane is slowly turning over, so slowly that one would think it was executing a maneuver. It was a Heinkel, and our gunner at the rear turret got it. Two other planes are fast disappearing in the distance. I lean out: two little holes in a wing, that's all. It is all finished, quite finished, and it lasted no more than three minutes.

Seated in one of the chairs that were taken out of the transport planes in order to transform them into bombers, the Basque mechanic begins to talk. He was a pal of Sergeant Iturbi. Iturbi is dead because of machine-gun bullets that weren't calibrated carefully enough. He had said calmly, "If my gun gets clogged, I'll crash my opponent." His gun clogged during an extremely unequal combat (a Nieuport, 180 kilometers per hour, against a Fiat, 300 kilometers per hour), and Iturbi dived straight into his adversary. The Italian pilot, Vincenzo Patriarca, was saved by his parachute.

"We Spaniards talk a lot—*muchas palabras*—but it isn't serious. We have no true *education*."

His words did not convey half what he expressed by his accompanying gestures and grimaces. He emphasized "education" with clenched fists and a sort of enraged look that left no doubt: he believed in education, all right.

"No, no. . . . One must be serious. . . . Look at the workmen here at the camp. They work twelve and fourteen hours a day, voluntarily, and they have refused payment for extra time. But the military, they haven't refused the advantages of war. . . . It is wicked. . . . As if it could be a question of money, today! . . . Ah, there are moments when I feel like putting a couple of bullets into my head!" And he went through the motion of aiming at his temple.

At seven o'clock that evening a bus takes the fliers from the camp at Barajas back to Madrid. In the bus there are about ten workmen. The one beside me asks, "How many planes have we?" Always the same question, everywhere. They know that it is one of our weakest points.

I answer as usual: "Very few, but we are getting along all right. Today we shot down a German plane."

A few moments before, my neighbor was serious, even sad. The news I give him electrifies him. "Terrific! This evening I'll have an extra drink! Who did it?"

"That fellow there in back."

He gets up and congratulates the gunner of the rear turret, passing on the good news to his comrades. The bus is in an uproar. For them a vanquished plane is a memorable victory, almost an ultimate one. They see things one by one, as symbols, not with regard to number, or weight, or size. A vanquished plane promises certainty that all the rest may be vanquished, and are potentially already vanquished. These people discover their own strength with an intoxication that makes them forget a great many things. It is the psychology by which, after having taken La Caserna de la Montaña "with their bare hands," as they tell you again and again (and that is absolutely so: successive waves of Madrileños—men, women, children, old people—overwhelmed the barracks, which were bristling with machine guns, with the force of their attack; the arms they possessed would have been quite unavailing), these people considered themselves not only victorious, but invincible through divine favor. The armies of Franco and Mola were planning to meet at Badajoz and thence to march upon Navalmoral, Talavera, Toledo. The people continued to revere the "miracle" of the Mountain, to consider defeats as unfortunate but inconsequential, to exclude a priori, as a frightening and unreal hypothesis, the possibility of a definitive disaster.

In 1809, before the victorious French invasion, Don Andrés Torrejón, mayor of Mostoles, a small village nineteen kilometers from Madrid, took it quite simply upon himself to declare war against Napoleon. He did it in the name of the people, and his mad gesture has remained not without echo or consequence.

In 1936, General Franco declared war upon the descendants of Andrés Torrejón. General Mola added the scornful challenge "The people can do nothing against the army."

His challenge was taken up not only with enthusiasm but with almost morbid exultation. To fight the generals on their own ground: that involved the pride of every man, woman, and child. Single-mindedly, they applied themselves to the task. The result was a surging mob—but a mob that completely stopped those who had thought it could be dispersed in a few minutes.

When the people take arms they become violent and unmanageable. They swarm about, singing, killing, and being killed; they storm batteries with pistols and knives, and flee because of a few airplane bombs which harm none of them. They are zealous in planning the most impossible ways and means, and at the same time they prevent the most routine measures from becoming effective or the most vital organizations from functioning. It is both sublime and absurd. And yet that was all the Spanish Republic had to save it.

One cannot speak of *organizing* a crowd. One organizes what is already arranged or established; one does not organize that which is in a state of constant flux, spreading simultaneously in every direction. Moreover, this mob that refused to yield to the organized army, and shouted its hatred of that "collective" organization, was obliged to transform itself into an army, to create for itself the organization of war.

In the beginning there was originality, with all its creative force and despairing weakness. Each syndical federation in each region organized its combatants. Each detachment was placed under the authority of a special "regional committee," whose connection with the other committees as well as with the central government was, naturally, rather weak. Under the command of the political leader most versed in military affairs, these detachments left for Zaragoza, for the Sierra de Guadarrama, for Guadalajara, for Sigüenza. They stopped when their driving force was no longer sufficient to master the enemy resistance, without much regard, as will be readily understood, for strategic considerations. The sum total of the different points at which this first drive was stopped constituted the "front." And thus the war began.

The most important thing was not strategy; it was confidence in Fernando de Rosa. From this confidence, and from it alone, arose the "October" battalion, one of the best among those that fought on the Sierra de Guadarrama. A young man, twenty-eight years old, small, blond, with a clear and decisive look, always on the *qui vive*, such was Major de Rosa, *el italiano*. He had proved himself on the barricades of Madrid in October 1934 and before the court-martial that condemned him to thirty years in prison after he assumed all responsibility for the insurrection, to save Largo Caballero, under penalty of death.

"*El italiano es un hombre con dos cojones.*" It was with this enthusiastic and more or less untranslatable statement that the soldiers followed Major de Rosa when he led the attack with the shout "Who is coming with me?" Because *his* voice reassured them, *"No pasa nada"* ("It is nothing"), his men remained in their places under the same bombardments that caused panic among comrades near by. Bullets did not unnerve de Rosa; therefore his men were not unnerved. The bond between officer and troops was a sentimental one, violent and yet fragile, with little of the military about it. The method this courageous youth employed in holding his men was nothing more or less than the technique of making every moment count and of capitalizing on lucky breaks.

One day two prisoners, self-styled Socialists, asked if they might join the October battalion. De Rosa did not hesitate to accept them. But his soldiers, suspecting treachery, protested, "To take strangers, without even making inquiries . . ." De Rosa agreed. "Indeed, we ought to make sure. I shall see for myself tonight." That evening he left for night patrol alone with the two recruits. Halfway up the mountain, de Rosa stopped a moment, removed his revolver from his belt, and gave it to one of his companions. "Carry it—it's in my way." And he continued his patrol that way. "You can rest assured, they are absolutely safe," he declared to the anxious soldiers who awaited his return.

The October battalion lasted right up to the moment when de Rosa, standing on a promontory during an entire attack to prove that not all bullets kill their men, was killed by a ball through the forehead. Filing into Madrid behind his coffin, the soldiers of the October battalion, guns on their shoulders, wept like orphans. The battalion was dissolved; it could not live without de Rosa.

It was such battalions that stemmed the first attack of the Fascist generals—and lost Toledo and

Castille. Thrown into confusion by the violent and unexpected drives of the Moroccans and the legionnaires of the Tercio—soldiers well armed, well protected, well directed, having on their side, in addition, the overwhelming advantage of mechanical resources —the militiamen found themselves scattered upon the highway to Estremadura, in groups of fifty, thirty, fifteen.

"What are you doing?" they were asked.

"Where are our leaders?" they countered. "We want Mangada. With him we will recapture Talavera." Mangada was a beloved general, but he could not be wherever a handful of men claimed his presence. They had neither sergeants nor corporals—no one who could reorganize them or assure them that they were not entirely abandoned. And here they were demanding a general!

Soldiers continued to turn traitor. Alongside the road lay the body of an officer of the civil guard. "I just shot him," announced the major of the Fifth Regiment of militia. "He had been entrusted with a battery, and he turned it over to the Fascists."

There were fifteen-year-old boys among those disbanded soldiers—they made one think of the drummer boys of historic armies. But if the Moors had taken them they would have ended in the common grave with the rest. Tired, hungry, dirty, a pause for a cigarette by an open field freed them from care. And the women—peasants and workers, sturdy, courageous, their dusty hair caught up under soldiers' caps—carried their guns like farm tools. In their pockets, among the cartridges, were needles, thread, and extra buttons.

It was a woman who, at the head of two hundred militiamen, directed the last defense of Sigüenza—a fierce and useless resistance. On the tenth of October the city was occupied by Fascist soldiers (there were many priests among them, especially Jesuits). The population was massacred without discrimination, in spite of the fact that the victims were, for the most part, of clerical leaning. The two hundred who lay wounded in the hospital, including doctors, were wiped out with knife thrusts.

It was under these conditions that Comrade Etcheverry decided to open up a way to the cathedral, so as to wait there for the reinforcements which had been asked for. By means of dynamite cartridges she succeeded in taking over the church with her men. During the fight her husband was killed. Some three hundred women and children had already taken refuge in the cathedral. A machine gun was placed in the tower, and the interior was barricaded. To the demand for reinforcements Madrid answered, "We can do nothing. Resist if you can." Comrade Etcheverry resisted. From morning till evening for six days, eight trimotor Junkers dropped bombs on the church. Not a drop of alcohol, not a bandage, to care for the wounded. Comrade Etcheverry gave the order to kill the dying. On the seventh day they decided to abandon the church and try to escape under cover of night. Once again enemy lines had to be crossed. For four days those who had the courage returned the way they had come, in groups of twenty or twenty-five, opening up a passage once again with dynamite. In this way Comrade Etcheverry was saved. She is now in Madrid.

The Catholic priest Juan García Morales wrote these words in August 1934: "For centuries Spain has been a nation of starving people who, souls alight with the Christian faith, have raised up the spires of Gothic cathedrals, and have covered with gold the cloisters of Avila and Salamanca. Today Spain's army of the starving no longer demand charity. They demand justice and the right to live decently. Unemployment is not alleviated by the dole, and the plan of the agrarian descendants of the ancient lords to provide for the construction of still more charitable institutions is an anachronism, like everything else which is the product of their minds. To treat the problem of human suffering in the twentieth century as did Saint Vincent de Paul in the seventeenth is to make of Spain a gigantic and permanent poorhouse."

In the same year a deputy presented a report to the Cortes in which he gave this instance of the working conditions in Castile: "At Salamanca, a group of landowners presented a plan for agricultural contracts paying 2.50 pesetas a day [less than thirty cents], with the workers obligated to return this pay if they were fed by their employer. That is, these workmen earned only their food. The contracts were approved by the provincial *junta*. Not only that, but they were later replaced by others in which it was added that certain classes of workers, as specified by contract, would have to pay .50 pesetas a day to their employer if he fed them during the working period. Work then became a privilege granted in consideration of money."

In the winter of 1935, the mayor of Boas de Segura sent the Minister of Labor the following telegram: "Unemployed workers in Boas de Segura in unendurable situation. Hungry crowds begging in the streets, soliciting charity by force. Please send emergency funds." That hatred has sprung from deep roots, in a land so harassed, is not particularly surprising.

In 1936, after five years of hesitation and delay, the Republic was finally forced to reflect seriously upon the situation. The generals appealed to "Grande

Espagne," to the shades of Philip II, to the "defense of the Faith." They caused Moors, Reichswehr, and Black Shirts to unite. And there you have "Spanish Fascism"—which nobody had believed possible.

"What is Fascism?" I asked a peasant of La Mancha one day.

"It is something for those who don't care for liberty."

Alone in a vast ward in the Escorial, which had been transformed into a hospital, a man lay seriously wounded. His tanned face bristled with whiskers. He looked at us with an expression of hostility, almost of rage.

"Where are you from?" we asked.

"From Alicante. I'm a farmer. There are seven of us brothers—when we're at home. All at the front." And, having noticed a slight gesture of astonishment on the part of his questioner, he hastened to add, with scornful impatience, *"Vivir ó no vivir, sin libertad, es igual"* ("Living or not living, without liberty, is all the same").

One sometimes has the impression among these people of being in the midst of a crowd of Patrick Henrys. "Give me liberty or give me death" seems to be everybody's motto. They have the common urge to liberate the whole world from the Fascist menace. This is often expressed by boasting and posturing. But there is also faith—a fanatic faith based upon this perfectly simple concept: a nation living in freedom, a society of honorable men obliged neither to go hungry nor to be clothed in rags. Could anything be simpler?

Atlantic Monthly, March 1939
(Trans. Anon.)

3

Lost Italians

Toulouse is the capital of the French southwest, and the southwest is the chosen land of Italian peasants coming from the great valley of the Po. In relation to France it is a southern region, but in climate and in the pattern of its culture it is very like the north of Italy. Men coming from Cremona will think that Saint-Sernin, the cathedral of Toulouse, looks like the cathedral in Cremona—except, of course, that their cathedral at Cremona is finer. And so the southwest came to be not only a region for Italian immigration, but also the center of exiled Italian Socialism. It was there that the memory of the agricultural syndicates of Parma, Reggio, and Molinella lived on. The only other comparable achievement of civilization in Europe was the municipality of Vienna. These men in exile had remained Socialist not as people remain believers in a religious faith, but simply as people remain honest men. Nothing could wipe out the memory of the days when the "apostles," Prampolini, Massarenti, Baldini, were the able administrators of prosperous co-operatives, the days when the ideal had become a tangible achievement and a visible source of hope, when the normal work of each day was normally profitable, when there were agencies that would place a man looking for work and organizations through which a man could buy and sell and obtain a loan. All that had been set fire to, destroyed and pillaged, but to no avail; a peasant never forgets those things that he knows he has built and paid for himself—with the same pertinacity and effort with which he has made his field and his house and paid for them. You can make an Italian forget or disown many a theoretical concept, but you cannot make him forget one single good that he has seen with his eyes or touched with his hands.

And so it came about, at the time of the great disaster that befell France in June 1940, that most of the Italians who had settled throughout the country turned their steps toward Toulouse. In Toulouse there were comrades, there were *compaesani* who could speak one's dialect, there were friends of friends; a man would find a bed, something to eat. They came from everywhere: from their homes, from foreign regiments, from labor battalions, and from concentration camps; from Lorraine and from Alsace as well as from the neighborhood of Paris, from Belgium, and even from England—via Dunkirk.

We all gathered around a table in a dilapidated basement, and there was never enough room at the table, or enough chairs. Yet out of the abyss of disaster spaghetti had been resurrected. A dining room had been organized. The secretary of the local Socialist section had decided that this was far more economical and rational than giving out subsidies: to feed men is something simple and useful; when you hand out money, you can never tell where it will go. And so those who had no money could eat without paying, and those who could pay paid a little extra, and the section's treasury made up the difference and made things balance. Furthermore, at night the basement could be used for those who had nowhere to sleep. On the most elementary basis possible—the necessity to eat—a little community had immediately grown into existence, or, rather, a family of sorts had grouped itself together.

Of course, the Belgian refugees and the Poles had their group kitchens, too. But it was not at all the same thing; they had big refectories for a hundred or a hundred and fifty people, while with us—apart from the fact that we would not have had the means to set them up—we had never even considered the possibility of letting it grow beyond the proportions of a large family. If occasionally we were thirty or so at table, there was instant chaos, ill temper, complaints, and argument. About twenty was the ideal number— enough for company, enough to feel among friends, but not so many that one would feel, in spite of their numbers and in their midst, alone. There was, too, a tremendous difference in organization between us and the men of the northern countries. They had budgets and directors, and they ran things on a timetable. With us it was a question of being able to improvise, or, rather, to reimprovise everything as each day came. Even in 1940 the problem of getting food to live on was none too simple in Toulouse—with sixty thousand refugees in a city of two hundred and fifty thousand inhabitants. Finding money to buy food in the market, finding something to burn in the stove, and finding oil for cooking, those were the problems that had to be solved anew every other day.

Eventually we found what we needed, and it was always thanks to a favor of Providence or to some sleight of hand—but, above all, it was due to the knowledge of an infinity of little roundabout ways of approach. It was due, in brief, to that fundamental experience Italians possess, by which they know that, in the life they lead, nothing is ever gained by traveling the main and obvious road, but that the little one can snatch from circumstances is attainable only by following the side roads and the hidden, secret, and intertwining lanes. The French know how to find their way around, but it is not the same thing. They are too accustomed to thinking that anything one wants will eventually turn up on the main highway of routine; their resourcefulness lies in finding the right trick at the right time, in ingeniously improvising some perfect little contrivance in a moment of need; but if the necessity to trick and contrive were ever to become a permanent condition and rule of life, that would be exhausting indeed and, clearly, no longer worth while. Italian resourcefulness is an instinct, sharpened and distilled, which discovers a track through the jungle of existence, and this path is at once a magical creation and a daily necessity. You will understand what it is if you have ever lived in the land of the Arabs, where, whenever something is difficult or impossible to find, people say to you, "If you want to find it, go and see the Arabs"—just as they would tell you to go and consult the sorcerers. After the disaster that tore their country asunder to its very roots, it was extraordinary, and almost irritating, to see the French, surrounded by ruin and chaos, in the immense despair that filled every heart, intent on one sole aim above all others: that of returning to normal daily life, in order to reconstruct, no matter how, that mechanism of normality without which they cannot conceive of life as being possible. But for Italians—for the Italian people—normal life is no more than a habit at best, a hair's breadth removed from disaster; and after disaster, as before, the necessity for intense resourcefulness remains.

As for the comrades of whom I speak, a normal life—well, it had been a long time since they had known anything of the sort. Foreigners without papers in France, volunteers in Spain, soldiers once again in the French army, or prisoners in French concentration camps—not to mention the years they had spent in Italian prisons—such had been, for almost all of them, the stages in their careers. And this life had left on their faces the imprint of an excessive physical fatigue and of an excessive patience and enduring. Their condition was not like that of their Spanish comrades: they did not have the same nervous despair and sadness; in their eyes you did not see the look of men who have seen "the heavens in which nothing shines," a look that has remained in the eyes of so many of those who have come out of Europe's hells alive. They were very tired, and, worse, they were very disappointed; but, when all is said and done, they sought only to forget, if that was still possible.

There was one man among them who had come from England. He had been at Dunkirk, as a volunteer in a French foreign regiment. Planes, tanks, the Germans three hundred yards away, and cannon from the British vessels, broadside along the beach, shelling them. For three days no one had attempted to cook, and no one had wanted to eat. Ultimately the Italian had decided that one could perfectly well make soup out of horse meat, and certainly there were plenty of dead horses. And he had lighted the stoves. The next day a burst of machine-gun fire from a plane tore the kitchen apart. This made little difference, for it was time to go. It was the Italian, too, who managed to find a boat, which had been left behind in a hut. At first there were only four men who wanted to try to reach England in a rowboat; but when the rest saw the four of them going off into the night, the four counted themselves and found they were ten. After half an hour on the water, the others were seasick and only the Italian was left to row. He had no idea in which direction England lay. A man in the bow, lying on his stomach with his head nearly in the water, kept repeating, "See that star? That's where you want to go." And he would point at the sky. In point of fact, they rowed for thirty hours, and they reached England.

They were so exhausted, sprawled on the ground, that women came to them and gently put bits of sugar in their mouths. They were taken to London, and in London they were housed in a jail—with all manner of politeness, but locked up, just the same, all day, except for two hours outside in the morning and two in the afternoon. After a week, their French colonel came to get them and take them back to France. They landed at Le Havre, where the Germans were just about to arrive. In spite of that, they were set to work unloading planes from a ship and loading them back on board again. Then quite suddenly the officers were nowhere to be seen. And so they built a raft with gasoline drums, and for two days they made their way down the coast. Out of all this adventure there remained in the Italian's mind a definite and dominant impression that he had been made a complete fool of, for he had volunteered to fight Fascism, and he had been left in the lurch on a road to nowhere.

I am convinced that, among the volunteers of the International Brigades in Spain, the Italians alone had the courage, between one battle and the next, to take a woman and have children—so irresistible is their instinct to take root and establish a family, in whatever country they may find themselves. For instance, there was Tommasi, the cook at the mess, a workman from Treviso, a serious boy, so serious that he looked like a preacher, who had brought a wife and child with him from Spain. The woman was now in the hospital with an eye disease, and, although he had no employment at all and not a penny in his pocket, he somehow managed to keep the child healthy and cleanly dressed.

Carletti's case was sadder still. His wife and child had been shot down beside him during the retreat from Catalonia. After that, in France, it had been the concentration camp: three thousand square yards, twelve hundred prisoners, iron discipline, for these people were "suspect." A policeman had once said, "You will never get me to believe that anyone who gets out of here is still a man." During the war, precisely in order to get out of there, Carletti had asked to enlist in one of the militarized labor battalions that had been organized with a view of putting these foreigners to some use, somewhere. They had been set to work building roads in the neighborhood of Dunkirk. Caught in the battle, each one had managed as best he could. For two whole weeks Carletti had stayed hidden in a shell hole, with an antitank girder above his head to shelter him from the bits of steel that were coming at him from every direction. At night he would go out to look for something to eat. Happily, there were trucks near by that the English had left behind; in them one could find a lot of first-rate provisions. Then the Germans had come and had put him, and the others, to work burying the corpses, digging pits and filling them with a layer of quicklime, a layer of corpses, quicklime and corpses, corpses and quicklime—for four days. In the end, identifying himself as a subject of the Axis powers, he had succeeded in getting his release and a pass to the unoccupied zone. But the Spaniards had been taken away to work in Germany. And that was another commodity found ready-made in France—thousands of men without a country, with whom one could do what one wanted in all tranquillity of mind.

Sometimes, sitting in the café, Carletti would try to explain what was deepest and innermost in his way of looking at such experiences. On these occasions he would recite in a low voice the poems of Gori. Gori's poetry cannot be found in any anthology; he flourished at the turn of the century, was the poet of Italian anarchism. Notably, he wrote a long poem that is a sort of rhapsody of anarchy—in *terza rima,* like *The Divine Comedy.* The poem sings the misery of the proletariat contrasted with the insolent opulence of the rich; the worker's pity for women whom the evil power of money has brought to ruin; the sanguinary attempts of obscurantism to put out the light—and the poem ends with a final vision of humanity's painful advance toward ultimate liberation. The whole thing is of a sentimentality so theatrical and so naïve that it ends by being poignant. Two generations of Italian proletarians were nourished by that poem, and its verses were passed on from mouth to mouth. Not that the words fully expressed what these men felt, but they expressed the essential element and character of their faith—which had much in common with the strong emotions men feel at some sudden turn in a play. The element of surprise in their drama was the appearance of hope on the horizon of simple and uneducated men who were unsatisfied and resigned. And that could also be expressed as their poet expressed it, by the Ideal, written across the skies in great flaming letters. As for the language, it was the language of grand opera, the only form with which they had some familiarity. Then, too, there had been no one to speak for them in more delicate terms. Gori was the poet of anarchy. The "Worker's Hymn," written by honest Filippo Turati, the prophet of reformism, expresses in slightly more prosaic words, and in slightly worse verse, exactly the same world of feeling—simple, clumsy, and dressed in its Sunday best.

This was the nature of the ideal that, for twenty years and all across the world, Francesco Loprete had carried faithfully with him, from his native Apulia to Buenos Aires, back to Apulia, then on to the trenches of the Carso, from there into prison, and from prison into civilian life—just long enough to breathe once or twice—and then again to the prison cell and the wardens. That was an Italian odyssey—complete. It was in Toulouse, as it happened, that I received a postcard from him. It came from the Vernet concentration camp, and it said, "I hope that you are all right and that all our friends are all right, too. I would like to tell you what it's like here—and someday I hope I will tell you. I am very hungry. All my best wishes to you and to our friends." And then came another postcard, from the "Campo di Concentramento di Polizia di Fabriano (Ancona) Italia." When the Italian Armistice Commission had passed through Vernet and asked the detainees whether they wanted to return to Italy, Loprete had opted for Italy, the more readily because the Italians had been promised that in Italy they would not be bothered by the police—a promise in which he probably put little faith, but still . . . concentration camp for concentration camp, it made little difference.

He had come to see me in Paris in the fall of 1938. He was just out of prison—eight months in France, six months in prison, because he had no papers. He had not been able to stay in Milan; he was arrested every two weeks for the simple reason that, having once been convicted as a "subversive," he could get no work. Since he was not working, they arrested him for vagrancy, and if he found a way to earn a few lire selling fruit or flowers on the streets he was arrested for violation of police regulations. And so one day he had set off on foot for Switzerland, carrying in his pocket a sample of the bread the government gave people to eat in Italy, a sample to show to the anti-Fascists in Paris, who would write something about it in their newspapers. He had gotten to France, but only to be arrested as soon as he set foot in Belfort. After serving his time, things had gone fairly well—from 1938 to 1939; he had even found work, and he began to feel once again at ease with the world. But when war is declared, a foreigner without papers risks serious trouble. Someone advised him to go to the authorities and offer his services for the duration. And so he did, but they arrested him and gave him six months in jail. Always for the same reason. What annoyed him most in retrospect was having made the great mistake of offering to enlist. This time, again, he carried away the "evidence": a little fold of paper in which he had placed three worms found in the prison bread. That was in February 1940. At the beginning of May, he was offered work as a farmhand in the neighborhood of Versailles, for French farms were short of help. All he needed now were proper papers, and finally, when he had his contract signed and in order, it seemed certain that he would get them. He applied to the prefecture at Versailles; he was arrested and sent off to the concentration camp at Vernet.

All this seems like an entirely exceptional sequence of misfortunes. But it is exactly the kind of misfortune provided for poor devils born in southern Italy; fate seems to have settled the pattern once and for all.

I am certain that today, in the concentration camp at Fabriano, Francesco Loprete, obstinate as a stone, is waiting for things to change. In other words, he is awaiting the millennium. Only he would like to have his friends write to him. For that would help him to think—as he puts it.

Commonweal, October 31, 1941
(Trans. Anon.)

4

Paris 1951

I am writing this piece on a desk I had to buy two years ago at the flea market, because the object you are most unlikely to find in a furnished apartment in Paris (or in a hotel room, for that matter) is a comfortable desk, that is, a surface stable enough to stand the thumping of the typewriter and sufficiently large to allow for a minimum of disorder: the blank paper, a couple of magazines, the ash tray and cigarettes. I need a pencil to mark something down I want to include in this "letter," I open the right-hand drawer, and I am seized by a familiar feeling of nausea. There are three or four pencil stubs, a piece of seersucker material, blotting paper, envelopes, a couple of those tiny notebooks from the Forty-second Street five-and-ten. In a few days, all this will have to be collected and packed, together with the rest of our odds and ends. We have to move, for the third time in twelve months. The first time, it was because of the greed of a high-class bitch who had found an American diplomat willing to pay three times as much as we did for the apartment. The second time the separation was amiable and agreed upon in advance. This time, it is the City of Paris itself that forces us out. Nothing doing. It is written in the statutes: no subletting. We are subletting, of course, like two-thirds of the foreigners who have come to Paris after the war (the other third being made up of those who can afford to buy a place or pay a lot of money for the *pas de porte*—"key money," that is). We are in a flagrant state of delinquency, and even more so is the old lady who was counting on the money we gave her every month to pay for her room and board, and who now will have an apartment and no board, while we have to look frantically for another opportunity to commit the same offense.

The case is purely academic. No individual greed is involved. There will be no profit for anybody, except for the prestige of the written rules of the HBM, the Habitations Bon Marché, an institution founded by the City of Paris in 1920, at a time when the administration was not so administrative and, in addition to enforcing rules, built a number of moderately priced apartment houses. Strict rules were then set forth, and never suspended or modified thereafter. It has merely become impossible to find a place to live without violating some law. But *Lex Vincit Tempus*, threateningly says the inscription carved on the building of the Police Judiciaire, Quai des Orfèvres. We shall move out.

This business of moving in and out gives me nausea, as though I were living on some wretched boat and not in this most lovable city. I have no desire to write, or read, or talk, or do anything at all, except lie down on the couch and dream of wilderness: Arizona, Lower California, Patagonia. But even Long Island would do, or anyplace that was at least fifty miles from the crowds—and the rules. I wonder why I am living in Paris at all. What do I get out of it?

I get *Le Figaro* every morning, plus another paper, preferably a leftist one, to strike the balance and puzzle onlookers, since the paper you buy in Paris is not just a paper, but also a flag and an ensign. I used to get *Combat*. But *Combat*'s third reincarnation, under Louis Pauwels, is so discolored that I now get *Aurore* and *Franc-Tireur*, by turns. The first gives me the best crime reportage, much better than the *Daily*

Mirror's in dramatic value. Two of the stories, lately, were excellent.

One was the story of the *machine à étrangler*. A *rentière* in her fifties had rented a villa she owned in the Midi to a Monsieur in his late forties. The Monsieur was *très bien,* since he paid a high rent with admirable regularity. One day, he sent the lady a letter offering to buy the villa. The *rentière* was enchanted and went to talk things over with the gentleman right away. They met in the *salon,* debated the price, agreed. Then Monsieur took out of a drawer the *machine à étrangler.* The contraption was both simple and ingenious; it consisted of the revolving drum of a Colt to which a piece of steel wire of a convenient length was attached. Monsieur explained to Madame how the thing worked: the wire was passed in the form of a noose around the throat of the patient, then in the proper way around his arms and chest, the length of the whole, and especially of the noose, being automatically controlled by the revolving drum in such a way as to strangle the person in question as soon as a certain peg had been reached. Keeping the upper part of his body still, except to breathe, was vital for a person wearing such an ornament. Clear?

And now would Madame mind following Monsieur out into the garden? In the garden was a shack, all padded inside. There Madame remained locked for three days, without food or drink. The third day Monsieur came back and proceeded to the application of the *machine à étrangler* to Madame's exhausted body. Thereafter, the poor *rentière* appears to have become nothing but an inert instrument of the criminal's plans. She was forced to call her lawyer and instruct him to send all her stocks and bonds to the bank; then, still shackled, she had to go to the bank, sell her property, and collect the money. After which the couple went to a restaurant, where the inventor of the strangling machine had a good lunch, while his victim didn't dare move a finger. Finally, the two went back to the villa, where Madame was, at last, released from the fearful shackles, sworn to secrecy, and set free, while Monsieur simply stayed on. Back home at her sisters', the poor woman remained dumb for two days. The third day, the truth burst from her lips. The police went to the villa, found the gentleman and his machine, took both away. A few days later, the inventor of the *machine à étrangler* committed suicide in his cell by hanging himself with his bedsheets.

Many aspects of this story seem to me typically French: the laborious cleverness of the conception; the ingenuity that went into the construction of the crazy homemade gadget; the rigorous simplicity, and even cleanliness, of the execution. But, above all, the story is a little masterpiece of sadistic imagination. No physical violence was employed at any moment, only psychological terror. The problem was how to crush a woman's will in order to achieve a definite purpose. It was solved successfully. If, as some people might suspect, sexual charm and seduction were used to bolster the prestige of the diabolical machine, that was not against the rules, was it?

The second story was about the dangers involved in trespassing on French property. The proprietor of one of those *petites villas* that make up so large a part of the *banlieue* of Paris, and of which the equal in bare ugliness exists nowhere on earth, realized, on one of his weekend visits to his domain, that the house, *his* house, the painfully acquired appurtenance of his Ego, had been violated by burglars, or, rather, one should say "intruders," since nothing serious was missing except some *apéritif*. Three soiled glasses on a *tabouret* and some mud on the carpet bore witness to the defilement. The following week, the same profanation had obviously been repeated. One can easily imagine the rage of the insulted proprietor, alone in his desecrated home, hissing like an infuriated cobra at the phantoms of those three bums. The fact is that he went out, bought a bottle of Pernod and a good dose of strychnine, poured the strychnine into the Pernod, and left for Paris and his office desk. The third week, he had the satisfaction of seeing the usual three soiled glasses on the *tabouret*, and the Pernod bottle half-empty near them. Triumphantly he went to the police, to tell them that if they wanted to arrest three roaming burglars all they had to do was to look in the Paris hospitals for cases of poisoning by strychnine. One of the delinquents was thus discovered. He was one of those wretched Algerians who starve and sometimes also rob and kill in the streets of Paris. He was dying.

Newspaper reports of the occurrence were remarkable in that most of them did not seem to consider that, by pronouncing the death penalty against the drinkers of his Pernod and by applying it on his own, the worthy *petit propriétaire* had clearly gone beyond the limits of the legitimate defense of his property. Only *Franc-Tireur* published a humanitarian protest against such excesses. But, after all, has not a *propriétaire*, in his own house, the right to put strychnine, or curare, or hell-fire, if he wishes, in his own Pernod? And can any power on earth restrain the passion aroused in a French heart by the violation of his own individual right to private pleasure, private property, and privacy unlimited?

Every evening I read *Le Monde*, easily the best newspaper in continental Europe. *Le Monde* has taken the place of *Le Temps*. The difference between the two papers is symptomatic indeed. *Le Temps* was the organ of the Quai d'Orsay and the Comité des Forges, well informed, austere, and corrupt. Deciphering its editorials required a preliminary period of training in reading between the lines. If you graduated from it, *Le Temps* would give you a daily glimpse into the secrets of the powers that be. During the fever that preceded Munich, and in 1939–1940, if one had not been carried away by emotions and just reasoned on the assumption that *Le Temps* did, indeed, represent official France, one could have predicted step by step the behavior of the French ruling class up to Pétain. *Le Monde* is a very different kind of paper. It is a liberal Catholic organ, and rather on the intellectual side at that, as is shown by the fact that some of its most important comments on current events (those on "neutrality" in particular)* were written by Etienne Gilson, the Thomist scholar. It does not exactly represent either the Quai d'Orsay or vested interests, or, for that matter, the high bourgeoisie, although, of course, it is perfectly respectful of all these institutions. If it is the organ of a class, *Le Monde* is, or means to be, the organ of the intellectual part of the bourgeoisie: professors, professional men, cultivated business people, and also a certain fringe of the ruling class, temperate but nevertheless critical of present policies. Its editorials summarize a topical question, rather than express a definite opinion on it. Not having a fixed policy, *Le Monde* can let a variety of opinions be expressed in its columns. The range of this variety, however, is revealing. The publication of Gilson's articles on neutrality was significant indeed. And so was that of a number of strong criticisms of the Indochina policy. Finally, *Le Monde* is the organ of a liberal bourgeois opposition, which is dissatisfied with the present state of affairs while perfectly aware that it has no immediate solution to offer. Hence, it waits, it sees, and, from time to time, it sends up cer-

* The policy of neutrality between the Soviet and American blocs. —Ed.

tain trial balloons, like those on neutrality and against rearmament. The moods of this opposition deserve to be watched attentively, because they are much more serious than, let's say, Monsieur Moch's proposals on German rearmament. In any case, *Le Monde* is a civilized paper. It goes very well with the Fourth Republic, the first of the four in which the republican principle itself goes unchallenged, but also the first that has no conquering faith and no vision of the future. Hence, some people feel it should at least stick to reasonableness and dignity of style.

But neither the newspapers nor the level of political life, neither the literary magazines nor literary and artistic life, would be sufficient reasons to remain in Paris for more than a few weeks. I am stuck here, that is the truth. I am stuck because I can't get rid of the thought, conceived many years ago, that if something unexpectedly human happens in history, it must either happen here or find here its true significance, its most appropriate dramatic form. That's it. I am fascinated by the French stage, by the way the French, all of them, from the concierge to the Sorbonne professor and the famous actress herself, act out the comedy of life. Everyone with complete conviction and with nothing held back, always in the limelight, everyone demanding the same fidelity to the role from himself and from the whole cast, and everyone suppressing ruthlessly the superfluous, any impulse that does not fit into the plot as it develops. Looked at from a certain angle, French civilization appears as a fabric woven of three main threads: the School, the Office, and the Theater. Everything that has to do with knowledge and the formation of the individual belongs to the School. Everything that concerns material life is taken care of by bureaucratic order. The Theater is the final result, embracing all that pertains to social life and to life *tout court*. It is the most important part, the ultimate test of the whole.

Having observed the French play the comedy of life with a seemingly total absence of innocence, serious persons have again and again repeated that the French are a frivolous people, all artifice and insincerity. And it might well be true, in the sense that artifice and insincerity might be the price the French pay for their virtues, just as other people get crudity and muddle in exchange for their spontaneity. If the French are wrong, however, they are wrong in a very big way. Taking life as a play in which one is called to impersonate remorselessly a role entirely his own is a very serious and very radical attitude. It means to be thoroughly committed, but with a vengeance that is human. The only serious objection is that comedy will inevitably be the result, never tragedy. At least, not tragedy in the Sophoclean sense. Also, a certain kind of wonder is dispelled, since the meaning of the whole show is somewhat taken for granted so that one can proceed with the plot, as it were.

Marivaux has been the fashion in Paris for some time, both at Barrault's and at the Comédie-Française. Now, I am afraid, the vulgarization has come, with Anouilh's latest play, *La Répétition, ou l'amour puni.* It is the music-box perfection of Marivaux's plays, in fact their rigorous thinness, that attracts the contemporary spectator. There is more substance than that, however, and more poetry, in Marivaux's eighteenth-century chitchat. In a review of his second *Surprise de l'amour,* Thierry Maulnier attempted a parallel between Marivaux and Choderlos de Laclos and went so far as to mention Sade. Marivaux, it seems to me, is neither cynical nor cruel. But he is pitiless, in that he cares only for the rules of the game and for grace. The game is life, and it cannot but take the form of a play, since its rules concern polite society and it states that as soon as a sensitive person (one who is supposed to be motivated by feeling, desire, and love of life; notice, not of the social scene) begins to express himself, he starts a plot of whose development he is not the master, a game whose rules he must obey to the last if he wants to win, or, rather, to be happy. The most charming show now on at the Comédie-Française is Marivaux's *La Double Inconstance*. It is the quintessence of Marivaux. The play is about Harlequin and Sylvia, who are young and in love, a real, natural, absolute love. But do they know what they have started by being in love? They don't. They think the plot of life begins and ends with their mutual love. It is their only fault, and it is sweetly punished in the end by Sylvia's falling into the arms of the Prince and Harlequin's embracing Flaminia. It all began with love, and went from love to love. The same tune, but, from variation to variation, another melody was born.

I wonder whether, listening to Marivaux, Hamlet would mutter, "Words, words, words."

As for Anouilh's play, it is modern *marivaudage* around Marivaux. Some highly improbable, although entirely up-to-date, people in a *château* are staging *La Double Inconstance* for the entertainment of their neighbors. While they are rehearsing, the same plot that develops musically and sweetly in Marivaux takes place harshly, and with all sorts of jarring nastiness, among the "real" characters. It is a highly polished piece of theatrical work, clever, shrewd, witty, and everything, but much less spirited and inventive than Anouilh's previous plays, and finally pointless because so much more pretentious.

Published as "Paris Letter,"
Partisan Review, January–February, 1951

5

Albert Camus

A man is dead: you think of his living face, of his gestures, his actions, and of moments you shared, trying to recapture an image that is dissolved forever. A writer is dead: you reflect upon his work, upon each book, upon the thread that ran through them all, upon their vital movement toward a deeper meaning; and you seek to form a judgment that takes account of the secret source from which they sprang and which is now stilled. But the picture of the man is not made up of the sum of your memories; nor the figure of the writer of the sum of his works. And one cannot discover the man through the writer, or the writer through the man. Everything is fragmentary, everything is incomplete, everything is the prey of mortality even when destiny seems to have granted both man and writer the gift of living to the limit of his forces, and of giving everything humanly possible, as in the case of Tolstoy. The story of a man is always incomplete; it is sufficient to think of what could have been different—almost everything—to know that his story can never contain the meaning of a human life, but only what that existence was permitted to be and to give. The truth was the living presence; and nothing can replace it. Immortality is an illusion for thought and art, as for man. They are nothing but relics mutely surviving time's erosion and history's disasters, like monuments of stone. But it is in this very fragility—which equates the humblest existence with the one that we falsely call "great" and is simply one that had the luck to express itself—that there lies the meaning and value of human life. And that value is eternal.

Albert Camus appeared in my life in April 1941, in Algiers, where I had come as a refugee from France. I met him soon after my arrival, for in Algeria he was famous: the leader of a group of young journalists, aspiring writers, students, friends of the Arabs, enemies of the local bourgeoisie and Pétain. They lived together, passed the days on the seashore or hillside and the evenings playing records and dancing, hoping for the victory of England and giving vent to their disgust with what had happened to France and to Europe. They also put on plays, and in that period were preparing a production of *Hamlet* in which Camus, in addition to directing, played the leading role opposite the Ophelia of his wife, Francine.

He had published a volume of prose poems entitled *Noces*, they told me. I did not read it, not because in those days I was not in the mood for prose poems, but chiefly because his company and the company of his friends was enough. In their midst I found the France I loved and the pure, clear warmth of French friendship. I attended the rehearsals of *Hamlet*, went to the beach with them, took walks with them, talking about what was happening in the world. Hitler had just occupied Greece, and the swastika waved over the Acropolis. I suffered continual nausea and solitude in the face of these events. But, solitary and shut off as I was, I was the guest of those young people. To know the value of hospitality one must have been alone and homeless.

I try to recall details, as if through them I could relive those days and learn something more about the young writer with whom I actually spoke little, since he felt no more like talking than I. I remember being totally obsessed by a single thought: we had arrived at humanity's zero hour, and history was senseless; the only thing that made sense was that part of man which remained outside of history, alien and impervious to the whirlwind of events. If, indeed, such a part existed. I considered this thought my exclusive privilege; I felt that no one else could be so possessed by it; yet I yearned for someone to share it with. But there was no one. It was not an idea compatible with normal life, let alone with literature—or so it seemed to me.

However, I did have something in common with this twenty-eight-year-old writer—love of the sea, joy of the sea, ecstatic admiration of the sea. I discovered this one day when I was his guest at Oran and we went by bicycle to a deserted beach beyond Mers-el-Kebir. We spoke little even then, but we praised the sea, which does not have to be understood, which is inexhaustible, and which never palls. All other beauty does, we agreed. This agreement sealed our friendship. Camus told me then that he was writing a tragedy about Caligula, and I tried to understand what could attract a modern writer to such a subject. Unfettered tyranny? But contemporary tyranny did not seem to me to have much in common with Caligula's.

From Oran I continued my journey to Casablanca, from where I had been told I could embark for New York. I said good-bye to Camus and his wife, knowing that we had exchanged the gift of friendship. At the core of this friendship was something very precious, something unspoken and impersonal that made itself felt in the way they received me and in our way of being together. We had recognized in each other the mark of fate—which was, I believe, the ancient meaning of the encounter between stranger and host. I was being chased from Europe; they remained, exposed to the violence that had driven me out. I carried away with me the impression of a man who could be almost tenderly warm one moment and coolly reserved the next, and yet was constantly longing for friendship.

I saw him again in New York, in 1946, on the pier where I had gone to meet his ship. I saw him like a man coming straight from the battlefield bearing its marks, pride and sorrow. By that time I had read *L'Etranger, Le Mythe de Sisyphe,* and *Caligula.* In those black years the young man from Algeria had fought and conquered. He had become, together with Jean-Paul Sartre, the symbol of a defeated France, which because of them had imposed itself victoriously in its chosen domain—intelligence. He had won his position on the stage of the world; he was famous; his books were brilliant. But to me he had conquered in a more important sense. He had faced the question that I considered crucial and that had so absorbed me during the days when I first met him. He had mastered it and carried it to extreme and lucid conclusions. He had succeeded in saying, in his fevered way and in an argument as taut as a bow, why, despite the fury and horror of history, man is an absolute; and he had indicated precisely where, according to him, this absolute lay: in the conscience, even if mute and stilled; in remaining true to one's self even when condemned by the gods to repeat over and over the same vain task. In this lay the value of *L'Etranger* and *Le Mythe de Sisyphe* for me.

With an almost monstrous richness of ideas and vigor of reasoning Sartre had said something similar. But when he arrived at the question of the connection between man and history today, between man and the choices that impose themselves today, Sartre seemed to have lost the thread of his reasoning, to have turned backward to realism, to categorical obligations imposed on man from the outside, and, worse, to notions of the politically opportune. Camus held firm, at the risk of exposing himself, defenseless, to the criticism of the dialecticians and of seeming to pass brusquely from logic to emotive affirmation. It is certain that what induced him to remain firm was not an ideological system, but the sentiment, so vehemently expressed in *L'Etranger* and in some pages of *Le Mythe de Sisyphe,* of the inviolable secret that is enclosed in every man's heart simply because he is "condemned to die." That is man's transcendence. That is man's transcendence in respect to history; that is the truth that no social imperative can erase. Desperate transcendence and truth, because they are challenged in the very heart of man, who knows that he is mortal and eternally guilty, with no recourse against destiny. Absurd such transcendence and truth—but, absurd as they were, they were reborn every time Sisyphus descended "with heavy, but equal, steps, toward the torment whose end he would never approach. . . ." This secret, like the "eternal jewel" of Macbeth, can never be compromised or violated without sacrilege.

Albert Camus had known how to give form to this feeling and to remain true to it. Because of this, his presence added to everybody's world, making it more real and less insensate. And because of this, not of his fame, the young writer from Algeria had "grown" in my eyes, worthy not only of friendship but also of admiration. It was no longer a matter of literature, but of directly confronting the world. Literary space, that *trompe l'oeil* that had been invented in the nineteenth century to defend the individual artist's right to be indifferent, was broken. Camus (and, in his very different way, Sartre), by the simple act of raising the question of the value of existence, asserted the will to participate actively, in the first person, in the world; that is, to challenge directly the actual situation of contemporary man in the name of a conscience whose rigor was not attenuated by pragmatic considerations. With this, one might say, he returned to the *raison d'être* of writing. Putting the world in question means putting oneself in question and abandoning the artist's traditional right to remain separate from his work—a pure creator. In the language of Camus, this signifies that if the world is absurd, the artist must live immersed in the absurd, must carry the burden of it, and must seek to prove it *for the others*.

This was the real and the only valid meaning of *engagement*. Such a choice carried within itself the threat of the cancerous negation that Camus called nihilism. One had to go through the experience of nihilism and fight it. The simplest act of life is an act of affirmation; it is the acceptance of one's own and others' lives as the starting point of all thinking. But living by nihilism is living on bad faith, as a bourgeois lives on his income.

In 1946 Camus was invited to speak to the students of Columbia University, in New York. I have kept notes of his talk, and am sure I can reconstruct it without betraying his meaning. The gist of the speech was as follows:

We were born at the beginning of the First World War. As adolescents we had the crisis of 1929; at twenty, Hitler. Then came the Ethiopian War, the Civil War in Spain, and Munich. These were the foundations of our education. Next came the Second World War, the defeat, and Hitler in our homes and cities. Born and bred in such a world, what did we believe in? Nothing. Nothing except the obstinate negation in which we were forced to close ourselves from the very beginning. The world in which we were called to exist was an absurd world, and there was no other in which we could take refuge. The world of culture was beautiful, but it was not real. And when we found ourselves face to face with Hitler's terror, in what values could we take comfort, what values could we oppose to negation? None. If the problem had been the bankruptcy of a political ideology or a system of government, it would have been simple enough. But what had happened came from the very root of man and society. There was no doubt about this, and it was confirmed day after day not so much by the behavior of the criminals but by that of the average man. The facts showed that men deserved what was happening to them. Their way of life had so little value; and the violence of the Hitlerian negation was in itself logical. But it was unbearable, and we fought it.

Now that Hitler has gone, we know a certain number of things. The first is that the poison which impregnated Hitlerism has not been eliminated; it is present in each of us. Whoever today speaks of human existence in terms of power, efficiency, and "historical tasks" spreads it. He is an actual or potential assassin. For if the problem of man is reduced to any kind of "historical task," he is nothing but the raw material of history, and one can do anything one pleases with him. Another thing we have learned is that we cannot accept any optimistic conception of existence, any happy ending whatsoever. But if we believe that optimism is silly, we also know that pessimism about the action of man among his fellows is cowardly.

We opposed terror because it forces us to choose between murdering and being murdered; and it makes communication impossible. This is why we reject any ideology that claims control over all of human life.

It seems to me today that in this speech, which was a sort of autobiography, there were all the themes of Camus's later work, from *La Peste* to *Les Justes* to *L'Homme révolté*. But in it there remained, discreetly in shadow, the other Camus, the one that I can call neither truer nor artistically superior, for he is simply "the other," jealously hidden in his secret being—the anguished, dark, misanthropic Camus, whose yearning for human communication was perhaps even greater than that of the author of *La Peste;* the man who, in questioning the world, questioned himself, and by this testified to his own vocation. This is the Camus of the last pages of *L'Etranger,* and especially the Camus of *La Chute,* in which we hear his deepest being, the self-tormenting tormentor, speak, resisting all forms of complacency and moral self-satisfaction. He wrote, "I was persecuted by a ridiculous apprehension: one cannot die without having confessed all one's own lies . . . otherwise, be there one hidden untruth in a life, death would render it definitive . . . this absolute assassination of the truth gave me vertigo. . . ." With these words, it seems to me, the dialogue of Albert Camus with his contemporaries, truncated as it is by death, is nonetheless complete.

Dissent, Summer 1960
(Trans. Miriam Chiaromonte)

6

The Student Revolt

Some three years ago, in an article in *Tempo Presente* called "Rebellious Youth," I came to the conclusion that only one thing seems to have shaken the political inertia that characterizes our age and to have aroused political passions and a real sense of participation; and that is the idea of freedom. The Hungarian uprising, directed by intellectuals and fought by the young and the very young in the name of unadorned freedom, was the main and most memorable example of this. Before that there was Poznan and the "Polish October," where, in the main, intellectuals and young people were demanding their freedom. In Italy, there was July 1960; more significantly, there was the upsurge of action and opinion in France against the Algerian war. Then, in July 1963, there was the miners' strike in Asturias, in which the demand for freedom of association and of speech was raised before the question of wages, and was much the more important demand. And I also dealt at length in that article with the revolt of American students against racism and the war in Vietnam.

It was perfectly clear that freedom was again the leaven in the political struggle, and that the young find themselves quite naturally in the vanguard of the movement, without waiting for the politicians to finish their calculations, organize their tactics, and put out their slogans.

But I felt that it was not enough to rejoice that a

wave of rebellion (or rebelliousness), rather than some "realistic" conformity, seemed to have engulfed young people immediately after the war: "We must also consider each manifestation of rebellion case by case. . . ."

All right, then, let us consider what is happening in this rebellion of the young—and not only of students. Since 1965 it has spread across Europe, indeed, across the world, from North and South America to China; in China, with the approval of its intellectual hotheads and hangers-on, the remarkable event known as the "Cultural Revolution" has increasingly appeared to be an astute operation intended to unleash the rebelliousness of the young against the party machine, to the greater glory and support of Chairman Mao, and with the army to prevent things getting too much out of hand. In Europe, the young are in revolt in nearly all the countries of both East and West, including Scandinavia and Britain, on the one hand, and the Soviet Union and Poland, on the other.

But we must distinguish between these various forms of rebellion and consider their differences.

First, the Russian students' and intellectuals' protests against the regime's repressive refusal to listen and the open revolt of students, teachers, and intellectuals in Warsaw, to the cry of "freedom," are not at all the same as the uprisings of students in Turin, Milan, Florence, and Rome against their respective vice-chancellors, teachers, and ministers, even though the Italian students may challenge the whole of society in their slogans and manifestoes, may talk about a "total rejection," refuse what they call "concessions," and declare their wish to change everything from top to bottom, independently, with their own methods and according to their own standards. The freedom the Polish students are demanding is a clear, specific challenge to a clearly and specifically oppressive regime; whereas the "global confrontation" the Italian and German students are talking about is a formula as vague as it is violent. If we are speaking of the universities, then a challenge to their academic power means, at most, asking for the students' direct participation in discussions and decisions that affect their studies. Whereas if we are speaking of society as a whole—"the famous consumer society"—then "total rejection" means rebellion against everything and against nothing.

In fact, apart from their extremely significant refusal to accept guidance from the political parties, what the rebellious Italian students seem to be protesting against is mainly the war in Vietnam, and what they approve of are men and events wholly alien to the situation, both educational and political, in Italy—men like Guevara and Castro, or exotic figures like Mao Tse-tung. Freedom, in fact, is the last thing they consider or even care about.

On the other hand, apart from violent clashes with the police (sometimes deliberately sought) and painfully confused stands taken by members of the academic establishment—who are either warily submissive or toughly determined (and occasionally both, in quick succession)—the students have done as they pleased, and continue to do so. One is still waiting to see what direction their revolt is going to take and what objects it really aims at, and not merely who is going to lead it and in what direction. But it is obvious that there is no question of seeking freedom—rather, its opposite: anger at the lack of authority and at the lack of any established order that commands respect.

We have yet to see what the Italian students are capable of doing, after this great wave of revolt in which indignation against the scandalous conditions of the universities and of schooling in general in Italy, and against the brutality and madness of the American war in Vietnam, went with a cult (not unlike that of film-star fans) of Che Guevara and an enthusiasm for Mao Tse-tung, a dictator and thinker whose authority stems more from his power of command than from any qualities of his thought. It is impossible not to see in this revolt, however, an urge toward violence fatally combined with the idea of obtaining, at once and through direct action, what it is impossible to obtain at once and through direct action—namely, the reform of education and the reform of society. Impossible, that is, without total guidance by the hand of a dictator—and where that leads we know all too well.

The Italian students may have been doing as they pleased, but they have used this freedom of theirs for serious ends—or, at least, they are meant to be serious. Their revolt was a result of their anger toward and contempt for a so-called ruling class that primarily rules the affairs of the political parties into which it is divided and subdivided; and in this it was fully justified. But until now theirs have been mass riots, in which the voice of reason was drowned; and anyone who wanted to know what the whole thing was about had to go and listen to individuals, one by one.

But why was the students' revolt so confused, both in its ideas (or, rather, in its slogans) and in its behavior? It was justified by the facts, in particular by the Italian Parliament's shameful refusal to pass the reform that would have abolished the most scandalous privilege in present-day Italian universities—the right of deputies, senators, and ministers to hold academic chairs purely for prestige. Was it because of their youth? We are told to understand and not dis-

courage the muddled enthusiasm of the young (because if we discourage it this means we want everything to continue as it is, corrupt, inert, torpid). And
so we should, on condition that we reject absolutely
the idea that the young must be right simply because
they are young. It was on this principle that Fascism
advanced, and something equally evil might grow out
of it today, whether its label is socialist, anarchist, or
simply humanitarian. We have already had the star-
tling spectacle of teachers in their fifties rushing to
join the rioting young, urging them on to "total rejection" and even to violence, in the certainty that they
are marching with history.

But the young are in revolt not merely to reform
the universities. As they themselves admit, their protest goes further than that. Indeed, it seems likely that
the wretched conditions of education in Italy today,
the teaching cliques, the academic charlatanism, the
physical impossibility of following courses or even of
seeing the professor's face except at exams, are all
secondary reasons, excuses for rebellion, rather than
its primary cause. That lies elsewhere, and it is, I
think, very simple: it is the fact that the young—those
born after 1940—find themselves living in a society
that neither commands nor deserves respect, a society
whose authority merely weighs on them and so seems
to license every kind of lawlessness and rebellion,
open or covert. This is so from the top of the social
hierarchy (if there is still such a thing, apart from a
hierarchy of power) down to the forms of political life
and the circumstances of everyday Italian life. But the
most irresponsible and corrupt group of all is, I would
say unhesitatingly, today's intellectuals. They follow
the crowd instead of setting an example, quibble instead of thinking, offer political factionalism instead
of critical guidance, hold forth on undigested ques-

tions of ideology, and, in fact, instead of acting as the voice of a people of which they are part, themselves make up a special party, one that furthers their own particular aims and needs.

It is against this lack of moral guidance and of an authority worth respecting that young people are rebelling today, all over the world; and it is a serious matter, not to be answered by police attacks or tricky maneuvers. This explains why, in the absence of anyone or anything to respect—and of an authority that can be either respected or hated, but which at least exists—the Italian young, like the young in France or Germany, create exotic myths out of Che and Ho and Mao. These myths are by their very nature either empty or totalitarian; they lead either to nothing or to mass demagogy and, sooner or later, to a technocratic authoritarianism cloaked in ideology. This authoritarianism—which is today's, *not* yesterday's or the day before yesterday's, which is generally called up as a bogey—does not even demand a charismatic leader; all it needs is the existing state of affairs, the endless complexity, the vast inertia, and the enormous, almost supernatural authority of industrial society, a society borne up not so much by the *capitalists,* as the current cliché maintains, as by the very ideas to which those in revolt have appealed. For has modern man, in his collective existence, laid claim to any god or ideal but the god of possession and enjoyment and the limitless satisfaction of material needs? Has he put forward any reason for working but the reward of pleasure and prosperity? Has he, in fact, evolved anything but this "consumer society" that is so easily and so falsely repudiated?

In these conditions, it is suspiciously romantic to talk about "revolution." How will it be achieved except by a *coup d'état* executed by a highly placed few, and in secret?

Are the young mistaken, then, in their revolt? No. But neither are they right. You can talk about right only when you talk reasonably, person to person. A rioting crowd never reasons, nor can it ever be right; it is an explosion and nothing more, an event that may have its proper causes and reasons and so logically cannot be either approved or disapproved except in detail, case by case, individual by individual. You do not approve of an earthquake; you try to clear things up afterward. But as regards the earthquake of which the revolt of the young is only *one* symptom, the present Italian ruling classes (indeed, the present rulers of the world in general, for the whole business is universal) show no sign of clearing anything up, only of aggravating the difficulties.

If there is a remedy at all, it lies elsewhere and is a very long-term one. In my view, it consists of a determined secession from a society (or, rather, from a state of affairs, since "society" implies a community and a purpose, which is exactly what collective life nowadays lacks) that is not actually evil by nature (indeed, may well be improved), but which is neither good nor bad, only indifferent—and that is the worst thing of all, and the most deadening. From this society—from this state of affairs—people must detach themselves, must become resolute "heretics." They must detach themselves without shouting or riots, indeed, in silence and secrecy; not alone but in groups, in real "societies" that will create, as far as is possible, a life that is independent and wise, not utopian or phalansterian, in which each man learns to govern himself first of all and to behave rightly toward others, and works at his own job according to the standards of the craft itself, standards that in themselves are the simplest and strictest of moral principles and, by their very nature, cut out deception and prevarication, charlatanism and the love of power and possession. This would not mean detaching oneself from either the life of like-minded others or the life of politics in the real sense of the word. It would be, all the same, a nonrhetorical form of "total rejection." The French student revolt, by sharply attacking the principle of centralized authority and demanding a reorganization of collective life from the ground up, has raised precisely this question.

Published as "Letter from Rome,"
Encounter, July 1968
(Trans. Anon.)

7

The Death of Gandhi

"You can wake a man who is really asleep;
if he is merely pretending your effort
will have no effect upon him."
—GANDHI

"The picture of that half-naked fakir ascending the Viceregal Palace makes me mad." The one so aggrieved was Winston Churchill, in 1931. But the intellectual, the ideologist, the politician, the priest, the "average man" of the West, all were mad at the "fakir," fundamentally all for the same reason. That man, Gandhi, fancied things to be too damn simple. Civil disobedience, nonviolence, the spinning wheel. You gather a crowd, walk to the seashore, go through the motions of breaking the Salt Law, get yourself arrested assuming that in the meantime the Viceroy is beginning to feel ashamed of himself, et cetera, et cetera. "It is inconsistent with Truth to use articles about which or about whose makers there is a possibility of deception. Therefore, for instance, a votary of Truth will not use articles manufactured in the mills of Manchester, Germany or India, for he does not know that there is no deception about them. Moreover, laborers suffer much in the mills. Use of fire in the mills causes enormous destruction of life besides killing laborers before their time. . . . Further reflection will show that use of such goods will involve a breach of the vows of non-stealing and non-possession," and so on, and so on. What a way of dealing with the problems of modern industry and capitalism! What backwardness! Life is not that simple. Not in the West. And the contrary assumption is very maddening.

Take the 1922 trial—Gandhi's telling the British judge: "The only course open to you is either to resign your post and to dissociate yourself from evil, if you feel that the law you are called upon to administer is evil and that in reality I am innocent; or to inflict on me the severest penalty if you believe that the system and the law you are assisting to administer are good for the people of this country and that my activity is therefore injurious to the public weal." He didn't get the severest penalty. He didn't get the judge to resign. He got six years and many expressions of respect. Does the performance remind one of the trial of Socrates? Well, that's the trouble with it. Simplicity, where the question is not simple. The British Empire is not Athens. The world is not a city-state, where the personal appeal might have some practical meaning. Suppose the judge had resigned. Would the system have been seriously affected? Would the Indian masses have been better off? Moreover, we know beforehand that in modern times judges do not resign or otherwise respond to ethical appeals. Because, as the British judge who sentenced Gandhi pointed out, they consider the law a rule to be applied for the sake of the regular functioning of a certain mechanism of which they themselves are part, and not at all as something connected with such metaphysical problems as good and evil. The mechanism might be defective, but until it is subjected to the proper changes, through the proper channels, it is the lesser evil. If you want to make it better, you have to get to work on the system as a whole, not on this or that changing aspect of it. Gandhi overlooked entirely this question of the system, which is the only rational one. His was a touching but simple-minded search for ethical effects. Good for the mystical East (but how good, really, is still a question for the social scientist to determine). As for us Westerners, we know only too well that our judges wouldn't even bother to be polite if we were taken before them and started raising questions. Moreover, we are not sure at all that we would know what questions to raise. Our situation is too complex. And we can only be convinced by a complex approach.

A parallel with Tolstoy will make the point clearer. Tolstoy was a great artist tortured by moral problems. He, too, was a simplifier. As Lenin has said, he was the great voice of the Russian peasantry, but unaware of the problems of the industrial proletariat. We know, however, that while preaching chastity he was harassing his wife with a most demanding lust; while excoriating the meat eaters he went to the kitchen at night to eat meat secretly; and he never succeeded in extricating himself from his social position as a famous writer, a landowner, and a pater-familias. This is complexity. We can sympathize both with the ethical effort and with his failure. Or we can smile at both. We can wonder and admire. In any case, we feel entitled to think that it would be wrong to take ethical responsibility too seriously, since Tol-stoy's example seems to prove that the ethical is no real independent dimension of life, only a name for contrasts that might be encountered but don't have to be solved, because apparently they are not susceptible of a real solution. Tolstoy's message of nonresistance to evil went completely unheeded among us, and in its native land it was answered by a holocaust of twenty million human lives just in order that the Russian proletariat might break its chains. It must be that Tolstoy's was an intellectual and aesthetic vision, rather than a moral truth or a possible social attitude. Nevertheless, it's nice that somebody in our midst should have had such thoughts. It enriches our culture. The conclusion does not make things any better for us or for our civilization. But it reinforces in us our dearest wisdom—to care without caring, and finally to trust the event for suggesting what our response to it shall be.

Gandhi is completely refractory to such considerations. In 1903, he took up "the problem of further simplifying my life and doing some concrete act of service to my fellow men," and from then on he cared unceasingly, and unremittingly did what he found to be right, which was always, in the last analysis, *the simplest*. He banked his life on one single idea: to *test* the force of Truth on man. An "experiment," as he said himself. To carry out the experiment, he exacted from himself and from others the most rigorous conditions he could conceive of. From chastity and vegetarianism to being beaten and jailed without resisting—that meant asceticism. And it is very apparent, when you read Gandhi, that to him asceticism was equivalent to an effort of the whole being to "simplify" further and further, in order to isolate with more and more rigor the core of the matter, the ultimate source of human energy, Truth, and to unleash as much as possible of it in acts. Is it too much to say that it is difficult to think of another man in all known history for whom thought and deed were so utterly inseparable as for Gandhi? Gandhi's God fed absolutely, not on mystical ecstasies, but exclusively on deeds, on what the Mahatma called "readiness to reduce principles to practice." And between his

God and his mission to make true men of four hundred million individuals, he drew absolutely no distinction. So that this absurd man, who declared himself "ready to die for the Cow," was nothing but a *political* man, a man all of whose thoughts and acts were for the sake of his immense community, and also a man who found value only in *common sense*, literally. So that there is poetic justice in his very death. He was not sentenced by a tribunal, not executed in the name of a state that had found him intolerable. Apparently, tribunals and governments could only be disconcerted in dealing with him and reacted mechanically according to the letter of the law. Only an individual, and one of his own people, could be made really angry and bloodthirsty by him, who in his turn professed to be nothing but an individual among so many. So a man was killed by a man. No protest is possible, no righteous indignation, no indictment of systems or institutions. We are just back where we started: the strife between man and Truth.

All this makes Gandhi profoundly unintelligible to us in the West. Not because he was a mystic, which he was not, but because he was such an utterly consistent, such an absurdly logical man and carried his own reasons to preterhuman extremes without ending in failure and bad conscience.

In spite of so many words of his, which were only simplified reiterations of ideas familiar to the West, Gandhi has no real message for us. Possibly only a single question.

"Are you really asleep?"

politics, Winter 1948

CRITICISM

8

Three Lines from Dante

Cosi la neve al sol si disigilla
Cosi al vento nelle foglie lievi
Si perdea la sentenza di Sibilla.

So does the snow unseal itself in the sun,
So in the wind on the light leaves
The Sibyl's utterance was lost.

Many will recognize these lines, 64–66 of Canto XXXIII of the *Paradiso*. They follow three tercets in which the poet has tried repeatedly to convey the impossibility of communicating or even of holding in memory the beatific vision of God procured for him by Mary through the intercession of Saint Bernard. And here the poet's fourth attempt ends in two images of consuming power and in three of the most beautiful, harmonious, and profound lines of the *Comedy*. What was to be conveyed—the inevitable oblivion—has finally been conveyed; and with it much more, as is always the case when a poet touches that height of rapture and abandon where words are transcended and almost swept away by the meanings they bear, while at the same time they begin to glow with their own light.

Without attempting to explain the beauty of these lines, let me try to discover the grounds for both the emotional and the magical power they exert. The first thing to be said is that if emotion and enchantment are alike "subjective" (in the sense that they are felt by us in the moment of our reading and cannot be compared with the emotion and magic another reader may feel), there is nevertheless nothing subjective about the lines' inherent poetic quality, their "beauty." When we read or repeat them to ourselves, their resonance, even in our own minds, may be different each time, or may vanish altogether, yet their actual quality, as we perfectly well know, remains unaffected. And we know that if the lines arouse a different emotion in others (and thus, in a sense, have a different resonance in every reading for every reader), this wide variability has a precise and objective limit in the verbal and melodic form of the lines and in their meaning, which is one (or tends infinitely toward unity), although the ways in which we may receive, interpret, and evaluate it are innumerable.

In other words, the lines exist in and for themselves and are totally resistant to distortion. Nobody could make us read them as a celebration of stability and permanence, and nobody could reduce them to pure evocative harmony independent of the meaning of the words. Yet these words—*neve, vento, foglie, disigillarsi, perdersi**—have in this context a value different from their usual instrumental one; and the difference is, in its turn, controlled by their necessary, rigorously clear ordering, which frees them from the equivocations of the common language and compels them to a single, unique significance, absolutely decisive in its indeterminacy. The tercet is truly an object in itself, independent of the echoes it may arouse in the mind of this or that reader at this or that time, and independent of the interpretations that may be made of it. In this sense we may treat it as a pure form. In

* Snow, wind, leaves, unsealed, lost.   —Ed.

this sense, too, it shares in what certain contemporaries tell us is the chief characteristic of the "modern" work of art, namely, existence as pure "object" without any other purpose than that of freely affecting sensibility. There is, however, an important difference. For, while modern art claims to have no reference to anything other than its own words or signs, the three lines in question here, though they transcend the world of ordinary meanings, do refer to a world we recognize as ours, if only by means of a luminous and meaningful image. In other words, Dante's lines convey a truth about the world of which they themselves are only a vague echo, or whose tangible aspect they seek to grasp by means of the tangible signs of words. We cannot say that of a work of modern art—at least, not of its explicit intent—since it presents itself as a special fact among other facts, thereby constituting its own truth.

But how do people read these lines today? In what frame of mind or spirit? The answer seems clear enough: generally as "pure" poetry, with the assumption that the values of sensibility outrank all others. Poetry is to be read and enjoyed for the emotions it arouses and for its manner of arousing them; the ideas, conceptions, and moral attitudes, as well as the social implications borne by all articulated expression, are secondary. Aesthetic theories aside, this is the way our culture has accustomed us to approach poetry. It is a legitimate and in some senses an inevitable way. It is, however, by no means a purely aesthetic one; rather, it is loaded with intellectual and moral presumptions, and perhaps even with a particular and complex world view, as I shall try to show.

The reader or critic who uses such an approach may find much to say about the beauty of the *Paradiso* verses. So much, in fact, that he may neglect altogether the rather dry context in which they emerge, like a sudden burst of pure lyric inspiration, out of the effort to express the inexpressible: the vision at once concrete and intellectual of the divine unity. But it is not only the theological-rhetorical context he may so neglect; it is also the immediate sense of the words. For, beyond the metaphor Dante uses to convey the inevitable fading of the vision, and beyond the image of dissolution and loss in the immensity of the world, we find a still vaster and more expansive meaning in those lines: all that passes away, every precious, fleeting moment, every effort to conquer time, every life, is comprehended and implied in those leaves inscribed by a divine impulse and lost on the wind as snow melts in the sun. And the two images coalesce into one, infinitely imbued with meaning while yet as elusive as the snow, the leaves, the hermetic utterance no human eye has ever read.

The relation between the several elements here—on the one hand, the lightness and variation of the images, and on the other the Aristotelian-Thomistic conception of the cosmos, Dante's faith, the *Comedy*'s structure—is obviously not a necessary one. It might, indeed, seem that if we are to feel to the full the magic of the verses, we ought to pay it no attention. Except that if we do so, in order to cull the perfect flower of pure poetry, we ignore the simple fact that these lines are placed *there, thus,* and in *that* context, and not otherwise. A like meaning expressed in a like manner might perhaps be found in other poetic contexts, but it could not possibly be found divorced from any context, in a "pure" state. To ignore that fact or try to circumvent it with aesthetic arguments is to single out one partial aspect of poetry (verbal magic and its resonances in the reader's mind) as though this were all.

The point is a delicate and important one, first, because, whether we are guided by aesthetic theory or not, we have, as I've said, been accustomed for some time to reading poetry this way; and, in the second place, because we do so without considering precisely what such an approach means. To abstract poetry from poetry in this fashion is not merely to try to isolate the poetic phenomenon for clearer identification and appreciation. It is also, and above all, to bestow on sensibility and its modes a primary importance among the mind's faculties and the modes of apprehending the world, and thus to make reason and intellect secondary. Such privileged placing of the "pure" aesthetic fact implies, as has been noted, a choice neither exclusively nor primarily aesthetic, but, rather, intellectual and moral, because based on a principle of preference for what is perceived by the senses. What concerns me here is not whether this choice is right or wrong, but that the quest for "pure" aesthetic quality is a consequence of such choice and not a primary and simple criterion. Such choice involves a conception of poetry as a reflection of real-life emotions and sympathies—a conception that remains substantially naturalistic even when it takes on rarefied and apparently intellectual forms, as in Mallarmé. The aesthetic criterion, then, aside from resting on a rather obvious sophism (art is to be judged as art), limits us to the surface of poetic form by the very fact that it confines itself to the sensuous resonance of language, assuming language to be an enclosed, self-sufficient object and not a conveyer of meaning. Pindar tells us that the music of the golden lyre heard by Zeus's eagle causes sleep to fall on the eyelids of the divine creature as he shudders with pleasure, "possessed by the magic of the sounds." But that isn't enough for man. Whatever the pleasure, the human mind cannot rest in it, nor in attention to the fact that begets it. The mind still feels a need to judge the sense and value of that fact, that is, to put it into proper relationship with everything else, with all experience, with the world's image as it appears to a man through his own experience.

And so that sense of universal transience that moves us so deeply in Dante's tercet, without requiring that we share either the religion or the philosophy of the poet, cannot be separated off, isolated, abstracted. Instead, it moves us all the more because it comes to us in just such a vision as Dante's, founded on the sense of eternity, on the changeless truth and unassailable stability of the order willed by God. Not only the pathos but the very beauty of the three lines arises from this contrast, just as the pathos and beauty of Francesca's canto are born of the contrast between the poet's stern recognition of divine justice and his limitless tenderness of compassion. But in the *Paradiso* tercet, as in Canto V of the *Inferno*, there is something more and different. Beyond dogma and theology and concern for the symmetry of the universe, there is direct and free contact with an aspect of the cosmos more stable and real than any dogma or architectural symmetry: the inconstancy of the mind —established in the one case through the sense of evanescence and in the other through the arcane, heavenly-earthly essence of amorous passion.

It is when poetry reaches such heights, passing beyond dry cogitation and religious, moral, or social prejudices, that, according to the aesthetic view, it becomes universal, absolute, and pure. Those heights are seen as the outer limits of the poet's own privileged sensibility, where the experiences of ordinary life—amorous passion, sense of the ephemeral, sense of immensity—acquire the luminosity, musicality, lightness with which the poet alone can clothe the rough material of existence. So viewed, poetry would consist in the transmutation into gold of the base lead of ordinary actions and words, and this conversion would be the subjective work of an extranormal sensibility and of an ability—a *techne*. It would correspond to nothing objective, but would stand as a shining and gratuitous addition to the world's facts.

Now, such an understanding of poetry, if it can to some extent be applied to forms based on sensibility, sensuality, and a certain egocentrism (as are, in a different way, romantic and symbolist poetry), is not only inadequate but also irrelevant to such poets as Dante and Shakespeare. Not because they are "great," but because their work is marked by the true characteristic of all authentic poetry: a mastery over the senses and feelings by the mind—by the *mind*, and not the *techne* alone—together with an immediate and substantial contact of mind with the being of things. The reality revealed by Dante and Shakespeare is not a sense-perceptible one, a summary of ordinary tangibles, nor is it a purely verbal one; it is an intelligible reality perceived only by the mind's eye, a real and permanent aspect of the world uniquely accessible to the intellect, as all meanings are.

Returning now to the *Paradiso* tercet, let us note its combination of natural facts—the snow, the sun, the melting of snow—with an image borrowed from the *Aeneid*, the Sibyl and her leaves lost in the wind. Such a combination is both typically Dantesque and characteristically medieval; but the precise placement of this pair in the poem is an essential cause of the emotion it stirs. Outside that context and apart from the struggle to express the inexpressible (an obstinate struggle, waged for an additional seventy-eight lines, in spite of the poet's initial admission that it cannot be won), the impact of the image would be feeble. It is as impossible to abstract it from its place in the final canto as from its cultural context.

How, finally, do we explain that the radiant

power of this image so predominates in our minds over natural and cultural origins, as well as over the religious, philosophic, historic, and personal situation from which it arises? Not by invoking "lyric synthesis" or "poetic genius." Poetry, in order to be recognizable, must, after all, have reference to something beyond its natural and historic roots—something the poet shares with other men, contemporary or future. It must refer to a common *reality*, an enduring one, and one communicable in language even though language can do no more than point to it. For if by chance words could fully convey it, it would not be so much a common reality as a single, personal event. And this reality must have its existence in the mind and yet at the same time its enduring place in the world, representing one of the permanent meanings of life. It is here that the Dantesque vision reveals itself to be as much conditioned by its natural and historic context as it is free of all strictures and bonds. Standing beyond the faith, convictions, and prejudices of the author, its concern is not with this world, but solely with the fixed yet varying meaning of our being in the world.

The poet in his most inspired moments testifies to the ineradicable freedom of rapport between man and his world; and in so doing he refers us to a free, firm, and inexpressible reality that, though independent of his beliefs or premises, is yet the very thing that levels him to the common condition and allows his "frenzy" to become communication. And thus Dante, when most intent on expressing the absoluteness of the "eternal light," gives us one of the most beautiful of all images of a totally different absolute: the absolute of transience and of mortality.

Tempo Presente, February 1964
(Trans. Irma Brandeis)

9

Pirandello
and Humor

In 1908, Luigi Pirandello, forty-one years old, already a novelist but not yet a playwright, published a long scholarly essay entitled *L'umorismo*. His first concern in this essay was to define the meaning of the Italian word *umorismo*, and, despite the opinion of eminent philologists of the day, he rightly rejected the notion that it came from the word *umore*, with its various derivatives *bell'umore, malumore, buonumore*. His second concern was to try to determine, essentially following the lead of the German Romantics, the real idea contained in the word. He ended by affirming that *umorismo* is a distinct aesthetic attitude, not to be confused with irony or satire or sarcasm.

With this essay Pirandello took a position in direct conflict with that of Benedetto Croce. When Croce, in the *Estetica*, faced the difficult problem represented by so essentially ambiguous an artistic term as humor, of which it was impossible to say (as he said of art in general) that it was pure "intuition" or pure "lyricism," he adopted the view of the French literary historian Fernand Baldensperger: *"Il n'y a pas d'humour, il n'y a que des humoristes."* This Solomonic judgment left the question unanswered.

Pirandello's essay immediately won him the honor of being sharply criticized by Croce, and the clash led to a lifelong rupture. It was from this discussion about humor that Croce derived the opinion that Pirandello had none of the faculties of the true artist, that, instead of following natural intuition and searching for purity of expression, he simply argued, scoffed, and dabbled in philosophy. And it was this same theoretical dispute that gave Pirandello, besides a personal aversion to the Neapolitan philosopher, the conviction that he himself had attained not only an original vision of things in general, but an original idea of art. Indeed, he came to believe that he had discovered and defined a new form of art: humor. Insofar as Pirandello considered himself a philosopher of aesthetics, with a theory of art to challenge Croce's, he was mistaken. It was true, however, that he had understood humor in a completely new way and had succeeded in making explicit the element of ambiguity that was implicit in the concept. Despite its academic form, which only occasionally permitted the author to expound his theory clearly, Pirandello's essay can be regarded as the most original statement of literary principles made by any Italian writer since Alessandro Manzoni. It is, moreover, highly indicative of the purposes of Pirandello's art as a writer, and more particularly as a dramatist.

It was in his reply to Benedetto Croce in 1920 that Pirandello managed to develop the really original kernel of his theory and to extricate it from the mass of literary-historical considerations with which it had been decked. The result was not simply a lucid explanation of the meaning of his art, but almost a manifesto in favor of an Italian literature unfettered by rhetoric, by aestheticism, or by sentimentality. It was a plea for a literature in which intelligence and consciousness would at last be accorded their rightful place and would be freed from artificiality, false naïveté, lyrical impressionism, and dilettante sensualism. What Pirandello wanted was a thinking, reasoning, critical literature, the opposite of what was being produced by men like D'Annunzio or Pascoli, who still dominated the literary scene and who, it must be said in all fairness, found in Benedetto Croce one of their sternest critics. This is yet another demonstration of the misunderstandings that arise in Italian cultural life—and, more generally, in Italian society— hen the almost inevitable dogmatism of a man who has arrived at an uncompromising vision of things meets the egocentricity that is bound to overcome the man who feels he has an original conception of the world and finds himself obliged to defend it against, and impose it on, a society that resists being shaken out of a moral torpor that lets it undergo its own history without participating in it. I am not saying that Benedetto Croce and Luigi Pirandello were made to get along with each other as intellectual personalities. But we cannot help seeing a comedy of errors of sorts in the fact that the philosopher who tried to introduce an interest in ideas and a concern for intellectual consistency into Italian culture and the writer who wanted to restore the dimension of the intellect to art should have been adversaries.

What did Pirandello mean by humor? In the first place, he meant that (to use his own words) "the faculty of reflection is not *hidden* in the composition of a 'humorous' work, it is not invisible, it does not remain a form of feeling, like a mirror in which feeling gazes at itself, but it comes to the forefront like a judge and discomposes the mirrored image. From this analysis, from this upset image another active feeling is born— a feeling which we could call, and which I shall indeed call, a *sense of the opposite*."

One of the examples Pirandello gives of a "humorous" sight is the spectacle of a garishly painted old lady acting like a young girl. We are aware of the caricature and consequently want to laugh. "I realize," says Pirandello, "that the lady is the opposite of what a respectable old lady should be. The situation is comic because of our *awareness of the opposite*." But if we look more closely at what we see, we realize that under the grotesque exterior the human element is hidden—the human, and humanly pathetic, struggle not to acknowledge old age and to drive away the idea of death, not just from one's mind but from one's appearance. "It is by reflecting on that first *awareness of the opposite*," says Pirandello, "that I pass on to the *feeling of the opposite*."

Actually, we see from what Pirandello says later that we do not so much pass from "awareness" to "feeling," but that a change takes place in our level of consciousness and our way of seeing things. What started off as a realistic observation becomes radically intellectual and, to use a slightly hackneyed word, "metaphysical." The first impression made by the sight of the old lady was comic. The second is not impression but reflection, and it is the opposite of comic. It is pathetic and saddening. Our initial attitude was ironical and took only appearances into account; it did not go beneath them. The emotion incurred by reflection is not only compassion but also a feeling for what is universally human. It does not just take into account the single visible object and the momentary impression, or even a general human quality of the person in question. It does far more than this. It takes into account that person's relationship with existence, bringing into play the almost invisible, but very real, factors, such as the passage of time, old age, and death, which are inevitable elements of every human existence and not just component parts of the absurd mask that suddenly appeared before our eyes. Let me give an example. Pirandello's humor is the very opposite of the ferociously sarcastic attitude Flaubert displays toward Charles Bovary from start to finish, noting in detail not what he is or has, but what the wretched doctor is not and has not.

Yet compassion cannot eliminate our consciousness of the grotesque, just as our consciousness of the grotesque cannot destroy the feeling of compassion. And so, surprised and almost dazzled by reality, the mind remains uncertain, perplexed, and, says Pirandello, "it no longer knows where it stands."

This, according to Pirandello, is the situation of the humorist—a situation in which the acute and constantly *critical* awareness of reality ("critical" in the two senses of lucid discernment and unstable uncertainty) is accompanied by an irrevocable feeling of distance from reality itself and, at the same time, of extreme proximity to the person who suffers the vicissitudes of reality. Far from being cold and abstract (adjectives often misapplied to Pirandello's work), the attitude of the humorist is very human. It is that of a writer free of the egocentricity and self-love that accompany every artistic attitude based on gratification of the senses, exploitation of momentary emotions, and fascination with pure form. The artificial objectivity of the so-called "realist" may be cold; the irony of the comic or satirical poet may be abstract and his words may be cruel. But the humorist, according to Pirandello, is a man who knows that human reality does not exhaust itself in any of the ways in which it appears (or in which it is "imprisoned," as Pirandello would say) and that to approach it with any preconceived scheme—any ready-made "ideal," whether positive and optimistic or negative and polemical—is an error. The humorist detaches himself not from what is human, but, as Pirandello himself says, from "all the fictions of the mind, all the creations of feeling," so as to look reality in the face.

In a piece he wrote about his *The Late Mattia Pascal*, Pirandello replied sharply to the critics who attacked his art "in the name of a humanity with which they seem to be perfectly acquainted" and, more particularly, who considered Pirandello's characters deficient in humanity because they reasoned. "For," answered the writer, "it seems that the critics identify *humanity* with feeling rather than with the capacity to reason. . . . The duty of beasts is to suffer without reasoning. Whoever suffers and reasons (precisely because he is suffering) is regarded by the critics as not being *human*. For," Pirandello concluded, with rather heavy-handed sarcasm, "it would appear that whoever suffers is nothing but a beast, and that only the man who is a *beast* is really *human* in their eyes."

So, according to Pirandello, humor is the intrusion of reason into the so-called "humanity" of naturalistic or aesthetic literature. Rather than intrusion, it would be more exact to speak of a *return* of intellect and reflection to the domain of art, where they have always belonged by right, as is testified by Homer, Shakespeare, Leopardi, Tolstoy, and all the writers who, "great" or not, are "complete." As examples of truly "humorous" writers, Pirandello singles out Cervantes and Sterne among the non-Italians and Ariosto, Bruno, and Manzoni among his countrymen. On the subject of Manzoni, and more particularly of Don Abbondio, he has written the best pages since De Sanctis—and is, I am inclined to say, even more perceptive than De Sanctis.

Who is Don Abbondio? asked Pirandello in *L'umorismo*. "He is what you find in the place of what you would have wanted to find," he replies. Reality. It is in vain that Cardinal Federigo and Manzoni himself, insofar as he wants to believe the Cardinal's arguments, oppose to Don Abbondio the ideal of the perfect priest. Don Abbondio is there, and, being there, he is the living proof that, as Pirandello says, "it is only very exceptionally that we find an incarnation of the ideal." Manzoni is fully aware of this; or, rather, he is fully aware of how alive and how real Don Abbondio is, this "opposite" of what he thinks a priest worthy of his mission should be. Indeed, perhaps Don Abbondio is truly real just because he is so representative of common humanity. It is this awareness of the "opposite" that enables Manzoni to create his most convincing character. For, had he looked down on Don Abbondio and described him in terms of the theological and canonical conception of priesthood, he would have created a puppet.

"What," Pirandello asks, "does the author feel about Don Abbondio? Contempt or compassion? Manzoni has an abstract and noble ideal of the priestly mission in the world, and embodies this ideal in Federigo Borromeo. . . . If Manzoni had hearkened only to the voice of the ideal, he would have represented Don Abbondio in such a way that everyone would have hated and despised him. Instead, he turns inward and also gives ear to the voice of human weakness . . . his concept of the religious, priestly ideal splits, and between the twin flames of Fra Cristoforo and Cardinal Federigo, Manzoni sees the wary and crestfallen shadow cast by Don Abbondio. And, at a certain point, he allows himself the pleasure of confronting and contrasting the active, positive feeling with the negative reflection . . . the lofty, abstract sermonizing of altruism is snuffed out by the pedestrian, concrete counsels of self-interest."

Does Manzoni feel "good-natured, sympathetic indulgence" for his priest? "Just a minute," says Pirandello. "Manzoni does indeed feel compassion for poor Don Abbondio, but it is a compassion that also happens to tear the churchman to shreds. Only by laughing at him and making him a figure of fun can Manzoni pity him and make others pity him. . . . But by laughing at him and pitying him simultaneously, the author finds himself laughing bitterly at poor human nature; the more pitiable the wretched priest, the more dubious human worth. . . . And what is the effect? When we look at Manzoni's priest from this perspective we can no longer laugh at him. At bottom, that pity is pitiless; the congenial indulgence is not so good-natured. . . ."

There are two points to be noted in Pirandello's interpretation of the relationship between Manzoni and Don Abbondio. The first is the direct intervention of the writer in his work, not as a *deus ex machina* but as moral judge of his own creation, an interested party, himself a character in the novel. It is in the portrait of the frightened and inept priest, who does not dare resist the mighty and is incapable of thinking about anything but his own peace and quiet, that the human authenticity of Manzoni's Catholicism appears most clearly. However they may try, Cardinal Federigo and Manzoni never manage to dismiss the living objection that is Don Abbondio. The sublimity of Catholic morality remains in doubt. Here the paradox that quickens Manzoni's creation emerges clearly, for his awareness of that fact is what forms the basis and the true strength of his morality. Manzoni is fully conscious of the "opposite" of his ideal Catholicism, and this consciousness generates what is truest in his art.

In other words, Manzoni questions his own idea of Catholicism in the character of Don Abbondio, and it is by questioning this ideal, by making it a matter of reflection and discussion and not merely a "representation," that he gives it life. In this way he creates a dramatic relationship with himself and with the basic inspiration of his work—a relationship consisting of dichotomy, conflict, and bitter criticism. In Manzoni's novel the conflict is resolved by means of the mysterious designs of Providence, but for us the solution remains uncertain. The mere presence of Don Abbondio prevents it from being thoroughly convincing. The best proof of this is the concreteness of the character of the wretched priest, compared with the abstractness of Cardinal Federigo and Fra Cristoforo, characters derived from Bossuet and from speculations on ethics and theology, rather than from an authentic sense of what the embodiment of the priestly ministry could be in modern times. Don Abbondio, the product of a "negative" feeling and a doubt, not only is real; also, his limitless pusillanimity inspires us with the sense of "what he should be." But the other two characters, who incarnate Manzoni's idea of the true nature of the priestly mission, remain "ideal" figures. The truth is, they never manage to refute Don Abbondio; all they can do is silence him, while his shadow, "wary and crestfallen," continues to spread over the whole novel. Yet it is the very fact that the solution is doubtful—that Manzoni's Catholicism is dichotomized and unsure of itself ("humorous," as Pirandello says) and that the writer can assume a reflective and critical attitude toward his own apologetic purpose—that makes the "representation" of the whole problem so effective.

The second point to note in Pirandello's interpretation of the character of Don Abbondio is that the most concrete, the truest, and the most "realistic" of Manzoni's characters, the character born of the "feeling for the opposite" and the negative faculty of reflection, establishes an endlessly dramatic relationship with his author. Manzoni's Catholicism never stops trying to come to terms with Don Abbondio, with "what you find in the place of what you would have wanted to find," with *reality*. Don Abbondio is a question mark that neither the solemn words of Cardinal Federigo nor the liturgical sublimity of the *inni sacri* can erase. But, as I have said, this question mark, this doubt, this denial, strengthens, rather than weakens, both Manzoni's artistic vision and the persuasive power of his Catholicism. At the same time, there would be no dramatic tension or conflict if Manzoni had "given in" to Don Abbondio, if Manzoni had not continued to resist him in the name of an "unreal" ideal far truer than that sorry human specimen the timorous priest.

Manzoni's explicit Catholicism, manifest in the figures of Fra Cristoforo and Cardinal Federigo and in the "useful lessons" that close the novel, is not particularly substantial. But the attitude of reflection, judgment, and humanity expressed in Don Abbondio, in the ironic view of the mighty, in the sympathy for the humble, in the sense of the absurdity of history that pervades the entire novel, is nothing less than the active reality of the writer's consciousness—and that cannot be refuted so easily.

Now, to return to Pirandello: a writer is "humorous" when his attitude is one of reflection, judgment, and humanity, in other words, when the writer is a living presence in his work. A distinctive feature of the "humorous" writer is the rejection of the mask of objectivity (or of pure art, which comes to the same thing). The "humorist" inevitably becomes the main character in his own work. He is just as involved as the fictive characters and is responsible for the world he creates and the opinions he expresses. Moreover, according to Pirandello's definition, the "humorist" is in an ambiguous situation with regard to his own work, his own characters, and even his own thoughts, for they, too, after all, are "what you find in the place of what you would have wanted to find," one fact among others. The "feeling of the opposite" that Pirandello stresses is not an aesthetic attitude; it is of the essence of the writer's situation as a living human being. Behind the writer's mask, this feeling will always continue to strip him bare, to lead him back not to his own egocentric "part" but to the primordial equality that binds him to every other man through the immutable and basic facts of existence. It will always force him to question "what you find." In order to reach this point, the writer must accept the fact that he is an "uninhabited soul," *psychèn éremon*, to use the term Eugenio Levi applied to Pirandello (a term originally found, curiously enough, in a fragment of a lost Greek tragedy, Neophron's *Medea*).

Most of Pirandello's critics have realized the importance of *l'umorismo* in his work, but few have recognized the necessary connection between the "humorous" concept of art and the impulse that led Pirandello to express himself in dramatic form even before he started to write plays. One who has is Leone De Castris. In his *Storia di Pirandello*, published in 1962, he points out that Pirandello's view of humor was responsible for the writer's transition from the "rejection of personality, in the romantic and bourgeois sense of the word," to the "adoption of the *persona*, in the ancient sense of the word, as revealing the tragic suffering of man." This is where Pirandello's originality as a dramatist lies. This is why the various statements that have been made about him and by him—with regard to the contrast between life, which changes and flows, and form, which freezes; between living and seeing oneself live; between folly and reason—however correct, do not grasp what is most vital and fertile in Pirandello's innovation, the aspect that still has something to teach us and that has not yet been fully understood. Leone De Castris indicates it when he points out that the transition from "personality, in the romantic sense of the word," that is, from the individual as the naturalistic writers understood him, to the "*persona*, in the ancient sense of the word," frees the theater from the conventions that have fettered it since the sixteenth century and allows it to return to its true origins. This does not mean Greek drama (however difficult it may be for Europeans not to regard it as the original form of the theater) so much as the primordial dramatic impulse, the impulse that induces the individual to address himself publicly to others in the name of a common situation. In *Pirandello e la sua lingua*, also published in 1962, Filippo Puglisi makes some relevant remarks about the distinctiveness of Pirandello's style even before he started writing for the theater. "What is it . . . that strikes us . . . in the language Pirandello uses to express himself?" Puglisi asks. "First and foremost, his penchant for dialogue. . . . Pirandello needs to talk, to write as though he were talking, to address . . . someone else, to project his 'self' outside himself (as we usually do when we are alone and talk to ourselves) in order to have a question-and-answer dialogue with himself."

There is no doubt that this penchant and this need are at the root of Pirandello's dramatic art, and they would not be there if they had not existed within him all along, like an instinct—that universally human instinct which is the theatrical instinct and which Francis Fergusson convincingly calls the "histrionic instinct." And the theatrical instinct, in its turn, necessarily implies the reflective and dichotomous "humorous" attitude, the attitude Pirandello deals with in his essay. He cannot be said to have created an actual theory of the "humorous"; he simply sustains it, explains it, and illustrates it with great acuteness.

In *L'umorismo* Pirandello establishes irrefutably the radical difference between the supposedly candid and natural artist (who may never have existed at all) and one who aspires to be an authentic artist, that is, one who genuinely communicates from within the present situation of our moral universe. It is not a difference of form or a difference of attitude toward the formal problems of art, but a difference of substance, a difference in the artist's feeling for life and in his conviction about the place of art in life. According to Pirandello, the true artist is really committed to his art, and his art is the question he raises—cannot help raising—about himself and the part he plays in life in front of others. Such an artist will no longer resort to the alibi of a reality outside himself that he can represent objectively. For him, reality consists of the questions reality arouses within him—the very question of reality itself, of the validity of the world of duties, beliefs, and ideas in which he is involved. He does not have to oppose any "ideal" whatever to this reality, but only the awareness of what Pirandello calls that "living reality beyond the range of human sight," an awareness the artist has attained in solitude and which makes the normal aspect of things always appear ambiguous, suspect, and eminently problematic.

Is this realism? Certainly not, if what we mean by realism is the placid (or even anguished) acceptance of things as they appear in their material bulk, consecrated by authority or by inertia. But, on the other hand, where and how, if not through rhetorical artifice or passive sensuality, has the reality of things ever manifested itself other than as reflection on things and people, a feeling of the "opposite," a sense of contrast, a clash with the world, and, finally, as drama?

The situation of the modern writer, as described in *L'umorismo*, should preclude his recourse to any ready-made ideal. But he does have the right to challenge, in the name of reality, the illusions of sentiment, utilitarian fictions, and the claims of conventional truths. For what is real to him is not a constantly varied and changing spectacle but an ever-recurrent and never-resolved drama—the drama of human things regarded, as Pirandello said, "with an absolute respect for their naked virginity."

This sort of drama needs no rules, no plot, no effects of any sort. Nor does it need to be "theatrical." It asks only to manifest itself freely.

Tempo Presente, May 1967
(Trans. Alastair Hamilton)

10

Theater
in Utopia

The theater is not for everybody; it is only for those who love it. Today, in an urban environment, among so-called cultured people, these are few, and it is for these few and with these few that the theater must be made.

No sooner have we said this than we hear the progressives and aesthetes grumbling, "This means denying art to the people," or "What becomes of the universal character of art?"

But saying that the theater nowadays is not for everybody is not to deny it to the people. It simply means that there is no point in devising a theater for an audience that does not exist. Nor is there any point in catering to the mentality, habits, and tastes of a bastard mass of individuals who thrive on movies, television, and popular songs or, less still, in adapting the theater to that medley of literature, cinema, and debased ideologies to which the literary world and the sophisticated bourgeoisie are now so partial.

Surely, to say that art is universal makes sense only if we mean that true art is accessible to anybody who feels its attraction. It makes no sense if we maintain that it must be so fashioned as to be within everybody's reach, on the level of a public service. The truth is that we never create, act, or talk for everybody, but solely for those whom we love—or hate—enough to want to communicate with. There is no such thing as a language for everybody. The fact that we use the same language does not mean that we understand each other. It is only the texture of an existence and an experience genuinely shared with others that charges words and forms with a substantial significance and makes them capable of influencing the existence and the experience of whoever listens to them or contemplates them. Beyond this point, communication is illusory; culture is a useless burden. The horizon illuminated by a particular language—that of Plato, Giotto, or Molière, as well as that of each one of us when we talk passionately about something that really matters to us—seems to shut in on itself, even though, like the infinite circle of the terrestrial horizon, it is never closed, never really separated from other languages, describing as it does an imaginary boundary perceived only by the man who does not want to cross it.

This is the law of every human language and of every communication between members of a community. We talk for those who understand us and for nobody else. Otherwise, speaking does not mean communicating but striving to arouse some psychic effect by means of an artificially contrived language: a form of indirect persuasion. This may be an end in itself, assuming the semblance of art or thought; or it may have further aims—propaganda and publicity. But in spite of appearances it will never be the language of reason.

A phenomenon peculiar to our time is the multiplication of these artificial and persuasive languages, to the detriment of authentic communication. Of these languages the most widespread and effective is the language of the image, and especially that of the moving image: the cinema.

A great deal could be said about the relationship between word and image. The main thing, however, is that we must not confuse the one with the other, or the laws ruling the former with those regulating the latter. The most important, the most elementary, and today the most neglected of these laws is the one requiring that words be governed by a grammatical, syntactical, and logical principle. This means that words serve essentially to communicate the "motions of the spirit" and the dispositions of the mind. Image, by contrast, is intended to indicate objects and actions, and is therefore governed by what we can call the law of effective succession. By this I mean that the best way of making a series of images "talk" is to organize them according to the general effect we want to obtain and not according to any formal principle. We could also say that words evoke meanings and that, consequently, their most important qualities are appropriateness, clearness, and the order in which they are pronounced, whereas the image *provokes* emotions, so that what counts most for the image is obviousness, effectiveness, and force of impact.

This distinction leads to the conclusion that what impoverishes and sterilizes the theater today is not the competition of the cinema, which was never important, but the confusion between theater and cinema, word and image, between theater as drama and theater as spectacle—a confusion created primarily by producers and playwrights themselves. It is in the theater itself that nontheatrical or antitheatrical elements prevail or persist; stagecraft predominates over true dramatic development, external movement is confused with significant action, and the essential is sacrificed to the clichés of realism and rhetoric.

If the theater is simply spectacle, external movement, staged anecdote, if it has no other choice than between action that happens to be accompanied by words and words that are immobile, if we forget that its essence is precisely *reasoning action,* it is hard to see why one should not prefer the cinema. For the cinema is nothing but action devoid of reason and aimed at arousing the emotions. If we confuse the image with the word and think that the cinema is expressing ideas when it provokes realistic emotions, the theater obviously has no reason to exist.

I should point out that I am not trying to defend the text against its "theatricalization." To argue in favor of the verbal at the expense of the visual and spectacular elements of theater is too simple; moreover, it conceals a purely literary concept of drama, which can easily be refuted by the man of the theater. But if drama is essentially reasoning action, the theater is the embodied word, and they are two inseparable aspects of the same phenomenon.

We cannot oppose the purity of the word to the tyranny of the director and the tendency to turn the theater into something purely exciting and spectacular as if the stage were the setting for rhetorical tournaments. In defense of our views, we can only advance the significance peculiar to the theater, its richness, its complexity, and the basic fact that the plot of, for example, *Macbeth* or *L'Ecole des femmes* is the external aspect of an inner movement, not a combination of miming and words. Strictly speaking, therefore, stage production implies the bestowing of physical evidence on the inner movement.

The richness and complexity of the theater have been obliterated by a certain contemporary tendency that began, significantly, at the same time as that new character the director appeared on the stage, at the beginning of the century. The tendency is to restrict the entire phenomenon of the theater to the stage and its effect on the stage, and to assert that the play itself does not exist independently of the performance. This extreme thesis is what present-day adepts of the "theater of cruelty" have made of the views of Antonin Artaud.

The specious fortune of Artaud's ideas, or, rather, his suggestions, is a striking example of the confusion between the dramatic and the spectacular—a confusion that has overcome so many people searching today for a way out of the critical, or at least ambiguous, situation of the theater.

The other aspect of this confusion is the commonly held idea that the cinema, with different means, can express the same things as the theater—ideas, thoughts, and moral problems. Let me repeat that if this were true the theater would obviously lack its main reason for surviving in this day and age. It could simply be reduced to a kind of live cinema, a cinema of flesh and blood, and its essential purpose would be to arouse the same sensations and emotions we experience in everyday life, except that they would be selected and produced on the stage.

Now, the truth of the matter is that the cinema has never managed to convey moral ideas and problems. At most, certain films have tried to *illustrate* moral situations. But this is not the same thing.

Of the films that have attempted to represent an idea, the one that seemed to me the most effective was André Cayatte's *Nous sommes tous des assassins*. The film set out to demonstrate the inhumanity of the death penalty. In fact, it does something quite different. It is a series of images presenting in the cruelest detail what it is like to await the guillotine in the death cell of a French prison, and we were indeed horrified, but by the condition of the man sentenced to death, not by the death penalty. There is a difference. While those images horrified the spectator, they also satisfied a horrible, and horribly impersonal, curiosity about the physical details of the condition of the condemned man. Ultimately the death penalty was presented as a spectacle; it was not denounced.

This was inevitable. The cinematographic image can show with disconcerting, but also very transient, effectiveness the physical aspect of things. It can also show the physical equivalent of the "motions of the spirit," to the extent that motions of the human spirit have a physical equivalent. But it cannot render thought, consciousness, or ideas, for the simple reason that the camera does not catch these modes of reality, but, rather, their material and external aspects.

The death penalty, political oppression, and the evils of war are questions between the individual and the society in which he lives. They are moral questions, questions of ideas, questions of justice and injustice, of good and evil, which are meaningful to the extent that they are freely discussed through the instruments of reasoned debate, *logos;* questions whose purpose is not to provoke immediate reflexes and transient emotions, but to gauge the complexity of facts and their final significance, the force of feelings, and the clearness of ideas. To imagine that there can be a cinematographic equivalent of these moral problems is to have a very poor sense of man's inner life, of the quality of feelings, of the nature of moral problems, of that whole area, which is so inaccessible, and which is called the human spirit. But the tendency to underestimate inner life and moral phenomena is one of the salient characteristics of modern barbarity, as well as one of the most obvious effects of the cinema on the psychology of the masses.

Let us return to the theater and consider one of the contemporary plays that claim to be part of the "theater of cruelty": *The Brig,* by Kenneth Brown, originally staged by Judith Malina and performed by the Living Theater.

Here we have an excellent example of the kind of theater that exhausts itself completely in the performance and of a drama that does not exist apart from the almost physical effect it has on the spectator. As a dramatic work, *The Brig* is simply the stage representation of the prison regulations of the Third Regiment of Marines, taken article by article, as they are applied from reveille, at four-thirty in the morning, to lockup, at seven-thirty in the evening. The plot consists of the simultaneous and frantic enactment of nine regulations by seven prisoners supervised and bullied by a sergeant and three noncommissioned officers. There is nothing else, only the perfect performance of the regulations by the prisoner-actors and the relentless application of the same regulations by the warden-actors.

To apply the term "naturalism" to such a play would be just as wrong as to call the plot a piece of social criticism. The style of the Living Theater is to naturalism what one of Marcel Duchamp's "ready-mades" is to the real object, which in fact it is. For the two hours of the performance, we are not spectators at a more or less realistically presented dramatic action, but unexpected visitors to one of the countless compartments that make up the world in which we live. The effect Judith Malina is trying to achieve is not art, but reality.

Such a conception of the theater takes us not only beyond naturalism or realism, but also beyond photography and the cinema. For photography and the cinema give us the illusory image of a real object, while making us aware that it is illusory and not real. In *The Brig*, however, we have no illusions. We are there, witnesses to a crude, sordid, blind, and naked fact—but a true fact, which takes place before our eyes and which is an irrefutable proof of its own truth.

There is no more to it than that, and that is the limitation of this particular type of theater. *The Brig* means absolutely nothing except itself. It is a perfectly constructed object, which we can view with our eyes but which our mind cannot penetrate, because there is nothing to say about it apart from establishing that it exists. Contrary to the assumption on which this kind of theater rests—the assumption that the denunciation will be all the more virulent the more boldly we present the fact we are denouncing—*The Brig* is not a denunciation, but the neutral presentation of a fact half-monstrous, half-bizarre. In this case, at least, the "theater of cruelty" turns into a sort of supercinema; while it tries to involve both the spectator's sensibility and his judgment, it in fact leaves him outside the action, in an area of emotions that may be violent but that remain superficial.

At this point, I would like to return to the distinction I alluded to earlier between the "reasoning action" peculiar to drama and the "emotional action" typical of the cinema and, more generally, of every spectacle intended to excite intense but transient emotions.

What do I mean by "reasoning action"? To start with, I mean, very simply, an action guided by an inner necessity and one that progresses from its point of departure to its final end according to an ordered and stringent logic, not just any old way.

Several years ago Francis Fergusson formulated a definition of drama, following Aristotle, that may clarify my meaning. He described drama as "an imitation of action in the form of action." By "action" Fergusson does not mean an external action, but a moral action. He believes true drama consists of a process of moral revelation by which the hero, finding himself involved in a given situation, discovers progressively, in encounters with his fellow men and his companions, the significance of what he has had to do and suffer. By discovering this, the dramatic hero— whether he be Oedipus, Macbeth, or Uncle Vanya— also discovers the significance of existence and of the world.

What is important in Fergusson's definition is the clear transference of emphasis from the purely "poetic" meaning of drama to the fact that it represents a specific action or movement of the plot toward its fulfillment. In other words, drama is a symbolic way of representing moral experience in the act of forming itself, of representing the nature of the world in the act of revealing itself in person, as it were, through human acts.

I must add two observations to Fergusson's definition, with which I basically agree. The first concerns the relationship between external action and moral situation. What characterizes drama, it seems to me, is not that a moral revelation is effected by an external event, for the same can be said about the novel. It is the fact that from the very outset a moral situation and its inescapable logic have been identified. The second observation is that this logic develops in the form of conflict and argument, that is, by reasoning, if by "reasoning" we understand something other than abstract ratiocination. In drama, what is at stake is the meaning of the protagonist's actions and therefore of his existence, and so it is reasons, not states of mind, that confront each other—not feelings and passions but, if anything, their logic.

It is in this sense that drama can be defined as a

reasoning action. This is not an exhaustive or rigorous definition, of course, but one that only attempts to bring out as clearly as possible the eminently intellectual nature of dramatic language. "Reasoning" in this sense means, above all, "necessary," and "necessary" is the opposite of arbitrary, casual, even of "likely." Whether it be *Agamemnon* or *Six Characters in Search of an Author*, what matters in a dramatic action is its necessity—the rigor with which it proceeds toward its outcome and the inevitability of the outcome in view of the premises and the development of the action.

Let us consider this concept of necessity in connection with a play that remains the finest example of a rigorous dramatic action: *Oedipus the King*.

What do I mean when I say that the action of *Oedipus* is necessary? Not just that the plot is well constructed from a formal point of view, certainly, or that Sophocles has adhered to the essential and avoided anything secondary or incidental. The necessity of *Oedipus* lies mainly in the fact that Sophocles has developed and displayed the situation of Oedipus the man, not his psychology. And this, in its turn, means that in developing the action the poet has not considered the countless possible reactions of a man in Oedipus' position in order to select the most interesting reaction, but has concerned himself solely with the terrible nature of Oedipus' guilt and the alternatives he faced of accepting or rejecting the consequences.

To make King Oedipus, a proud man and self-confident to the point of excess, acknowledge his own guilt and then to show him shattered by his guilt but not diminished, indeed, risen to the full dignity of man—this seems to have been Sophocles' aim in composing his masterpiece. But in order to conceive the drama in this way, in order to lead Oedipus from his initial arrogance to his fall into disgrace and thence to the greatness he acquires by accepting his own destiny, the poet had to be guided by a view of the nature of things and of man's place in the cosmic order that enabled him to grasp the necessity of Oedipus' action and to adhere to it, regardless of the numerous but vacuous possibilities of "likelihood."

Without a firm conviction about the nature of things, even if the conviction is that nothing in this world is stable or unambiguous, there is no possibility of drama, because there is no possibility of seeing any necessity in human actions.

The word "conviction" in this context does not mean a philosophical system or a political ideology, but strength and clarity of mind, a balance between feelings and ideas, maturity of judgment, and an inner order.

This is what I mean when I say that drama is a "reasoning action." The protagonist of the drama is not an individual but a particular state of things, a particular order or disorder of the world. The validity of a dramatic action can be measured by the clarity with which it represents this state of things, this order or disorder. The dramatic character, therefore, is not an individual suffering this or that misfortune, but a being to whom just one thing happens: the world is made as it is and not otherwise. His function is to show a certain form of destiny at work, not to express himself; when he is on the stage, the only part of him that counts is the part involved in the action. The purpose of drama is to remind us what kind of world we live in and to bring home to us the weight of the acts we perform in it. Its function is to teach the audience how to attain a just evaluation of human actions.

Unlike the novel, drama is governed by necessity.

Its action is guided and propelled by the supreme principle of reason, not by motives of psychological realism.

This is not a privilege of Greek tragedy, as is all too often assumed, but the characteristic of any drama worthy of the name. In Racine, in Shaw, in Chekhov, in Pirandello, there is always a particular principle of reason at work, which is simply the reflection of a particular situation of the world.

To repeat, it is in this sense that we can and must say that the theater is first and foremost the "word"; for consciousness, reason, and necessity are inseparable from the "word." But it is the articulated and reasoned word, the word in action, above all, the word not only spoken but embodied.

If drama is the word in this sense, obviously the stricter it is, and the fuller it is of poetic force, the less will it tolerate the spectacular element. The essential purpose of a production will be to bring out the argument underlying the plot, to modulate its various phases, and not to deck it with costumes and place it in bizarre or sumptuous settings.

All the evidence shows that this was the way stage production was regarded during the great periods of the theater. As to modern theater, the only "staging" required by the plays of Ibsen, of Pirandello, or of Beckett is the staging of the word, that is, the presence of an actor capable of interpreting the text in the right tone and with the right rhythm. The rest is mere accompaniment adapted to the sense of the words. And we can undoubtedly say that the only style of production suitable for modern theater is one of severe simplicity or even poverty.

If drama is the acted word and staging is not pageantry but the embodiment and the scansion of the dramatic argument, it follows that the presence of the spectator is not purely incidental, due to the lack of machines that would enable us to record images and words and take them wherever we like. The spectator is an essential element of the theater. Nor is it only the people present in the auditorium, but also those who never go near the theater, on whose way of life, ideas, and tastes the existence of the theater depends.

What is certain is that the spoken word cannot be replaced. The recorded word, the word of the cinema, the word of the radio, and the word of television not only lack a living presence, but are not real words; they are something else, something entirely different. They are artificial words, part of an artificial language valid for everybody and for nobody at the same time. The word accompanied by a living presence, on the other hand, is not only a clear word, which reaches us free of mechanical diaphragms; it is also, above all, an authentic word, addressed to us in particular and in the concrete, not in general and in the abstract. It is addressed not only to our ear but to our spirit, to our mind, to our consciousness, and it is therefore the only word capable of conveying a fullness of meaning.

Since it is the true word, the living word is not addressed to everybody, but only to those capable of hearing it and understanding it. There are few such people today, or so it would appear. And this leads me to conclude by repeating what I said at the beginning—the theater today is an art for the few, and should be practiced as such.

Tempo Presente, May–June 1965
(Trans. Alastair Hamilton)

11

Antonin Artaud and His Theater

Early in 1923, Antonin Artaud, stage and film actor, then twenty-seven years old, sent a selection of his poetry to Jacques Rivière, editor in chief of the *Nouvelle Revue Française*. On May 1 he received a note from Rivière saying he was sorry he could not publish the poetry but would like to make the poet's acquaintance. And so they met.

The very day they met, Artaud wrote Rivière a letter which has been frequently quoted but rarely given serious attention.

> I suffer from a fearful mental disease. My ideas abandon me at every stage, from the mere fact of thought itself to the exterior phenomenon of its materialization in words. Words, the forms of sentences, inner directions of thought, the mind's simplest reactions: I am in constant pursuit of my intellectual being. When I can seize a form, even if it is imperfect, I fix it for fear of losing the whole idea. I live beneath myself, I know, and I suffer from it, but I accept it for fear of dying completely. Those forms of expression, those infelicitous turns of phrase for which you reproach me come from the deep uncertainty of my ideas. . . . [I am] happy indeed when this uncertainty does not give way to the absolute nonexistence from which I sometimes suffer. I should like you to understand that it is not a question of greater or lesser existence resulting from what is commonly called "inspiration," but of a total absence, a real void . . . the few things I sent you are fragments I was able to conquer from complete nothingness.

Later, replying to a letter in which Rivière had tried to reassure and encourage him, Artaud again explained:

> The diffusiveness of my poetry, the defects of form, this constant failing of my mind are not to be attributed to a lack of practice or of mastery of the instrument I handled—but to a collapse of the soul at its center, a kind of erosion of ideas that is both essential and fugitive. There is something that destroys my thinking, something that prevents me from being what I could be, but that leaves me, as it were, in suspense. . . .

Let us not speak about the man's madness, for it would be too easy. Let us speak about the man tormented by an obscure malady who is conscious of living beneath himself, who knows that the defects of his poetry are not superficial but come from "a fearful mental disease," from "a collapse of the soul at its center," the man who is nevertheless absolutely determined to be published by the *Nouvelle Revue Française* (the most rigorous literary periodical in France), determined to be a *littérateur*. He persists in demanding whether or not "a defective poem with flashes of true beauty has less authentic literary value and less genuine power than a perfect poem without inner resonance."

We have before us a human crisis transformed into a literary problem, a crisis that the victim himself reduces to the banal question of whether a piece of writing perfect in form but weak in substance is preferable to an imperfect work that has "flashes of true beauty."

What is significant here is not the painful weakness of Artaud's position, which comes from his illness, but the ambiguity created by his falling under the spell of literature. This ambiguity wracked his entire life; and this ambiguity still dominates his legitimate and illegitimate heirs, including those who have discovered a guide to the theater of the future in his writings.

Although Rivière answered Artaud's earnest questioning with great kindness and understanding, he spoke as a man of letters, not as a physician or a sage.

> In itself the mind is a sort of cancer [Rivière wrote] spreading and constantly growing in all directions. . . . There is a whole literature . . . which is the product of the immediate, and, so to speak, animal operation of the mind. This literature has the appearance of a great plain of ruins; the columns still standing are supported by chance alone. It is chance that reigns there, and a sort of dreary multiplicity. One can say that it is the most precise and direct expression of the monster every man carries within himself and, most of the time, instinctively tries to bind in the twining weeds of fact and experience. "But," you will retort, "is this what one must describe as the fragility of the mind? While I complain of a weakness, you paint another disease that probably comes from an excess of strength." Here is my opinion more precisely: the mind is fragile, inasmuch as it needs obstacles. Without them it loses its way and destroys itself. It seems to me that this mental "erosion," these inner "harpies," this "destruction of the mind in its substance" are entirely due to the excessive freedom of your mind. To become taut the mind requires limitation, an encounter with the blessed opacity of experience. The only cure for madness is the innocence of facts.

At this point it is clear that Artaud's and Rivière's discussion becomes a dialogue between deaf men. For while Artaud speaks in the first person of a real condition, his "fearful mental disease," Rivière answers as a *littérateur* concerned with the control of his medium and proffers advice against giving the mind "excessive freedom" to a man who suffers precisely from a lack of any control over his mind's "freedom."

However, it *is* Rivière the man of letters that Artaud is addressing, for he wants to be recognized as

Artaud the writer. Now, as an editor to an aspiring writer, Rivière is absolutely correct in observing that a literature which abandons itself to the "animal operation of the mind" can only be "a great plain of ruins" ruled by "chance . . . and a sort of dreary multiplicity." But in doing so he remains fatally deaf to Artaud's cry, which is not simply the appeal of an aspiring writer but the call of a human being in distress.

Furthermore, Rivière overlooked an essential fact. In the republic of letters, within which he was an eminent judge, a law had been in force, ever since the time of Rimbaud, which held that every product of the mind, no matter how "animal" or unleashed (the more so the better), is meaningful and important in itself. His objections to Artaud, then, were really a matter of form, not substance. And Artaud was right in pointing this out to him, and in claiming for his faltering but humanly authentic writings the same recognition given works that are, perhaps, more controlled but less "true." Artaud was right; but that does not make his writing any better, nor does it save him from the equivocation in which he has been caught by his literary ambition. The equivocation is not formal but substantial: existential in the fullest sense of the term.

Artaud felt that writing and achieving recognition as a writer were the sole means he had of struggling against the menace of the "collapse of the soul at its center." He struggled against it by expressing it totally, letting it do all the havoc it could, and making it the distinctive feature of his personality. Today, it seems, the only way of asserting one's full individuality without restriction is to achieve success as an artist. Since Artaud could not make his mark in the republic of letters as a master of form, he was driven to push to the limit what Rivière termed the "animal operation of the mind," venturing in all possible directions until he reached the very boundaries of the meaningless. Given his condition, the fatal result was that the disease corroding his mind was purposely aggravated. By putting his illness at the service of his pen, he was forced to enter a closed circuit where mental turmoil produced verbal turmoil, which, in turn, augmented mental turmoil every time the current was turned on.

In short, by falling under the spell of literature, by becoming involved in the question of literary form (and its negation, a no less literary problem), Artaud betrayed himself and the truth he carried within him. Artaud's human situation was an absolute one. It defied expression, and the only solution it permitted was, perhaps, a religious one, a passage to another order of reality. It was this that he frenziedly searched for all his life through writing. But obviously writing could not lead him there.

In what tortuous straits Artaud found himself is revealed with painful clarity in the letter he wrote (May 20, 1924) to Jacques Rivière, who had suggested the publication of their correspondence under assumed names. "Why lie," Artaud begins by protesting, "why try to place on a literary plane something that is the cry of life itself? Why give an appearance of fiction to something made of the ineradicable substance of the soul?" However, his desire to see his writings in print evidently is too strong for him, and he adds, "Yes, but on condition that the reader is not given the impression of perusing a work that has been fabricated. . . . The reader must believe in a *real* illness and not in a *mal du siècle*."

It seems to me that the wish to have a role in the

literary world has rarely been expressed so ingenu-
ously. After all, in order for the reader not to be "given
the impression," to make the reader "believe," one
must work artfully, that is, pretend, lie, and "place on
a literary plane" something that is "the cry of life itself." There is no other way. Without simulation, you
cannot make really public a true illness and real
suffering. Shown to the public, one's inner life always
seems simulated—or, rather, only to the degree that it
is well feigned does it not seem so.

Driven by the ambition to have a unique and
privileged position in the world of letters, Artaud
strained his ideas and his spiritual life to their wildest
pitch. By making them the theme of a theatrical fiction, he consciously aggravated his malady. Aggravating it and simulating it, he became more and more its
prisoner.

How break the vicious circle? Artaud tried to do it
by prophetic outcries and by frantic abandon to the
spasms of his malady; he publicly exhibited himself
exactly as he was. "Antonin Artaud Acts Himself" is
the title someone gave to his last public appearance,
on January 13, 1947, and it is described with both
compassion and objectivity in André Gide's diary. No
one witnessing such a performance could have considered it a fiction, like certain public manifestations
of the futurists, Dadaists, and surrealists. Artaud's
performance was made up of genuinely disconnected
and incongruous gestures, painful grimaces, and in-
articulate cries. The proof of its reality was supposed
to reside in the fact that all those unrelated and
squalid signs were absolutely undecipherable, remaining, as they did, beyond the range of communication.
What he exhibited in public was a real illness; a fact
that was unintelligible, painful, cut off from the
world.

Artaud's effort to represent his own human plight outside the frame of any pre-established order and "mental point of reference" (his own words) ended in an impasse. It resulted in total and constant confusion between literary artifice and individual truth, theatrical fiction and real existence. "All I have done is to transcribe the pain of an abortive adjustment," Artaud wrote. And these words could well serve as the epigraph for his life as well as for his work.

The observations and proclamations contained in *Le Théâtre et son double* reveal Artaud's ambiguity in a less frenzied form than the contents of *Il faut en finir avec le jugement de dieu* and *Les Lettres de Rodez*. On the one hand, Artaud spoke of the theater from the point of view of the professional he was and wanted to be. On the other, he spoke of it as a private form of expression he had dreamed up, a medium that could save him from the abstractness and inanity of writing by permitting him to incarnate fully and publicly the only character he really cared about and that continually escaped him—himself.

If one does not keep in mind the ambiguity and impotence that pervaded Artaud's personality, then his ideas on the theater, or, rather, his insights and prophetic utterances, break up into congeries of confused and contradictory suggestions.

Those who have rallied to the call of the "theater of cruelty" with the illusion that the more they simplified the notion, the more revolutionary it became, have failed to consider the significance of a great number of Artaud's declarations and the meaning of the title he gave to his collected writings on the theater: *Le Théâtre et son double.*

The literal meaning of *double* is "an immaterial body that reproduces the image of a person." It is a term used in sorcery. In Artaud's letter to Jean Paulhan informing him of the title he had chosen for the book, Artaud explained:

> While the theater "doubles" life, life "doubles" the true theater, which has nothing to do with Oscar Wilde's ideas on the subject. The title refers to all the "doubles" of the theater I think I have found in these last years: metaphysics, the plague, and cruelty.

So the "double" of the theater—in other words, its origin and ultimate cause—is not life, which, fascinated by its reflection in art, imitates art (as Wilde suggested). It is, rather, the incorporeal or transcendent essence of existence and its ultimate meaning. In the theater it takes on a body, fills a space, and receives the gift of expressive gesture and of speech, while in real life it remains completely obscure and dispersed.

"Art is not the imitation of life. Life is the imitation of a transcendent principle with which art restores communication." So we are out of the realm of naturalism, realism, or any ideology. As a matter of fact, we are in the midst of what I shall call, for lack of a more precise term, Artaud's "gnosticism"—his bottomless pessimism about the nature of the real world and his hatred of it, as a place of shadows and evil, which can be redeemed only by the effort of creation, the act of incarnating and personifying physically; for creation is a drive toward the light and the good. But it can never redeem completely. For in order to incarnate and personify, the creative act must accept matter, which is the principle of evil, and the form of the world as it is.

"Life, since it admits extension, thickness, heaviness and matter, admits, as a direct consequence, evil and all that is inherent in evil and matter," Artaud writes. In a letter to Jean Paulhan explaining the meaning he attaches to the word "cruelty" as applied to the theater, he adds:

> I employ the word "cruelty" in the sense of . . . a cosmic rigor and implacable necessity, in the gnostic sense of a living whirlwind that devours darkness. . . . Good is desired, it is the consequence of an act. Evil is permanent. When the hidden god creates, he obeys the cruel necessity of creation which has been imposed on himself by himself; and he cannot *not* create, hence not admit into the center of the self-willed whirlwind a kernel of evil ever more condensed and ever more consumed. . . . A play in which there was not this will, this blind appetite for life capable of overriding everything, would be a useless and unfulfilled play.

Here we have an example of the intrinsic ambiguity of Artaud's ideas. He posits a creation that, while gravitating toward the good (and the light), cannot avoid admitting a "kernel of evil," which, however, is "ever more consumed." In the next breath, this voluntary, conscious creation, gravitating toward the good and the light, becomes a "blind appetite for life capable of overriding everything." Now, these two ideas obviously cancel each other, on aesthetic as well as logical grounds. Still, the tension in which they coexist helps to clarify not only the meaning of each but the relation between them. (It seems to me that on the whole it is the first of the two conceptions Artaud tends to stress; but the question is not important for the purpose of this essay.)

Artaud's "gnosticism" was the source of the apocalyptic horror he had of the endless proliferation in the modern world of *l'homme moyen sensuel* and his ideals. "We are enveloped," he writes, in a revealing passage,

> by a phantom humanity which is evil and malignant. It takes root in the bodies of ordinary men who at certain moments reveal themselves to be vampires and

> begin to act like them. These are the men who at birth did not kill the beast in themselves and who have refused to separate themselves from the beast which enslaved them. This beast is a bottomless eroticism, the lugubrious light of an eroticism coming from the farthest reaches of the world. . . . It is there that one sees the horrible world of lubricity glittering.

This is by no means the most violent expression of Artaud's disgust with everything material, animal, or sexual. But it should be enough to enlighten those who interpret his idea of "cruelty" as an exhibition of eroticism and sadism. His horror of that "phantom humanity which is evil and malignant" leads directly to his conviction that, since the French theater has been an expression of this type of humanity from the seventeenth century on, French drama has been nothing more than "storytelling psychology," with the result that "actors in France no longer know how to do anything but talk."

"The misdeeds of the psychological theater descended from Racine," Artaud asserts at the beginning of his essay "On the Theater and Cruelty,"

> have unaccustomed us to that immediate and violent action which the theater should possess. Movies, in their turn, murdering us with secondhand reproductions which, filtered through machines, cannot *unite with* our sensibility, have maintained us for ten years in an ineffectual torpor in which our faculties appear to be foundering.

This seems to take us back to what I would call the primitive conception of theater. Indeed, leaving Artaud's violence aside, how can we disagree with his idea that "the stage is a concrete physical place which asks to be filled"? In point of fact, the notion was not new even at the time Artaud affirmed it. The great Russian directors—particularly Meyerhold, who, in 1930, had brought his theater to Paris, where Artaud must certainly at least have heard of it—had made it the fundamental precept of staging. Moreover, the principle that in the theater speech must be a function of an action is obvious enough.

When Artaud declares that the cinema is the enemy of the theater because, instead of giving cohesion to our naturally dispersive sensibility, it makes it founder "in an ineffectual torpor," he seems to invoke a theater that is the very opposite of the cinema: a theater based on the direct and rigorous communication of the meaning of human actions, rather than their physical appearance. But it is clear that Artaud also had in mind a theater based on violence, on sounds and gestures whose only superiority to the cinema was that the gestures, sounds, and lights were not merely reproduced but physically present. Here he seems to be describing the spectacular theater envisaged by contemporary directors like Meyerhold.

We must not forget, however, that Artaud meant more than that. For he invoked a theater that "did not limit itself to showing intimate scenes from the lives of a few puppets, transforming the audience into Peeping Toms," but one that put the audience face to face with the fact that "everything that exists is cruelty." He went on to assert that "it is upon this idea of extreme action pushed beyond all limits that the theater must be rebuilt. . . . This cruelty will be bloody, if necessary."

From all of which one might conclude that Artaud seriously advocated the presentation of monstrous events on the stage. But he suddenly veered again and gave "cruelty" a purely figurative sense, identifying it with "a severe moral purity which is not afraid to pay life the price it must be paid." It is obvious that the only possible connection between

---

"bloody" cruelty and "severe moral purity" is metaphorical. One must not forget the deliberately extreme and often maniacal language he used. As a matter of fact, Artaud (in a letter to Jean Paulhan) made an attempt to soften the meaning of the "cruelty" to which he was so attached.

> It is not a question of brandishing the butcher's knife every minute but of re-introducing in each theatrical gesture the notion of a kind of cosmic cruelty without which there would be neither life nor reality.

"Cosmic cruelty" is obviously connected with what I have called Artaud's "gnosticism": his idea that since we are cast into a world of shadow and evil, since we strive to rise toward the light, and since we can act and create only in the world as it is, we are forced to collide with the laws of the body, matter, and evil, that is, with "cruelty." And if the theater is to tell the truth, *this* is the fact, he feels, that should be represented.

It seems to me that the most authentic and most penetrating of Artaud's insights is the idea that the theater, like the plague in ancient chronicles, is a ruthless revelation of the ultimate reality of existence, for it lays bare the true nature of the individual and the world in which he finds himself, thus causing the disintegration of social conventions. "Like the plague, the theater is a formidable summoning of forces, which, by example, guide the mind back to the source of its conflicts. . . ." And this statement is followed by a reference to the mysteries of Eleusis, which is connected with his assertion that

> the theater is, first of all, ritual and magic, tied to forces, and founded on a religion and on affective beliefs whose efficacy manifests itself in gestures and is *directly* linked to the rites of the theater, which are actually the exercise and expression of a spiritual need for magic.

Here we have not only the timeworn confusion of theater with religious rite, but also its confusion with magic and primitive myth. Yet we cannot deny that underlying all this was Artaud's serious idea of restoring to the theater its original and primary function: the public commemoration and celebration of the essential aspects of human destiny. It seems to me that he is calling us back to the same springs from which came the images of Oedipus' revelation and Macbeth's delirium, as well as Ibsen's passion for truth, Strindberg's obsessions, and Pirandello's vehement ratiocination. Furthermore, I find it quite arbitrary (even though seemingly justified by some of Artaud's declarations) to interpret his ideas as a prescription for "Happenings," dramatic improvisation, or the staging of violence. For, in such spectacles, anguish, which is so real for Artaud, becomes either an aesthetic object or a pretext for the unlikely—a far cry from the ideal theater, where "one stakes one's life."

My remarks should not be construed as a defense of the inert traditionalism of much of present-day Western theater, but as an attempt to treat with the seriousness it deserves Artaud's emphasis on the theater's essentially spiritual effect. (One might even speak in terms of "purification" or of the old, misunderstood catharsis.) "The theater must become a kind of experimental demonstration of the profound unity of the abstract and the concrete." Now, it is clear that such a demonstration cannot be conducted in a universe of gesture, scream, and fearful action. It can only be carried through on the level of the intellect, even if the means used is physical action.

There is a passage in Artaud that seems to me particularly pertinent. He is writing of the leap required to pass from real action (which is utilitarian and violent) to theatrical action (whose meaning lies precisely in its being gratuitous, made for contemplation and purely symbolic). In his essay "The Theater and the Plague," he says:

> An actor requires infinitely more power to keep from committing a crime than a murderer needs courage to complete his act. It is here, in its very gratuitousness, that the action and the effect of a feeling in the theater appears infinitely more valid than that of a feeling fulfilled in life. Compared with the murderer's fury, which exhausts itself, that of the tragic actor remains enclosed within a perfect circle. The murderer's fury accomplishes an act, discharges itself, and loses contact with the force that inspired but can no longer sustain it.

The actor's fury, however, Artaud points out, remains in contact with the nature of the world that inspired it.

The same idea is expressed in another essay. "Though a theatrical gesture is violent, it is disinterested. The theater teaches precisely the uselessness of the action, which, once done, is over, and the superior utility of the state of soul not consumed by an act and which, renewed, achieves a purification."

Yet we can find statements in Artaud's writings that completely contradict these passages and that really seem to call for a theater based on gesture, spectacular violence, and frenzy. But here we must pause and recall once again Artaud's point of departure and the direction he followed all his life. In the first place, he rejected realism root and branch. "To the crude visualization of what is," he said, "the theater opposes images of what is not." Of course, one might retort that this has always been the function of art. But Artaud's attitude requires elucidation. He refused to grant that contemporary "average men" and their empty, opaque existences had any reality.

Today we have reached the point of *applied life,* in which everything has disappeared—nature, images, and strength. We have reached a state of stagnation in which man lives on what he has inherited, with a reserve of feelings and moral attitudes that have not changed for the last century.

This is the situation that he felt must be undermined and destroyed. According to Artaud, realism both in life and in the theater was an essentially conservative force. He rebelled against modern man's pride in the realism of pragmatic thought and rejected all the ideologies that had fed Western society since the seventeenth century. In this world of utilitarian realism, man is conceived of as a series of psychological reactions which are to be adjusted to the objective social situation and its practical goals whatever they are. For Artaud, man belongs at the opposite pole, in the realm of abandoned freedom.

> We do not permit the obstruction of the free development of a delirium which is as legitimate and as logical as any other succession of human ideas and acts. The repression of antisocial reactions is as chimerical as it is unacceptable in principle. All individual acts are antisocial. Madmen are, by definition, the individual victims of social dictatorship. In the name of this individuality which is peculiar to man, we demand that these slaves of sensibility be freed.

This was written during the brief period Artaud spent in the ranks of the surrealists. With the passing of time he became more and more violent; for example, he accused modern medicine, particularly psychiatry, of trying to "rob man of his ego" and of "claiming the singular right to dictate the duties of each individual's conscience."

I believe this global revolt explains Artaud's passage from the notion of the theater as "a call to the forces that impel the mind by example to the source of its conflicts" to the extreme idea of a theater that "will no longer be based on dialogue; and dialogue itself, the little that remains, will not be written out and fixed a priori but will be put on the stage, created on the stage. . . ." Moreover, he asserts that the theater will be restored to itself only on the day when every dramatic representation evolves directly on the stage and is not a chewing over of a definitive, self-sufficient written text.

And we must not forget his declaration that "the theater, like the plague, takes gestures and pushes them as far as possible." Such observations are generally regarded as arguments for the idea of theater as total spectacle—a dramatic art form where gesture, movement, and sudden incongruous "Happenings" are violently stressed at the expense of the text and the coherent development of the action. It is probable that the insights of Artaud we choose to consider the most original and most personal ones are those, like the examples just given, where he strains his basic intuitions to the breaking point and reduces them to absurdity.

But, aside from the fact that elsewhere in his works more convincing and more penetrating reflections totally contradict the thesis of "total theater," we cannot accept it for other reasons. We know from his own utterances that Artaud's concern was not with staging but with the meaning and essential function of the drama. Moreover, the man who said "the spiritual infirmity of the West [can be seen in] man's confusing art with aestheticism" could not really be an aesthete and could not seriously attach great importance to aesthetic—purely spectacular—stage effects.

In truth, if we assume that Artaud's thinking is exclusively concerned with a theory of stage direction, we are forced to conclude that the theory is self-contradictory on the basis of his own writings. For it is based on two antithetical principles: (1) the substitution of the *mise en scène* for articulated language, and (2) the use of articulated language as a "means of expressing the *mise en scène*," that is, to make it "express what it generally does not express . . . *poetry*." It seems to me that this is trying to square the circle.

When Artaud attempted to clarify the meaning of his strictures against the emphasis on the text, he said, for example, "It is not a question of suppressing spoken language but of giving words the importance they have in dreams." This may be full of suggestions, but what does it mean to give words uttered on the stage the importance they have in dreams? It implies either a recitation of senseless phrases in somnambulistic attitudes or the opposite, a stylized, lyrical performance with words sounding as if they were dreamed, only because they take on a surrealistic quality entirely different from their value in ordinary discourse. As a matter of fact, it would be a return to a noble style of recitation somewhat similar to Arnold Schönberg's *Sprechgesang*. In that case, however, the words must be selected meticulously, *not* improvised.

If it is concrete suggestions for staging one is seeking in Artaud, one should examine the sections where he discusses the *"objective* unforeseen"—"the unforeseen, not in situations but in things, the abrupt untimely transition from an intellectual image to a true image; *e.g.*, the man who is blaspheming sees suddenly and realistically materialized the image of his blasphemy"—"or the sudden appearance of a fabricated Being made of wood and cloth entirely invented, corresponding to nothing yet disquieting by nature. . . ."

Excellent illustrations of successful use of the *"objective* unforeseen" are Pozzo and Lucky in Samuel Beckett's *Waiting for Godot* and Ionesco's creature in *Amédée* that grows until it overflows space. It is likely that these dramatists were influenced by Artaud, although we cannot be certain. In any case, such ideas were in the air even before the experiments of the surrealists. Moreover, Etienne Décroux's ideas about the use of pantomime and stylized, violent gesticulation were propounded as early as 1931. The young Jean-Louis Barrault, Artaud's friend and admirer, had gone to Décroux's school and, at the same time, had carefully studied Artaud's theories.

Of course, when Artaud called for the suppression of the spoken word he was, as usual, pushing his ideas to extremes. He did not mean all he said and immediately corrected or modified his position. But even if the devices identified with him can be considered relative innovations ("relative," for they were already known in Russia and Germany, if not in France), it is hard to see the connection between the use of pantomime and Artaud's vision of a theater that, freed from the chains of the average man's psychology and the bonds of realism, was to restore a sense of "moral danger" to the audience. If pantomime is made the most important theatrical element, the theater once again becomes all surface. The "aesthetic" factor, which Artaud genuinely disparaged, is accentuated. How, then, is his primary aim, the spiritual turmoil of the spectator, advanced—unless the "butcher's knife" is brandished, in which case we have a circus act, not pantomime. . . .

Be that as it may, pantomime does not lead us to the "metaphysical" theater of rigorous moral purity envisaged in *Le Théâtre et son double*. What, then, is the most coherent and comprehensive interpretation we can give to Artaud's miscellany of ideas on the theater? Can a clue to the underlying principle be found in the statement that the theater of the future should speak "a unique language halfway between the idea and the word"?

It is certainly the kind of phrase that appeals to modern sensibility, oscillating, as it does, between image and word—between the black magic of the pure sign, a simple, fleeting mark made by real movements, and the fascination of the evocative, symbolic, rhythmic words of coherent discourse. But it is a phrase that has no real application, except to the cinema and to the dance styles of contemporary adolescents.

After all, if Artaud's message is simply that a theater of immediate "sensation" is closer to us than dramas based on the inevitable, logical development of a human action that conflicts and interacts with other human actions, then it amounts to nothing more than a facile denunciation of conventional drama, which is already in its death throes, if not completely dead.

What can we finally say, then, about Artaud?

First of all, I think we must recognize the fact that his idea of the theater is not merely ambiguous but self-contradictory to the point of schizophrenia. On the one hand, his theater must strive for spiritual intensity and the purity of poetry. On the other, it must cling furiously to the corporeal, to the actual presence, to the brutal and exterior effect. If we separate these two drives, we reduce each of them to a series of banal propositions. It seems to me that the source of their significance and evocative power is the spasmodic tension between them and the irresolute immobility resulting from it. Otherwise, one is tempted to send Artaud's admirers back to a book published about a century ago, Friedrich Nietzsche's *Birth of Tragedy*, where the two conflicting principles are defined with considerably greater clarity.

Roger Blin, a man of the theater, Artaud's friend and (to some degree) his disciple, summed up his impressions of Artaud's work in these lines:

> A maximum of stylization, a maximum of antinaturalism, and not merely the rejection, but the destruction, of every canon of the bourgeois and classical theater. This is Artaud's great value. . . . However, I was never persuaded by the application of these principles, by the stress on brutality, cruelty, screaming. . . . For Artaud the stage is a space to be filled with gestures, not with words, because words exert a tyranny. In short, it seems to me that Artaud aimed at a surrealist theater that never existed.

The theater envisaged by Artaud's current discoverers is one that never existed and could only exist very artificially and very briefly.

As for Artaud himself, what he wanted was not just a theater that never existed, but one that *never could exist:* a medium of total regeneration, in which he could play the role of Antonin Artaud and give substance to the emptiness of the written word, thereby redeeming himself from the world of shadows that imprisoned him.

Published as "Antonin Artaud,"
Encounter, August 1967
(Trans. Miriam Chiaromonte)

12

The Political Theater

In a certain sense, the first known example of political theater dates very nearly from the birth of theater in the West. It is the famous case of the *Capture of Miletus*, by Phrynichus, a contemporary of Aeschylus, whose play was staged in Athens in 493 B.C. The tragedy, Herodotus says, enacted the fall of the great Ionian colony into the hands of the Medes, who massacred the male inhabitants and made slaves of the women and children. The production, Herodotus also reports, roused the Athenian audience to such wild displays of collective grief that the play was closed at once, the poet sentenced to pay a fine of a thousand drachmas, and the tragedy permanently banned.

We have here, it seems, a perfect example of political theater: the subject of a public nature and a burning topicality, since Miletus had fallen the year before; the violent emotion of the audience; the interference of censorship first and trial afterward; finally, the sentencing of a dramatic poet for having dared to make a play out of a national disaster, for "defeatism," so to speak.

The history of the Greek theater, moreover, offers numerous examples of political theater. Aeschylus' *The Persians* is a political tragedy; the Peloponnesian War is present in the form of allusions, sometimes quite transparent ones at that, in those of Euripides' plays that have the Trojan War as their subject; and, finally, the comedies of Aristophanes are openly political, so that he, too, had to pay in person for his opposition to Cleon, the demagogue whom he persisted in ridiculing so fiercely in *The Knights,* although he had already been the victim of Cleon's persecutions in court. And, as we know, the production of *The Knights* brought about the expulsion of Cleon by the enraged populace.

Even Shakespeare's history plays can be considered great examples of political theater. For some people, even *Hamlet* and *King Lear* are in substance political tragedies: Francis Fergusson has quite dazzlingly argued just such an interpretation of *Hamlet* in *The Idea of a Theater.* The romantic theater in the last century, from Schiller to Victor Hugo, was surely political; we can say (and this applies in part to the plays of Vittorio Alfieri as well) that the true protagonist of that theater is History, or, to be exact, the struggle is between the free individual and the forces of evil, darkness, and tyranny. A still more political drama—indeed, perhaps the drama to place at the origin of the modern political theater—is *Danton's Death,* by Georg Büchner.

If, however, we speak of political theater, the name nine out of ten people bring up is that of Bertolt Brecht. This is unjust. The creator of the formula and the founder of a theater wanting to be, explicitly and radically, not only political in the broad sense but also immediately at the service of a course of political action—the Communist course determined by the Bolsheviks—is Erwin Piscator, the director with whom Brecht collaborated for some time and by whom he was more than merely influenced, at least as to theory.

For Piscator, a Bavarian, like Brecht, and three years Brecht's senior, and for Brecht (as well as for what we can call the first Communist generation), the crucial experience was that of the First World War, in which Piscator had taken part as a common soldier. The horror at that unheard-of slaughter and at the blindness of those who caused it, stubbornly going on with it nearly to the exhaustion of "human resources," was the prime reason for the ferment that followed the war in Europe. Along with the Bolshevik accession to power in Russia, that horror was also the point of departure for the political theater of Piscator. In this theater (as, on the whole, in Brecht's as well), pacifism and revolutionary ideology blur into a single protest in the name of the individual crushed by brute force, whether of political power or of money.

"My personal epoch begins on the 4th of August, 1914." These are the opening words of Piscator's memoirs, to which he gave the title *The Political Theater*. The sense of his career as a man of the theater and of the firmly preconceived ideas (rather than theories) that were the basis of his theater is all in that one sentence. It expresses, besides the foundation of Piscator's Communism (which he himself dates from the reading of the message for immediate peace issued by Lenin and Trotsky on November 28, 1917), the idea that he had formed of the theater as a means of breaking with all art of the past, with the aim of making evident the problems of current history and urging action to "solve" them. The derivation of such an idea from the one that inspired the romantic theater seems direct enough, let us add parenthetically. The romantic idea of the theater is pushed here to its extreme. From such extremism derives Piscator's conception of the relation between director, actors, and authors, a relation that was, in his view, entirely subordinate to the political (or revolutionary) task in which the contemporary theater was bound to engage.

Just as it was taken for granted that the war and the Bolshevik Revolution had opened the ear of the proletariat and closed the ear of the bourgeoisie, so the political task of the theater was no more than the duty to reduce every theatrical theme to the most unimaginative topicality, represented in the most sensational way, with the aim not of moving the feelings but of provoking action.

According to Piscator, the theater had to be revolutionary because it was eminently the art of the present and of the topical. Conversely, no one could conceive of a topical art that would not be revolutionary. To bring about an authentic theater, it was not necessary to set out with this or that aesthetic, this or that idea of art, but, rather, to reject them all and be prompted solely by the will to transform the stage into a political forum (rather, into a Tribunal, as the first of Piscator's theaters was called), to participate in political events and influence them through polemics, accusations, and praise. This ought to be done even at the risk of turning productions into sheer propaganda pieces. But, argues Piscator with sophistical naïveté, the best art makes the most effective propaganda; bad art is not only bad propaganda but misguided politics as well, undermining and counterrevolutionary. Communism frees the theater insofar as it furnishes it with an ideology and thus opens up for the theater the paths of what Piscator calls "constructive thinking," denied to bourgeois culture, which is by nature utilitarian and consequently incapable of true thinking.

This is a convenient point to digress for a bit in order to clarify the difference between what we mean when we call Aeschylus' *The Persians* or Aristophanes' *The Knights* "political theater" and the meaning the expression takes on for Piscator and subsequently for Brecht and his followers.

The difference is far from complicated. In *The Persians* and *The Knights* politics comes in naturally; the choice of a public subject on the author's part is a spontaneous one. In Piscator, instead, the intervention is willful, and the choice of a subject is based upon a fixed ideology. Or, to put it differently, the Athenian playwrights bring politics into their tragedies and comedies the way, in Molière, Monsieur Jourdain brings in prose—simply because they were creating theater. "Politics," for them, meant "what concerns the *polis*," and the *polis* was not only the place of everyone, a free space protected by sacred laws, but also the place of *everything*, that is, of all that concerns man as a human being, and not just his private affairs; and, by the same token, not only the public events of the moment. In this sense, the Greek theater was political by nature. In writing the *Oresteia* and in writing *The Persians*, Aeschylus was inspired by the history of Greece and of Athens; but there was no ideology, no power, and no party that led him to deal with that subject rather than another. The stories of the House of Atreus and of the Trojan War were no less "political," they were of no less concern to the moral life of the community, than the victory of Salamis or the expedition of Cleon to Pylos. If anything, they were of greater concern, inasmuch as the plots of those ancient legends and stories allowed the community to recall and commemorate more extraordinary events and more significant characters than those of the present time. A current or recent event, such as the victory over the great fleet of Xerxes, had dramatic value to the extent that the poet was truly able to "give it distance," to contemplate it by raising himself above the emotions and passions of the moment.

The Persians is a splendid proof of that ability, the loftiest example of civic poetry that we know of.

"Our geometry applies only to matter, but the Greeks practiced it first of all in learning virtue," wrote Simone Weil in "The Iliad; or, The Poem of Force." Eight years after the triumph at Salamis, an Athenian poet caused his own townspeople to contemplate not the grandeur of their deed, but solely and strictly the law of the gods that had led to the ruin of the huge Persian force, the punishment of Xerxes' *hubris*, the harvest of sorrow reaped by a people because of the rashness of their king.

This is the highest note of the tragedy: the triumph of the poet's mind over the victory of his country and (if it is true that Aeschylus himself fought at Salamis) over his own victory. The victory with arms appears, in the drama, less important than its moral rightness. There is, to be sure, the famous account of the Messenger, and when he arrives at the point where the Greeks in fury strike their beaten enemies in the sea, "like tuna spilled from the nets," the savage thrill of victory in battle must have run through the audience. But the words in which the pride of Aeschylus the Athenian resounds are not those of the account of the battle of Salamis (whose function in the tragedy is, rather, to show with full emphasis the disaster of the Persians), but the meager bits of dialogue between Queen Atossa and the Leader of the Chorus, when she asks where Athens is and how armed and how rich and who commands the Athenians as their lord and master. The Leader of the Chorus replies, "They are no one's slaves or subjects"; at which the astonished Queen says, "How then could they resist the enemy invasion?" It is through her astonishment that Aeschylus gives us a sudden sense that it is Nemesis which has struck the barbarians and communicates to us that joy in victory which is truly liberating and purifying: the joy of being in the right, at one with laws more powerful than those that govern the world of material power. The largest force on earth has, in fact, been routed not by an equal and opposite force, but by that imponderable and sacred element which rules the course of human events and with which the Athenians were miraculously in harmony. The meaning of the victory and its merit consist in this.

We can measure the darkness of our present situation (darker than that of the period before Marathon and Salamis, when no Greek community felt protected from external violence) from the answer given today, in high and low places, to Atossa's question, an answer that is always completely in favor of force.

As a final comment in this digression on *The Persians* and on the lesson that Aeschylus wished to bestow upon his townspeople in order to celebrate the victory against Xerxes, perhaps it is not out of place to recall that the *choregus*, the citizen called on as a public honor to pay the expenses of mounting the production, was Pericles, not yet twenty years old; the same man who, forty years later, with the aid of the most lucid, even faultless, arguments, would persuade the Athenians to wage a war to the death against Sparta and therefore would lead Athens on a path of *hubris* just as ruinous as Xerxes' had been.

To my citing the example of Aeschylus, a Marxist could answer that it does not apply to our case, since the Athenian poet was in moral agreement with a society that, in its turn, conceived of dramaturgy as a civic function; whereas what distinguishes the capitalist society in which we are living is the impossibility of such an agreement, the inevitable alienation of the individual (and, with all the more reason, of the individual artist) not only from the constituted social order, but also from his own work and from himself as a human being. Hence the inevitably unhappy and, as a result, inevitably negative and embattled situation of the modern individual.

The objection has a basis of truth, but on a quite different level and for reasons a lot more complex than those a Marxist is likely to adduce. First of all, what matters in the example of Aeschylus is not the case of a poet "integrated" in his society and of a society capable of "integrating" the poet naturally, but the fact that in the dramaturgy of Aeschylus (as in that of Sophocles and Euripides) the real political or civic element is an organic part of a definite view of the meaning of existence, and does not prevail over that view and even less does it exhaust it. In the second place, if we are speaking of art, it is evident that what Marxists call "alienation" can be expressed in many and diverse ways; there is no imperative that forces us to give it the form of political or social polemics. And this for the simple reason that nothing can force anyone (a poet least of all) to *feel* a certain condition of things in a fixed way and to begin his discourse from a point established in advance. An imperative of this sort can come only from outside and from above, from the will to urge a definite type of political action. Such a will implies the conviction that the world ought to be considered from a given viewpoint and not from others, which amounts to possessing an absolute and absolutely authoritative truth. Such a will expresses, as well, the belief that political action is, until further notice, a categorical imperative, an absolute, the truest form of the relation between man and the world.

It is on this point that we ought to be arguing and not on the nature of the Athenian social order, in regard to which we can surely grant that there now remains no other relation with it except memory and that therefore it would be absurd to take Greek tragedy as a model for the dramaturgy of today.

On the other hand, not only is the modern political theater a theater inspired by a definite ideology and by a definite polemical cause (antibourgeois, anti-capitalist, anti-imperialist), but also it relies on a conception of theatrical spectacle that is the opposite of the Greek conception, as well as the opposite of the one from which the modern theater, from the end of the last century until recently—the theater of Ibsen, Strindberg, Chekhov, Shaw, Pirandello—has drawn its inspiration. And we could go on to the very present, mentioning Witkiewicz, Ionesco, Beckett, Genet, Gombrowicz. More than on the poetic word and on the dramatic or comic conflict, the political theater rests on the visual and auditory emotions: this is one of its salient features. In Piscator's productions, as in Brecht's theatrical inventions, it is a question of pointing and showing by way of plastic example, not of logically developing the contrast between opposed moral situations. Drama turns into fable. Hence the importance the staging takes on, even when, as in Brecht, it has apparently been reduced to the minimum.

It should suffice to mention here Mother Courage's wagon, of which we can say that it contains in itself the entire significance of the series of scenes imagined by Brecht on the theme of war.

In short, in the political theater it is the theater of stagecraft, the theater-as-spectacle, that asserts itself, finding in the aim of political edification support for the aestheticism that characterizes it. Why aestheticism? Because, by its nature, this theater transforms into a more or less phantasmagorical scenic image the incitement to action it intends to produce, so that the formal element naturally gains the upper hand. In speaking of Piscator, we should not forget the influence that directors like Vsevolod Meyerhold and Alexander Taïrov exercised on him—men who distinguish themselves by the attempt to translate the revolutionary idea into a language of scenic design derived from the aesthetics of the Russian artistic and literary avant-garde of their time.

Erwin Piscator's ideas are a mixture of mere intuitions and farfetched concepts, of a genuine sense of theatrical spectacle and a superstructure of ideology and advertising, of creative imagination and pedantry. From such a mixture sprang a form of theater as original as it was ephemeral. Ephemeral not because it has had no disciples, since, indeed, it still has some, but for the intrinsic superficiality of the effects it seeks to obtain. On the other hand, Piscator's originality derives from the unperturbed logic with which he breached the baroque and eighteenth-century theatrical patterns through every sort of staging device and technical resource, going from actors scattered on purpose amid the audience to the introduction of film, not only as background but as an integral part of the production.

But, as we have already hinted, the idea that Piscator carried to the extreme was not so much the one of political theater as it was the one of absolute supremacy for the production and the inventions of scene design over every other element of the spectacle, and, above all, over the word. The director, according to Piscator, had to be a sort of emissary (or commissar) of historical forces, the supreme arbitrator of the total *effect* of the spectacle. And that effect, naturally, would have to be upsetting and revolutionary. But, in reality, it was an effect pure and simple; and to this effect every other element of the spectacle had to be subordinate. All of which meant, to put it briefly, that everything had to be subordinate to the success the spectacle would have thanks to the sensation of novelty it provoked. Setting out from an extreme preoccupation with ideological content, Piscator thus arrived at the most extreme and self-defeating of formalisms. "The director and the author both have a single purpose: the success of the work," he proclaimed. He did not realize that, in making such pronouncements, he was giving a dogmatic form to the law that rules artistic production in a mass society. And, in fact, it is the advent of the mass media of communication (photography, movies, radio, yellow journalism), not the advent of Socialism, that the theater of Piscator really foretold.

As for Bertolt Brecht, it is well to remember that he began to put his conception of the theater into theoretical formulas only in 1934, when his career as a playwright was already established. We can, incidentally, note that the expression "epic theater" and the theory attached to it, which usually are considered Brecht's original ideas, not only were in the air but also had been written down well before him. And it is useful to stress another detail: "epic" in German simply means "narrative." In such a definition the meaning of Brecht's theater is already contained; it is a narrative theater, or, if you like, a theater of demonstration, not drama. The distinction is important.

For Brecht, in fact, it is the dramatic theater (no more or less than the Western theater from the fifth century B.C. to our time) that, in giving the spectator the illusion of witnessing a real action, involves him in the very action and fascinates him like a daydream, so that he loses his capacity for judgment. What distinguishes Brecht's "epic theater" is the fact that it consists of a series of objective illustrations of the "morality" that the author has in mind, produced on a bare stage and "distanced" (*entfremdet*) by an ironic performance. It ought, therefore, to leave the spectator aware that he is looking upon a fictive work and is free to draw his own conclusions from what is being performed. But we are still dealing with a "morality," or a "fable" if you prefer. Brecht's dice are loaded and are meant to be. For example, it is understood in advance that in watching *Mother Courage* the spectator will be unable not to conclude in favor of proletarian revolution and against warmongering capitalism. This does not, luckily for Brecht the artist, turn out to be the case; *Mother Courage* is in reality a pessimistic fable, indeed, nihilistic and misanthropic, much more than pacifist or anticapitalist. What is shown in it is not so much the degradation caused by war as the abjectness to which the human animal is willing to stoop just to survive the storms of history. If we imagine it taking place in Russia between 1919 and 1921, during the Revolution and the Civil War, the costumes would be different but the meaning would remain the same. The moral of another renowned epic composition of Brecht's, *Galileo,* is substantially no different from that of *Mother Courage.* In the final analysis, it still deals with the baseness of man, and the baseness is not condemned; it is, rather, considered a legitimate defense of the individual against the violence of arms or the implacable force of institutions.

The theory of the epic theater is therefore specious. No discussion shows this better than one by Brecht himself, in a famous passage quoted as classically convincing by his admirers, in which he defines the difference between the moral situation of the spectator before dramatic theater and before epic theater.

> The spectator of dramatic theater says: "Yes, I too have experienced this feeling—Yes, I too am like that—Well, this is natural—It will always be like that—The

suffering of this man moves me, because there is no other outcome for it—This is great art: all here is obvious, is evident—I weep with whoever is weeping, I laugh with whoever is laughing."

The spectator of epic theater says: "I would never have thought of this—You ought not to do this like that—It's surprising, almost inconceivable—It can't go on like that—The suffering of this man moves me, because it might have turned out differently!—This is great art: nothing here is obvious—I laugh with whoever is weeping, I weep with whoever is laughing."

Now, it seems obvious that, in Brecht's discussion, various kinds of theater and of possible reactions of the spectator in the theater are deliberately confused. For example, the observations on dramatic theater could apply to bourgeois comedy but certainly not to Sophocles, to Ibsen, or to Shaw. On the other hand, there is nothing particularly bourgeois in a play (like *Philoctetes* or *King Lear*) that makes the spectator say, "The suffering of this man moves me, because there is no other outcome for it"; while it is a very ordinary bit of sarcasm to imagine that watching a beautiful play (say, Kleist's *Prince Friedrich of Homburg*) makes him observe that it is "great art" because "all here is obvious, is evident." Again, almost all of Brecht's observations on what he defines as "dramatic theater" apply as well to certain scenes by Brecht himself: to the episode of Dumb Kattrin in *Mother Courage*, which is moving—but that is a poetic virtue, not a fault. Whereas everyone sees, conversely, how much distance or "distanc*ing*"—or, more simply, reflection —not only a tragedy by Aeschylus or Euripides imposes with complete naturalness on the spectator, but a play by Strindberg or Pirandello as well.

More specious still than the theory of the epic theater (though no one would deny that, as applied by

Brecht himself and by the actors of the Berliner Ensemble, it has yielded theatrically outstanding results) is Brecht's theory of the political theater. We can sum it up from the response the playwright-director gave in 1955, a year before he died, to the question "Is it possible to express the world of today by means of the theater?" The response was: "The world of today can be described to men of today only if one describes it as a world that can be changed." And Brecht added, "For men of today, the value of today's problems can be measured by the answers they get. Men of today are interested in situations faced with which they can act in some way."

Now, characteristically, this opinion of his contains more truth than it seems to at first glance, if we don't balk at the banality of the formulas; but, at the same time, it is a lot more false than a devotee of pure art might find it.

The truth is a truth of fact: it is true, that is, that nowadays men, taken in the mass, are not interested in contemplated action (that is, in *drama* in the true root sense of the word), but in action or potential action. That means a succession of images, movements, gestures, and (secondarily) words that arouse overwhelming emotion and possibly active participation (or physical imitation). It corresponds, in the most significant instance, to a ritual action, a dance or collective frenzy, in which we participate with limbs and nerves but not mind. And this occurs because what we look for in such actions is to submerge our self-consciousness in frenzied movement. In Greek, it was called *dromenon*, which indeed means "action," in opposition to *drama*, which is the action seen from outside, contemplated.

This means, however, that, taken in the mass, men nowadays are not interested in the theater, epic or dramatic, as the case may be. At the theater the individual cannot help participating with his mind as well as with the emotions of his nerves and his visual, auditory, and plastic sensibility. After all, Brecht said he wished to attain just this with epic theater, so that the audience, remaining outside the action, not charmed or roused to frenzy, might judge it and draw reasoned conclusions from it. In this respect, there is nothing new in Brecht's conception; surely every dramatist of any importance, from Aeschylus to Molière, from Molière to Strindberg, Chekhov, and Pirandello, understood theater in the same way.

On the other hand, Brecht's thesis is false for a very simple reason, which recalls the answer T. S. Eliot gave to those who spoke of the theater as a religious event: "If I wish to participate in a rite, I go to Mass, not to the theater." Similarly, if it is true, as Brecht asserted, that nowadays men are interested in the theater only insofar as the theater can describe the world as a world that can be changed, it is worth noting in the first place how obscure the debatable Marxist notion becomes when it is applied to theatrical fiction. Fiction is fiction, and such it remains, despite every edifying or didactic intention. A work of fiction never refers to the so-called "real" world, much less to this or that action one must perform, but always and only to the world of feelings, thoughts, meanings; the world of the spirit and of communication on a spiritual level, whose connection with the real world, and in a particular way with the world of actions, remains indefinite by nature. What sort of action is suggested by, let us say, not *Oedipus the King* or *Rosmersholm*, but by *The Threepenny Opera* or *The Caucasian Chalk Circle*?

In the second place, if it is true, as Brecht asserted, that nowadays men are interested in the theater only to the extent that the theater describes the world as a world that can be changed (which, please note, presupposes a fundamental optimism as regards the world itself and human nature), then, instead of going to the theater, they should go to "change the world," whatever the meaning of such a notion in theory may be and whatever may be the practical consequences that might possibly be drawn from it.

Dramatic or epic, as the case may be, we go to the theater in order to *contemplate* the world (that is, to find a possible meaning in men's apparently meaningless actions) and not to change it or to get the urge to change it. The moral and practical consequences of such contemplation are something else again, something having to do with the metamorphoses of the individual mind, which follow unforeseeable paths, never traced in advance.

Moreover, if it is Marxist in form, in substance Brecht's opinion matches the conservative's and the philistine's; it is, in fact, typical of the conservative and the philistine that they are interested only "in situations faced with which they can act," as Brecht put it. This is exactly the reason why the conservative and the philistine really dislike either the serious theater or any form of unbiased thought or free art.

Naturally, to impugn Brecht's theories does not mean to deny his talent as a writer and a man of the theater. As a writer and a man of the theater, Bertolt Brecht remains one of the most significant personalities of our time; but not for the reasons he gives, much less for those his adulators cite.

The limitations of directors like Piscator and of director-dramatists like Brecht do not stem from their desire to create a political theater, but from their rigid, pre-established idea of politics. This contradicts both the nature of theater and the nature of politics. To begin with, a theatrical action, however unreal, is an objective fact, and the preconceived opinions or didactic aims of the director or even the author cannot reduce it to the single meaning he would like it to have. This, let us add parenthetically, is the reef on which some presumptuous contemporary directors have foundered, insisting as they have on tendentious interpretations and overelaborate productions. The best inventions by Brecht (who tended, as a director, toward literal fidelity)—*The Threepenny Opera, Mother Courage, The Caucasian Chalk Circle*—are vitriolic, picturesque, and (I am tempted to add) picaresque fables about the elementary simplicity, hardness, and lowness of human instincts, and therefore about the rather distressing nature of human history. No effort on the part of ideologists can cause them to mean incitement to revolution or to be a demonstration of the class struggle.

There is no partisanship in the theater, whether of ideologist or of director, that can change the meaning of a theatrical situation, because, once it has been defined, it resists even its author's solicitations; in fact, the quality of a play more often than not can be appraised by the clarity with which the author was able to recognize the essential in the situation he began with and to stick to it, without allowing himself to be distracted by secondary ideas or rhetorical temptations. In the same way, there is no political ideology that can change the nature of the real situation, which is recognized by common sense even before politicians recognize it; and the best politician is not the one who persists in demonstrating that he was right, but the one whom the present state of things seems to prove right. In one instance as in the other, in theater as in politics, it is we citizen-spectators who are the arbiters. The dramatist who does not touch our common moral situation interests us as little as the politician who can impose his power and the power of his party but who does not care about the lot of real people. They are both remote personages, or, if you like, specialists whose language has validity only for their fellow specialists.

The contemporary political theater follows an entirely different direction from that marked first by Ibsen and then by Shaw. It is a theater that goes not from the situation toward its logical outcome through a more or less dialectical development, from action toward lyrical expression, or from emotion toward meaning, but, on the contrary, from a certain theme drawn more or less directly from current events toward the most spectacular and violent effect of stage-craft possible and from a certain pre-established idea toward a mimed symbol of it, plastic or vocal. And I say "vocal" to indicate that, in such a theater, the word tends to have a purely functional role, not unlike what it has in sound movies.

This is evident in Piscator and quite clear in Brecht; it becomes explicitly programatic in what today is called the "theater of confrontation," running from the Living Theater to Peter Brook's productions, passing through various minor American, French, and Italian efforts. The fact that many of these men of the theater go back to Artaud and interpret as they do the heterogeneous and contradictory ideas included in his formula of the "theater of cruelty" serves only to emphasize this tendency, which, all considered, abandons drama for a form of theater that is often called a theater of "gesture."

Such a tendency already appears clearly in Brecht, whose inventions, as we have already noted, have nothing of the dramatic, but are, rather, plastic symbols of a definite idea. In the best pieces by this theoretician of "epic theater," the idea takes the form of a staged ballad with a script to it. The script is almost always too long and wordy, almost always overburdened by the moral the author wants to force on it, which then remains truly hanging there, outside the theatrical image in which it ought to be embodied. Brecht's originality consisted in his ability to invent strongly expressive images for the stage, like the already mentioned wagon of Mother Courage.

In short, as regards Brecht's theater there are two facts to stress here. The first is that the "epic theater" is really a theater of stage effects, not of the word or of dialogue; therefore, it not only is not dramatic, it is not even ideological, since the concrete image on stage inevitably goes beyond any ideological intention and remains fatally ambiguous in that respect. The second fact to stress is that a theater like Brecht's ends in a sort of performance in which the political intention is transformed into a bantering fable whose meaning is essentially nihilistic. After all, it is really the nihilism—that mixture of dry cynicism and discomfort expressed better, perhaps, in some poems than in the theater—that constitutes Brecht's originality and modernity. It is to his nihilism and basic unbelief that his success in this postwar period is due, and not to the banal didacticism of his declared intentions.

The importance of Brecht's work as a playwright and director in the contemporary theater lies in his having contributed in an outstanding way to the transformation (which had already begun long before him, let us not forget) of the stage from the realm of the incarnate word to the site of more or less picturesque scenic effects and of polemical illustrations of preconceived notions. The forms of theater based on gesture, on realistic effects, on orgiastic frenzy that are presented just about everywhere today owe much to the author of *The Threepenny Opera*. "Productions ought to let the thing being performed take precedence," Brecht wrote. It is true that he added that the "thing being performed" would have to be "the common life of men"; but, theatrically speaking, this is a hollow phrase. The "thing" really being performed by Brecht is the concrete image that corresponds to the intention of his fable, and his method is the one of montage in the movies, which he himself contrasts with the principle of dramatic development.

Today, in the phraseology of a certain avant-garde, the political theater has become the "theater of confrontation" or of "protest" (or even "guerrilla theater"). We cannot, to be sure, see wherein the difference in subject matter really lies, except for the usually lesser talent of the new authors and directors. The attacks on the bourgeois mentality, the "affluent society" with its advertising, imperialism, racism, the American way of life, war in general and the war in Vietnam in particular, which are modish today on the stage of Europe and America, have this peculiarity: on the one hand, they smash in the doors that were already open, "confronting" ideas and facts that wear their weaknesses on their sleeve; while, on the other, they are simply rather weak forms of political theater, since they are reduced to turning in a circle around the thesis that evil is evil, good is good, war is ugly, peace is beautiful, and so on. The "confrontation" of Piscator and of Brecht, besides stemming from less simple-minded ideas, was in any case a great deal more artful and had quite a different charge of virulence.

But if we look carefully we see that the so-called "theater of confrontation" has no ideological intentions; it is addressed not to the mind but to the nerves. It aims at striking the spectator from the outside, with stage effects and pantomimes so shocking and violent as to force him (so the belief goes) to recognize himself as an alienated individual in a world void of meaning. In reality, however, it does not escape the aestheticism of which it is intended to be the absolute antithesis. Faced with the most provocative effects, the most orgiastic and realistic frenzies, the spectator still remains a spectator; the more frenzied the acts that seek to involve him, the more unrelated and the more rigid is his situation as a simple onlooker. A confrontation that is not moral but physical (which, that is, addresses itself to the nerves rather than the consciousness) confronts nothing. At most, it causes a temporary thrill and the illusion of participating, through such a thrill, in the struggle of good against evil.

The fact is that an authentic return from *drama* to *dromenon*, from contemplated action to enacted action, would imply that we had to deal with a real rite, not with theater; and this, in turn, would presuppose no more or less than the existence of a new religion. Now, neither in the individual soul nor in the life of society can political ideology take the place of religious belief. Grown inflexible, it can only transform itself into fanaticism. And fanaticism, for its part, can surely mobilize the spirit of sacrifice and of conquest in man, but as to moral life and artistic creativity it is sterile by nature. Particularly sterile, in this regard, is the still dominant and basically fanatical idea holding that the meaning of human life resides in the succession of historical events, that its substance is politics, so that the destiny of humanity will be decided on the terrain of political struggle. In such a case, naturally, political ideology—which in itself has to do with the field of action, the very terrain of the contingent and the relative—becomes an absolute of a religious type, and with it the state, the nation, the society, the party become ultimate and absolute realities. Such a belief is hostile by nature not only to artistic creativity, but to every kind of human activity that refuses to become its instrument; indeed, the divinities of this religion call for ruling hierarchies and rank slavery, not ritual ceremonies, liturgies, and festive celebrations.

Now, it is precisely from an ideology of this type that the contemporary political theater draws its inspiration. That explains its limits; and it explains, as well, how such a theater, even if it is almost inspired by genuine artistic intentions, ends by transforming itself into something that goes beyond ideological intentions, into a theater of gesture and of orgiastic realism. Whether such forms of spectacle can still be called theater is doubtful. But that is a question to take up somewhere else.

The discussion we are engaged in here does not at all imply the rejection of the idea of political theater. In a certain sense, no great theater is unpolitical; all great theater is concerned with the life of the community by way of individual cases. In particular, there is no doubt that, given the way we live now, plays and comedies based on family affairs, unhappy loves, and things of that sort have become impossible, rather than intolerable; as with realistic stories, their place is in screen and television plays, not in the theater. The only themes that withstand the test of the live stage are the ones concerned with the common fate, with the situation of man as such today. To use a slightly abused word, we can say that the contemporary theater tends to be a metaphysical theater; the few examples of original dramaturgy we have, from Beckett to Ionesco, to Genet, to Harold Pinter's best work, to the most recent Polish, Czechoslovakian, and Hungarian theater, move in this direction. But that does not deny that the formation of theatrical companies composed of writers, actors, and directors who dedicate themselves to transforming the political events of the moment into drama or farce would be an excellent thing.

The first, paradoxical, purpose of a political theater today would be to struggle against the tyranny of politics (of the absolutism of the state or party) over the life of society. But, paradox aside, such a theater would have two purposes. The first of these is to fight that deadly sophistry of our time according to which the only valid judgments on politics are those made by the experts, by the professional Machiavellians, and by the professors of Machiavellianism—in short, "inside" judgments—while all the rest is vain intellectualism and moralism. Since we want to banish them from the "stage" of politics, it would be extremely proper to have the intellectuals and moralists take the theatrical stage. There, they would play the role of that animal, man, which is in essence political but neither expert nor Machiavellian (at least, in Aristotle's view). This man, being the one who suffers the politics of the experts and the Machiavellians, will have at least the right to discuss it behind a mask and by way of theatrical fiction.

On the other hand, while it would give satisfaction to the ordinary person, such a theater would also try to do justice to the politician, the expert, and the Machiavellian, who are not, as we are often led to believe, just monsters, dolts, or egomaniacs, but, if looked at closely, are men as well.

The second purpose of such a political theater is

more strictly theatrical. It ought to be completely different from the one conceived by a Piscator or a Brecht, inasmuch as it is inspired by no damaging ideology but simply by the liberty to judge and satirize. To bring politics to the theater, to bring it there seriously, not smuggled in as if it was an advertisement, means (as we have already noted) to bring ideas there and drive out anecdotes, family affairs, psychological clichés drawn from daily newspapers, false spiritualism, and false moralism. An authentic political theater, something other than a cabaret theater, would not deal in a more or less journalistic way with the affairs of the day; on the contrary, starting out with the political and social events of the moment, it would bring to light the conflicts of passions, interests, and ideas that underlie them, while portraying them in a convincing manner.

Our times have been marked by the unleashing of force in its most ferocious forms; and in our experience of the violent and pitiless power exercised by man over man we have encountered the presence of the "numinous." So far, such an experience has been impoverished by stereotyped ideas, by ideological sentimentality, and by demagogy. Therefore, it is legitimate to imagine a political theater that, among other things, restored the sense of the tragic conflict, the awareness deep down that there are insoluble clashes and insurmountable limits in life, and that on this very awareness the dignity of man's lot is based. From such an awareness could spring a sense of life a little less degrading than the one evinced in the ways of thinking and acting that are widespread today.

It might be difficult for this theater to avoid the banal realism that still controls, in strange forms, contemporary writing. A political theater that rejects realism may seem a contradiction in terms. But it is not. There are two ways, both servile ones, of facing current events. The first is to follow, to copy, even, their "plot," simplifying it only insofar as deemed useful to the stage effect. This is the way of propaganda, more or less sophisticated. The second way, more intelligent, is to transpose them by means of ideology, replacing the real sequence of events with a more or less prefabricated logic; this is Brecht's theoretical principle, and it has the inconvenience of establishing an intellectually, morally, and aesthetically specious link with reality—which leads, by the way, to doubts as to the authenticity of the ideological intention of such work.

But perhaps there is a third way, one that begins with rejecting the first axiom of realism, according to which the significance of events and human actions is exactly parallel to the occurrence of the events and the performance of the actions themselves and, so to speak, is parallel in time as well, so that any intervention of the imagination, the intellect, the symbol, would lead to a weakening of the significance. Naturally, the contrary is true: it is truly impossible to render the *real* significance of a fact without having come to conceive it in the imagination. *The Persians* of Aeschylus, the comedies of Aristophanes, the history plays of Shakespeare, and the comedies of Shaw are surely outstanding examples of a political theater that is not realistic or even ideological and yet is genuine.

Here, to sum up, is the problem that the theater of Piscator, the theater of Brecht, and the present-day "theater of confrontation" do not solve, but obscure. Yet we have to admit that such forms of theater at least have the merit of posing the problem. And that, after all, is the crucial problem in the creation of a dramatic theater that is contemporary, not with the events of the day, but with our sensibility and with the questions that, in the depths of our consciousness, we address to ourselves and to the world we live in.

From *The Rarer Action: Essays in Honor of Francis Fergusson*,
edited by Alan Cheuse and Richard Koffler.
New Brunswick, N.J., Rutgers University Press, 1970.
(Trans. Richard Koffler)

13

The Worm
of Consciousness

Let us hear what Alberto Moravia says in *The Empty Canvas* (*La noia*) about boredom—that fundamental, ineradicable condition of all his work, which he treats explicitly for the first time in this last novel.

> For me . . . boredom is not the opposite of entertainment. On the contrary, I might even say that it resembles it in some respects, since it too produces distraction and forgetfulness, though of a particular kind. Boredom, for me, is really a sort of insufficiency or scantiness of reality. To use a metaphor, reality, when I am bored, has always had on me the disconcerting effect of too short a blanket on a winter night: pull it over one's feet and one's chest gets cold, pull it over one's chest and one's feet get cold; and so it is impossible ever to really fall asleep. Yet again, my boredom could be defined as a disease of objects consisting of a sudden withering or loss of vitality, as though I were seeing a flower bud, wilt and turn to dust all within a few minutes. The principal aspect of boredom was a practical matter: while it was impossible to remain in my own company, I was the one person I could not possibly be rid of.

This is the mood that Moravia called indifference in his first novel. But indifference applied not to reality in general but to other people. It was a young man's incapacity to share the feelings, passions, and desires that seem to give other people reasons for action that are, if not valid, at least clear and direct. It was accompanied by a sadness and a sense of guilt

---

the more depressing in that it had no ascertainable basis. One might say that the boredom felt by the protagonist of *La noia* is indifference extended to everything real, to objects taken singly and together, from the most vexatious object of all, oneself, to the object that is most abstract and omnipresent, the world, in which things and creatures should be intelligible but, instead, only mirror, in an endless multiplication, a senselessness that is always the same.

I have said "mood." Moravia's boredom, on the contrary, is an inner condition that is both without a cause and chronic, that not only undermines the very possibility of experiencing different or changeable moods but also infects the external world, rendering it uninhabitable and inadequate, not by reason of this or that deficiency but taken as a whole and, almost, without repeal.

At this point we pass from the "physical" (and naturalistic psychology) to the "metaphysical"; to a zone, that is, where for the observation and description of so-called facts is substituted the single haunting question of the relation, the seemingly unbridgeable gap, between the individual and objects, and where, for the image of the world as a place and source of events that are more or less happy, more or less painful, more or less unique, is substituted a feeling of weight, of the unbearable opacity of the world itself and of one's own existence in it. The world and its events seem a repeated experience of nonsense, our own existence a blind unalterable fact against which we rage in vain as we try to understand it. Perhaps there is nothing to understand, but we cannot help our rage.

Heidegger, in his essay "What Is Metaphysics?," gives an account of boredom that is particularly appropriate to this condition. According to Heidegger, the first, most elementary experience we have of the world is of its daily banality, in which things are presented one next to the other, one after the other, and all together, without giving us any over-all reason for their being there. Thus experienced, the world seems clear while it is opaque; it seems to constitute a whole while it only presents a collection of objects and facts; it seems to make sense while it only leads us stupidly back to ourselves and to the objects that are its components.

If we take Heidegger's discourse as a metaphor, or a kind of myth, we can conclude that, in a certain sense, all Moravia's work arises and is written as the result of the decision to accept the state of boredom as a fact; *he stops* at boredom and is incredulous of any further revelation. Therefore, he does nothing but reiterate that the daily world, the so-called natural and normal world which most people accept as the ultimate reality, is indeed the only reality, in that no other reality is given. Yet it is also a world of boredom, a *dead* world in the full sense of the word, a world that shuts us off from, rather than leads us into relation with, reality.

Moravia's stories and novels are stories of this dead world. They are not naturalistic, or even realistic, narratives, but repeated demonstrations of the unbearable reality of a dead world, a world in which consciousness is both awake and inert. In this sense, Moravia's realism is a purely moral realism, describing not things and events but their negative impression on consciousness; or, rather, their negation *by* consciousness, which obstinately, stoically, rejects them, holding them at a distance.

Moravia's realism, reduced to its essence, presents us with the image of a repeated, almost insanely senseless collision between consciousness and the banality of facts. It is a monotonous collision without catharsis, an end in itself. What Moravia actually describes again and again in the detailed treatment of facts is the insufficiency of reality (the blanket that is too short). Thus it is inevitable that each time, from the start, he should present us with the fact of consciousness, that he should make us feel the worm of consciousness at work. A book of his, therefore, is not a tale; it is above all an experience of truth. There are dozens of writers capable of describing outward appearance and sensation more clearly, more gracefully than Moravia. But there is no one to equal him in seizing the moments in which reality, piercing through the mist of velleity and pretense, begins to "exist" and to take on the meaning of its own overwhelming essence. These are the moments in which we feel the author's self-assurance, the self-assurance of a man who has plumbed the depths of his own experience, who, when he speaks, arrives immediately at the heart of the matter. It is then that Moravia succeeds in eliciting the feeling of extreme uneasiness and depression from a gesture, a physical contact, a glance, or the most opaque piece of matter. It is this, not the "joy of narrating," that gives the story its impetus, and it is toward this that the story moves. The plot is the "objective equivalent" of the irremediable condition of his soul. It arises from the author's desire to force it into the structure of a daily reality conceived as a "commonplace" of experience, not from a wish to depict the progress of a real action in the continuity of real time.

La noia seems to me an admirably concise, sharp, and energetic example of this fundamental, constantly repeated situation. In its moral and artistic economy, it is perhaps the most successful of all Moravia's works.

The hero of the novel is an abstract painter who

one day, "at last authentically inspired after so many attempts," hurls himself on the picture he is painting and slashes it to pieces with his knife. After this, he feels free either to begin all over again or to recognize frankly the fact that he has failed. "A failure, not because I was unable to paint pictures that were pleasing to others; but because I felt that my paintings did not permit me to express myself, that is, to delude myself into thinking that I was relating to things."

Here, then, is a man facing a truth that, though extremely disheartening, is yet better than an illusion. He is alone before an image of himself, "for various reasons unbearable," in an atonic world. He can do, or let himself go and do, anything at all. One day he finds himself beckoning to a girl. "As she passed under my window, I saw her look up at me, but this time without smiling. I raised my hand to take the cigarette from my mouth, but instead I found myself making an unmistakable sign to her to come back." That is how things happen, the writer seems to be saying; that is how we become involved in reality.

From this involuntary gesture, at once gratuitous and inevitable, the gist of the tale, the story not of love or eroticism but of the frustrated desire for possession and consciousness, takes its impetus. The relationship between the painter and the girl is naked, mechanical, and clean as a bone—or, better still, as a skeleton. No one has depicted a series of carnal acts, frenzied yet cold in their automatism—nudity, desire, and its outlet—with such complete lack of complacence, such impassive truthfulness. For Moravia does not describe bodies or their acts; he makes us feel their existence and their unreality at the same time—their refusal to be comprehended, their mechanicalness, their blind fatality. In the void of boredom, the triumph of physical love over every other vital impulse is represented with an annihilating vehemence that recalls the triumph of death and decay over earthly vanities and pleasures in the frescoes at Pisa.

> At first . . . it [physical love] seemed to me something very natural. . . . But now it struck me above all by its lack of naturalness, like an act that was in some way against nature, that is, artificial and absurd. Walking, sitting, lying down, climbing, descending and all such bodily actions now seemed to me to have a necessity, and therefore a naturalness of their own. Copulation, on the other hand, seemed to me an extravagant tour de force for which the human body was not made and to which it could adapt itself only with strain and effort. Everything, I thought, can be done easily, with grace and harmony, everything except the act of love. The very conformation of the two sexual organs, the female organ difficult of access, the male organ unable to reach its goal autonomously like an arm or leg, but needing, rather, to be aided by the whole body, seemed to me to indicate the absurdity of sexual intercourse.

Moravia does not say that this is love. He says that in the situation in which we find ourselves it would be dishonest to represent it in any other way. On the other hand, he seems to be saying that in the situation in which we find ourselves sex, denuded as it is of any vibration of the spirit, is also a truth, the only access we still have to nature. *"Etre la matière,"* the last words of Flaubert's Saint Anthony, expresses the only form of mystical longing of which modern man is capable. True hell is not there; true hell is in the unnecessary, in all that hides us from ourselves, hiding from us the fact that we are living in a morally dead world. This reality is described by Moravia, with unequaled ferocity, in the parts of the novel showing the relationship between the hero and his mother and describing the luxury, money, empty words, and permanent spiritual blindness of a being in whom possessiveness and greed are walled within the most deadly of the passions: inert self-satisfaction. It is from such places as the villa where this woman lives that boredom spreads out over the world.

Published as "Moravia and the Worm of Consciousness,"
Partisan Review, Winter 1962
(Trans. Barbara Loeb Kennedy)

14

The Ceremonial
Theater
of Jean Genet

For Jean Genet, more than for any other contemporary author or dramatist, writing plays and facing the publicity of the stage are moral needs rooted in the essential motive of his art. They are a means of escaping from the prison of the Self, the prison of an obsessive autobiography, in order to lay himself bare before the judgment of others while at the same time judging them.

Consequently, few contemporary writers share Genet's sense of the theater as a primordial form of expression, a medium by which the individual achieves an inner liberation, a "catharsis," through an *actualized* fiction. And because for Genet it is a pretense, a mask, it enables him to tell the truth and attain the sole reality man is granted: to mime his own situation in basic words and gestures and thereby give a purely formal, but also physically evident and public, consistence to something that would irremediably remain, in Pindar's words, "the dream of a shade."

In a note to his earliest play, *The Maids* (*Les Bonnes*), written in 1948, we find the outline of an idea of the theater that suggests the basic meaning of all Genet's plays and his reasons for resorting to the dramatic form.

The first point to be made about Genet's poetics is that they are accompanied by an invincible skepticism in regard to the possibility of ever achieving a satisfactory form of production on the stage today. As far as Genet is concerned, his model theater remains a Utopia, and this accounts for his clashes with producers, such as the one over the London production of *The Balcony* (*Le Balcon*) in 1957, which he regarded as intolerably realistic.

"We can only dream," wrote Genet in the commentary on *The Maids*, "of an art which is a skein of active symbols capable of addressing the audience in a language in which nothing is actually said, but everything is felt and anticipated."

Genet reproaches modern theater for the fact that, unlike Japanese theater or the ritual dances of Bali, it obliges the actors "to perform . . . not heroic stories, but dream characters." It is clear that by "dream characters" he means realistic characters removed from banal but substantial reality and rendered insubstantial by a pretense, a fiction, which, in its turn, is a servile imitation of a real situation.

According to Genet, the purpose of the theater should be "to bring about a dislocation in the rhythm of consciousness. This dislocation would permit the use of a declamatory tone and introduce the theater into the theater. . . . In other words the characters on the stage would simply be the metaphors of what they are supposed to represent."

To illustrate his point, Genet takes as an example the ritual of the Mass. Admittedly, this is a slightly hackneyed and misleading simile; we can hardly say that the gestures performed and the words pronounced by the priest when celebrating the sacrament of the Mass are "the metaphors of what they are supposed to represent." They are, more precisely, the ritually pre-established symbols of "what they are supposed to represent."

Actually, it is at the end of his brief commentary that Genet states the essence of his view of the theater. "In the western world," he writes, "which is increasingly affected by death and ever more directed towards it, [the theater] can only represent an increasingly refined reflection of a play within a play, of an image within an image. A ceremonious performance could render this exquisite phenomenon and move it quite close to invisibility."

At first these lines seem obscure. But they become clear if we bear in mind that, of all contemporary playwrights, Jean Genet is the one who has developed naturally and almost instinctively Pirandello's idea of a "play within a play," and if we pay special attention to the phrase about "the western world which is increasingly affected by death and ever more directed towards it."

It seems perfectly obvious that a theater that deliberately proceeds from "a play within a play," "an image within an image," to something "quite close to invisibility," in other words, to the most explicit and at the same time most rarefied pretense or fiction, is an extreme form of the "play within a play" as Pirandello understood it. Like Pirandello, Genet—and this will appear most clearly in *The Balcony, The Blacks (Les Nègres),* and *The Screens (Les Paravents)*—wants to give greater consistence to the theatrical fiction by openly declaring it to be a fiction, that is, by removing it once and for all from that equivocal situation in which the theater tries to give the illusion of reality, to create "dreams." The true and original function of the theater is to sever the community of spectators momentarily from that confused dream which is everyday life in order to place them before the reality of a human action to be purely contemplated and judged.

But, according to Genet, behind the "play within

a play" lies the most explicit sense of death. It dispels every reality presumed to be material, giving substance to everything presumed to be unreal simply because it is purely formal, normally invisible, belonging to what Genet in *Funeral March* (*Pompes funèbres*) calls his "shadow theater," in other words, inner life.

Yet to give consistence to something does not mean to give it reality; the theater remains unreal, "an image within an image," a game of mirrors carried to the point of rarefaction. And only if this fact is made as explicit as possible does the ceremonial game of the theater acquire its ritual meaning as a game of shadows, which, from the perspective of death, is life.

In other words, behind Genet's theory that his theater is not a spectacle but a "ceremony" there is the idea that modern man cannot give an artistic fiction any other consistence than that of a formally molded and measured image of the "dream of a shade," which is existence. And today, far more than in the days of Pindar, human existence is the "dream of a shade" because modern man believes only in present reality, object by object, moment by moment. Beyond it, as far as he is concerned, there is nothing—nothing, that is, other than death, which dispels and annihilates every reality, reducing it in earnest to a memory, an image, an "empty shade," as Ulysses says in Sophocles' play.

The only reality for man today is his own death. Death alone is true because it is the only final and absolute fact. Everything else disintegrates into solitude and nothingness.

In life, then, only what we live in the moment in which we live it has any weight or consistence. Above all, there is nothing else in which we can *believe*. The rest vanishes, becomes "nothing," loses all value and meaning. We may be able to see it, touch it, smell it, enjoy it, even suffer it, but we cannot believe in it; it does not help to lead us from the present to the future with the assurance that one instant, one fact, one action will connect with another and, together with the other, lead to a lasting meaning.

This implies savage and accursed egocentricity, for, naturally, all that exists and lasts in time, as long as time lasts, is the anxiety of the Ego, which pulls the individual brutally from moment to moment and from object to object.

But what is this Ego that pulls us along if not what others force us to be? We cannot be different from what others want us to be; we arrive in the world with our roles established. Whether we are good or bad, black or white, masters or servants, it is the others who tell us what we have to be. The process by which we exist in one way or another does not depend on us, and once we are established there is no escape. We can only decide to be what we are thoroughly, all the way, to accept ourselves as we are forced to be and live our parts as a destiny.

Yet this destiny is altogether indefinite and ephemeral. To be as others want us to be means being what we ourselves did not want to be and therefore what we are not; it means being as others want us to be because we have no alternative; at the same time, it means to rebel in the name of a being, a destiny, a role that we do not know. "As a child I admired the intractable convict who is always sent behind bars" ("*Je suis le forçat intraitable sur qui se referme toujours le bagne*"), said Rimbaud. But to want to be *the convict* also means that we feel we are in the right; it means that we want to be criminals *and* right at the same time, or, rather, that we do not want to be criminals but good men condemned to crime—in other words, men.

If we justify ourselves to others, however, we lose our identity and end up being nothing, living corpses, automatons, but without ceasing to be what others forced us to be. The convict cannot stop wishing to be a criminal, wishing the prison gates to close behind him once again, for fear of losing his identity.

These are the mechanics of Evil, according to Genet, and the mechanics of Evil are the mechanics of society. We are condemned because we live among others. There is no escape from this condemnation in reality, because in reality the only thing that is certain is this game of mirrors and the fact—the only true fact, because it is the only absolute fact—of death. If we could conceive of a transcendental Goodness the condemnation would end because it would redeem us from illusion and evil.

But in reality we never leave the prison. We do not leave it even in art, which is simply the shadow of life, that compulsory hallucination. This point is important, because it saves Genet from being suspected of aestheticism incurred by his self-indulgent taste for the "*mélange adultère*" of the repugnant and the exquisite, the abject and the angelic. And because it represents the fullness of unreality, for Genet art is the means of escaping from Maya's veil of appearances and therefore a means of moral purification.

Yet there is an essentially realistic art (more realistic than narrative and poetry, which pertain more than we may think to the domain of the egocentric dream) whose nature is to mirror the fundamental fact of existence, that is, our relationship with others, its fatality and the dialectics of evil and revolt that derive from it. This art is the theater.

In the theater the reality of existential condemnation becomes what it really is: a game of deception. The fear of death that encloses the individual in his perverse solitude becomes a weightless word and image; and Evil, with its paraphernalia of night-mares, becomes an image, too.

But, liberated from the weight of reality, the theater cannot claim to be anything but a commemo-rative metaphor, life remembered from the point of view of death. In order to be this (in other words, in order not to appear as an illusory reality), the theater must be a pretense within a pretense, a fiction within a fiction, a declared and stylized fiction, which openly denounces the condition of men's subjection to each other. It thus presents the spectator with true reality, which is the equivalence of all conditions in this ver-tiginous game of mirrors that constitutes existence.

Genet's theater is not a spectacle but a ceremony. Thus genuine catharsis can come about. In this true theater we are both aware of the fiction and fasci-nated by it. Moreover, it is through this theater that, by repeating his self-denunciation before others, the criminal assumes the human appearance denied him in reality. He is no longer wicked or good, guilty or innocent, a slave or a master, but the *other*, that part of ourselves which we are not, and he judges us when he appears before us, the judges. What we think of him will show what we are.

If Genet interests us as a dramatist, it is because of the exclusive passion with which he presents the human situation in varying guises and in its ultimate nudity, as a condition dominated by death and in which only death is real. Yet avidity, lust, violence, abjection, all men's desires rage no less furiously; in-deed, there is no limit to their enormity: they overflow in all directions. But, from the perspective of death, they are merely "sound and fury," forms of an exces-sive and vain clamor.

According to Genet, the theater should represent

the poetry of this ultimate evanescence and equivalence; it must be a game of metaphors and an allusive
ceremony, rather than a realistic fiction.

Little remains to be said about Genet's first play,
The Maids (1948), after Jean-Paul Sartre's analysis at
the end of that monstrous and brilliant treatise of
negative ethics, *Saint Genet, comédien et martyr.*
What Sartre explains very well is that *The Maids*
is the opposite of a traditional work of the theater: it
is a *lie* told by Genet. Genet fabricates a drama among
three people, each one of whom mirrors the other
while all three mirror the author. The author, for his
part, invents them in order to draw the spectator into
the recesses of a moral situation ("servility"), which
is reduced to a solitary and hopeless paroxysm—the
paroxysm of Genet, a pervert, a thief, and an in-
former, who cannot feel justified, innocent or true,
unless he feels enclosed in the frantic celebration of
evil, exposed to the reproofs of "honest" men, a hu-
miliated reprobate.
The Maids, written in Genet's turgid and com-
posite style, is a lyrical exaltation of the degradation
and the criminal desires of two maids who, says
Sartre, are really a single servile being in two people, a
single being split in order to disguise what is really a
monologue. Claire and Solange pretend to love each
other because they are servants. They hate each other
for the same reason. And they love and hate their mistress for the same reason. They want to be loved by
their mistress (the height of servility), and, out of
jealousy, they have denounced her lover to the police.
But, from the depths of their servile being, they cannot help hating the person who dominates them. And
so, out of revenge, they desperately want to kill her.
However, they cannot do it, not because they are ser-

vants but because everything takes place only in their mind—which happens to be the mind of the dramatist who invented them. So when Claire finally drinks the cup of poison refused by her mistress, we simply have the moment of exorcism that puts an end to the verbal spell cast by Genet. But the action could continue. We could again see, as we saw at the beginning, two maids trying on their mistress's dresses, pretending that one of them is the maid, the other the mistress, and, in so doing, fanning up the reciprocal and illusory passion that induces them to act out the crime they will always be incapable of committing. A hell in the true sense of eternal damnation and eternal deprivation of reality.

In his study, published before Genet wrote *The Balcony*, Sartre overstresses the element of mirage, schizophrenia, and solipsistic unreality that, he believes, characterizes Genet's plays. This is a slightly dubious thesis, which does not take into account one essential fact—Genet's purpose in writing for the theater (this is very different from the purpose of fabricating dreams and mirages), which we see in *The Maids*. To write for the theater means to expose oneself and one's mirages to the eyes of others. Consequently, whether the author likes it or not, that which was a solitary paroxysm in his novels becomes a significant moral problem. In witnessing *The Maids*, and even more obviously in witnessing the later plays, *The Balcony*, *The Blacks*, and *The Screens*, we find ourselves in the situation of judges who are judged, and this is the situation to which not only Genet but every true playwright from Ibsen onward wants to lead the spectator.

Genet himself regards his second play, *Death-watch* (*Haute surveillance*), as unsuccessful because it is too realistic. It represents a ceremony of criminal snobbery. In a cell three prisoners compete with each other in order to establish which one holds the true essence of criminality. At the same time they compete for the love of the absolute criminal, the man who is sentenced to be beheaded and who remains invisible in his infernal empyrean.

Snobbery, the dynamic essence of society, is entwined with erotic passion in a knot typical of Genet as a dramatist. The conflict ends with the strangling of the youngest of the three, the one who played the game with simple-minded exaltation, unaware of the violence he was unleashing. The impervious and inimitable model on the stage is Yeux Verts, murderer and rapist. But the true model, the chief of the chiefs, is the black man sentenced to death, Boule de Neige, the invisible First Mover of the action. The wretched victor is the weak, sad Maurice, who kills to win the murderer's wreath and is consequently despised by Yeux Verts. One is a murderer because misfortune turns one into a murderer, not because one wants to become a murderer.

The important point here is the snobbish inversion of the social pattern in the insane situation of those three men. But, perverse and insane as it is, this particular situation reflects the true nature of the social situation in general.

The patently ceremonial aspect of the action is also important. Victims of their mythomania, the characters lie and tell the truth; they live in a hallucination and act according to a rigid law of their own invention. So, in the end, the murder, like the suicide-homicide in *The Maids*, is both allegorical and real—a genuinely theatrical action.

But it is in *The Balcony* (1956) that Genet's dramatic imagination asserts itself fully, at least as far as the purely theatrical situation is concerned.

The Balcony is but a black mass celebrated unremittingly on the stage, in an atmosphere in which human misery is denounced with a ferocity that, never for a moment, allows us to indulge in the illusion that we are faced with reality. We are in a nightmarish masquerade, in the perverted world of Jean Genet, and we are watching Genet celebrate his hatred for "the things of this world." The masquerade is disgustingly similar to reality, and the spasmodically perverted world of Genet corresponds point by point, like a mirrored image, to the world common to everybody, to what each of us hides within himself.

The hypocrisy (or the moral presumptuousness) of the spectator is sorely tried in the course of these fourteen scenes. It is attacked from the depths of all that is most base and inadmissible with means that are atrociously grotesque. The three faithful and respected clients of Madame Irma's brothel do not, in fact, resemble any of us, but they bring into play the inner drama and the public mask of each one of us. One of them goes to the brothel to play the part of a Bishop, the solemn and sacred personage who absolves the sins of others, who lavishes anathemas and blessings, and who exercises a spiritual power as unlimited as it is imaginary, delighting in it to the point of orgasm. Another plays the part of a Judge, who goes to those clandestine assizes to sit in judgment and always condemn the same criminal. The third wants to be a great and victorious General and requires his partner to support his role over and over again. All three of them spend their secret sessions of illusion wearing the vestments, robes, or uniform of their station, perched on a pair of enormous buskins, the instruments of the ritual as well as the symbols of its illusory quality.

In the first part of the play, it is evident that the black mass imagined by Genet applies not only to each man's private world but also to society in general—what we call the establishment. One could say that *The Balcony* is a scenario of surrealist negation, but more consistent and far more radical. The play is animated by a derision and a violence that no surrealist ever attained, for, as far as the social order was concerned, the surrealists confined themselves to antibourgeois agitation and had a curb in the "positive" and optimistic myth of the Revolution and in Marxism. Genet's derision, when all is said and done, is that of a criminal and an individualist anarchist like Ravachol: it is carried to the extreme.

Genet imagines that a revolution breaks out in the world beyond the walls of Madame Irma's house. The revolution threatens to reveal the secrets and destroy the illusions perpetrated in that place of infamy, for the revolution is truth while the world over which Madame Irma reigns is that of a comedy based on money and slavery.

The rebels are on the verge of victory. An abject terror pervades the brothel, the terror of Madame Irma at the idea of losing her kingdom and of her three clients at the idea of being deprived of their immense and imaginary ranks, which they need in order to satisfy their lust. Along with certain superfluous and rhetorical episodes, like the love affair between the chief of the rebels and the beautiful Carmen, invested with a phallic fantasy typical of Genet at his worst, it is the terror that produces the intrigue which ends with Madame Irma being crowned Queen, with the Bishop being invested with supreme authority over souls, with the Judge being given real law courts over which to preside and real criminals to punish, and with the General being presented with the high command of the army, while the Chief of Police remains the *deus ex machina* of the whole business.

Man's consuming need to wear a mask and to

deceive himself, however base it may be, triumphs over truth and virtue. The revolutionaries were the real dreamers, who wanted to strip the world of fictions, while in fact the world can consist only of pretenses.

"Beware of nudity," says the Chief of Police at one point. And to the Bishop, who hesitates to assume his false rank in reality, protesting that he does not have the power to do so, he says, "Nobody has the power. When we were alone we were mere ghosts. Now we are visible."

A suffocating nightmare constantly challenged by consciousness, like all nightmares, *The Balcony* derives its strength not so much from its lyricism (which is frequently excessive and unbearable, as in the scene between the rebels and the Chief of Police) as from the undeniable truth it contains and proclaims. In this work, Jean Genet's "special" universe, which had previously been deliberately closed in on itself, finds for the first time an image that is universally valid and a meaning that can be fully communicated.

The Balcony was followed in 1958 by *The Blacks*, which is undoubtedly Genet's best play and one of the most original plays of the contemporary theater.

Genet called *The Blacks* a *clownerie*. It is a free improvisation on the theme of the relationship between Blacks and Whites. The real action consists of the confrontation between two types of men, and to interpret the work as an antiracist diatribe is to misunderstand it completely.

Stanislavski once said that in order to identify the theme of a play we must try to express the meaning of its action in a simple proposition with the verb in the infinitive. According to this principle, the formula of *The Blacks* would be "To discover what a Negro is."

This is the theme of Genet's *clownerie*. This play by its very nature must be acted out. Reduced to the written word, the essence of the play is lost, for the text is the outline of an action to be performed in public, not a piece of prose to be read in private, and this action is the confrontation between Blacks and Whites. *The Blacks* (*Les Nègres*), then, is conceived in genuinely theatrical terms. And whether or not Genet read Pirandello, this work is the best contemporary example of the type of drama started by Pirandello with *Six Characters in Search of an Author* (*Sei personaggi in cerca d'autore*) and continued in *Tonight We Improvise* (*Stasera si recita a soggetto*) and *Each in His Own Way* (*Ciascuno a suo modo*).

As often happens to inventors of genius, Pirandello remained a prisoner of his own invention after writing *Six Characters*. He looked on it as a theatrical stratagem and used it as a device, only to return to the conventional plots of his first plays. He did not realize that what he had discovered with his "Plays to Be Performed" was not so much a way of staging the dialectics of reality-fiction as a way of restoring the theater to its original form, which is that of the commemorative ceremony of the hero's sacrifice, on the one hand, and the comic *agon*, on the other—the two sources of Greek drama.

We must never forget that this freedom was brought back to the modern theater the day Ibsen questioned, on the stage, the *morality* of the part the individual plays in order to adapt himself to the society in which he lives. Pirandello, however, questioned the very *reality* of the part the individual performs in everyday life. What we finally discover is that we are prevented from acting our roles by the constant and inevitable drama of inner conflict between the part we find ourselves actually playing and the image we have of ourselves as free agents.

Man, then, is a theatrical creature by nature, not by accident. And the theater must represent this basic phenomenon: the relationship between the action in which the individual is confined and his consciousness, as well as the conflict between his consciousness and the fatalities of collective life. So the illusion of "reality" and verisimilitude, the likelihood of the plot are insignificant. What matters is the truth of the initial situation and the logic with which the playwright carries it to its final consequences. The dramatic action is not a make-believe game of truth, but a truth that openly pretends to be fictitious. This is the point reached by Pirandello. It is, therefore, with him that the theater became (or, rather, *could* become) what it was originally: an empty space in which we play at questioning the sense of human actions and passions. Provided that we know it is a game, freedom is complete. This is why naturalistic and moralistic prejudices are fatal to the theater; they prevent it from being a game, from speaking the truth.

But to return to Genet. As Sartre pointed out, Genet's existential situation is that of an "actor" obliged to act out the play of Evil. Only by exposing himself to the reproofs of "normal" people, and therefore by accentuating his imaginary role as a criminal and a pervert, can he feel "real." But when he feels real he also feels the victim of an unjust verdict and claims that he is innocent (or, at least, "justified"). Consequently, he finds himself entangled in the problem of Good and Evil from which he wanted to escape, and he is again compelled to play the part of the reprobate in the impenetrable world of Evil. He feels compelled to arouse in us a sense of nausea and condemnation, which makes him feel justified because it proves that our sensibility is purely conventional and our morality false. Yet this induces him to aspire once more to that innocence which he cannot accept without feeling deprived of the only reality that is truly his: the reality of evil.

According to Sartre, this is the role in which Genet is condemned to be imprisoned. But the role is real. Genet pays for it *in person;* he is not only an "actor," but also a "martyr" and a "saint." His sanctity, according to Sartre, resides in the fact that he shows contemporary man where the problem of true morality begins and what it is. In other words, he illustrates a problem that concerns every individual—and so Sartre tells us to put Genet to "good use," just as Pascal told the Christian to put his illnesses to good use.

In Genet's first plays, in *The Maids* and *Deathwatch,* Sartre saw the continuation and exasperation of the mythomaniacal act of Genet's novels. He regarded the theatrical situations and characters as travesties of Genet himself—travesties in which Genet carried the unreality of his own inescapable situation to the impasse of schizophrenia.

We may wonder whether Sartre would define *The Balcony* and *The Blacks* in the same way. For in these plays the situation is different. It seems that without falsifying himself or wanting to appear to be something he is not, Genet emerges miraculously from his nightmare and gives an objective, no longer a solipsistic and dissociated, form to the situation that fascinates him. It is through his plays, therefore, that Genet frees himself from his autobiographical obsessions and puts Genet to "good use."

The Blacks begins with the following note by the author: "This play, written by a White, is intended for an audience of Whites. But if, unlikely though it may be, it were ever to be performed in front of an audience of Blacks, a White, man or woman, must be invited to each performance. The organizer of the spectacle will welcome him solemnly, will give him a ceremonial robe, and will accompany him to his seat, preferably in the middle of the front row of the stalls. The play will be performed for him alone. Throughout the performance a light must be focused on this symbolic White. And what if no White were to accept the part? In that case white masks must be distributed to the black audience on their way into the auditorium."

This is a "prologue," and it clearly explains the theatrical game devised by Genet. An audience of Whites must feel itself judged, derided, and attacked by a group of Blacks. The Whites are spectators and the Blacks actors. So the judgment, the derision, the aggression are feigned, they are part of a game, of a festival, of a vacation from reality, and they should be accepted as such, just as at the Greek festival of the Anthesteria or at the medieval carnival people accepted the jokes and the diatribes of the men with whitened or masked faces. Once they are accepted as make-believe, the judgment, the derision, and the abuse become real—real judgment, real derision, real abuse. But if the spectator, within himself or with any outward sign, reacts as though they were truly offensive, he drops out of the game and not only finds himself in the wrong but also acknowledges the truth of those jokes. If, on the other hand, he pretends to regard them as pretenses, as unreal, of no consequence, he finds himself hypocritical. So all he can do is play the game, accept the words and gestures as if they were true, and search inside himself for the right answer—in other words, he must participate wholeheartedly in the theatrical ceremony.

The Blacks are actors. One of them, the Master of

Ceremonies, explains this as soon as the company has inaugurated the spectacle by dancing to the rhythm of a Mozart minuet—an opening scene that, incidentally (at least in Roger Blin's production in Paris), was one of the most beautiful in contemporary theater. The contrast between the lightness of Mozart and the furtive grace with which the Negroes adapted their steps to that delicate rhythm was both astonishing and moving, a perfect symbol of the basic significance of the action: the Blacks aspire to the most refined, as well as to the crudest, aspects of the civilization of the White oppressors.

So the Blacks are actors. But the actors are real Negroes. The spectacle they offer the Whites is a sort of alibi to hide something happening offstage, a conspiracy, a betrayal, which threatens them and which they finally manage to defeat by killing the traitor (always offstage). This, too, is a pretense, but, by alluding to the reality of the Blacks' rebellion, it makes the play doubly unreal. It turns it into a suspect and sinister game. The presence of the Negro behind the actor becomes explicit; the stage pretense is shown to be an illusion and an escape from a truly unbearable situation. The real truth, therefore, is also on the stage.

At this point Genet's aim has been accomplished. We are at real theater—not at the Dionysian or courtly theater, or in the auditorium of a bourgeois theater, but at the origins of the theater itself. We have reached the moment when theatrical make-believe turns from the festive rite of dances, songs, and wild jokes into the liberating institution that has as its rule the "truth game," accepted by the community as an integral part of its existence. It is a moment of complete freedom. The actors are free (and so is the playwright) to say everything, in the conviction that their words will be accepted for what they are, addressed not to the individual in the everyday mask he takes so seriously but to his real Self, to his consciousness, divided, doubtful, and therefore, naturally, open to the suggestion of the truth and eager to receive it. At the same time the spectators are free to receive the most upsetting revelations, aware that their purpose is not to wound but to arouse the part of themselves that is alive.

Is not this perhaps the sense in which we should understand the Aristotelian catharsis, which is usually taken to mean obliteration of the real in the imaginary?

The way in which Genet reaches this point in *The Blacks* may seem like a game of mirrors. And so it is. But it is the game on which the theater is naturally based and which is declared openly in order to break, *with theatrical means*, the inertia of nineteenth-century conventions. Anyhow, the spectacle never appears artificial, and the general effect is of such simplicity that we cannot but regard it as "moving."

As I said earlier, if *The Blacks* is abstracted from the actuality of the stage it appears as a somewhat insignificant text, inflated with a bombast that is permanently on the verge of smothering and obscuring the elementary simplicity of the action. In any case, the action can be summarized as follows: before a white audience, a group of black actors stage the relationship between Blacks and Whites as the Blacks see it and suffer from it. The Blacks are down below, and above, in a box, are the Governor, the Bishop, the Queen, and the Servant—whites, or, rather, blacks with white masks. The Blacks are commenting on a fictitious ceremony of theirs consisting in the ritual sacrifice of a white woman, a ceremony that hides the conspiracy. From this initial event, as in the capricious and frenzied improvisation of a jazz band, are derived dances, duets of love and jealousy, lyrical exaltation, sarcastic exchanges, and scenes that are simply farcical. At the end, fiercely and ludicrously, the revolt breaks out and terminates with the execution of the Whites, one by one. The Blacks have replaced the Whites. The play that now begins will be no different from the one that has just ended, except that the roles have been reversed.

This is an impossible conclusion, or perhaps we should say possible only insomuch as it is a pretense. In reality the confrontation, the judgment, and the rebellion never end. But the finale of the *clownerie* makes it clear that it is not a diatribe against colonialism or racism, but simply another attempt to illustrate, through the relationship between Whites and Blacks, the nature of social comedy as well as the ultimate similarity of destinies.

The crucial line of the play is: "If his suffering is too great let him turn to the word." This is what Genet lets his Blacks do: he lets them trust in the word to confess, jokingly, their own nature, and, in their confession, to judge and be judged. Underlying the game of mirrors and the buffoonery, there is an authentic moral dialectic, the tormenting dialectic of judgment to which our inner life, lived in the midst of others, is reduced. What is important here is the inventiveness that is released and given body by Genet's highly personal sense of the condition of men in organized society. It is this sense that drives him to "put on a show," almost as an act of retaliation.

The Blacks is less violently sarcastic but more convincing than *The Balcony* in the form and coherence of the action, an admirable example, unique in contemporary theater, of what a dramatic situation can lead to when it is created with a single-minded regard for its internal logic. What strikes us in *The Blacks* is the great freedom and lightness of the invention, compared with the obsessive and claustrophobic heaviness of Genet's novels. It is as if the theater were the agency through which the damned Genet obtains his redemption.

Redemption from what? From the muck of reality, from the obsession with everyday experience, from the insolence of the reprobate enclosed in his autobiography, determined to batten on the reproof of others without being able to answer them except by repeating to himself that he is a criminal and a pervert, segregated in Evil, and therefore inaccessible to the judgment of others. But simply by advancing onto the stage, by playing the game of the theater, there appears, instead, the possibility of a judgment that is not accompanied by condemnation and that is objective because it is purely intellectual; thus the imagination is liberated from autobiographical determinism. The novel was a prison that enclosed Genet in his narcissistic obsession. The theater provided an opening onto the world and the love of others.

Ultimately, then, *The Blacks* is an act of poetic love. For the Blacks, of course. But through the Blacks for every sort of reprobate, and through the reprobates simply for *the others*, for those who are different from us, those inaccessible and incomprehensible "others," as they are, with their deformities, their passions, their closed, private pain, the incalculable distance that separates them from us and the infinite similarity that ties them to us.

Genet's last play, *The Screens*, was published in 1961 but not performed in French until April 1966, when it was produced by Roger Blin at the Théâtre de France. It seems at first sight to have been inspired by the Algerian war, and this is why it had to wait such a long time to be performed in France. But those who give a strictly political interpretation to the work make an even greater error in judgment than those who interpret *The Blacks* in terms of antiracist polemics.

The Algerian war, the brutality of colonialism, the poverty of the Arabs are but the point of departure of *The Screens*. More than in Genet's previous plays, the true theme is the grotesque, sinister, and pathetic aspect of the social comedy and the equivalence of human destinies. This is poetically expressed in the final reunion of all the characters in the beyond, symbolized by the screens of tissue paper that each character breaks through as he arrives in that no man's land where nothing matters and where nobody feels he has to distinguish himself from anybody or oppose anybody.

Before they arrive in the antechamber of death and dissolve into nothingness, however, the characters have existed. Each has relentlessly played his own part, including the wretched Said, who, in his lifetime, could afford to buy only the hideous Leila for his wife. He drags his misery and the hatred of his own condition from scene to scene, finally betraying his racial brothers and ending up with the pompous colonial, Sir Harold, and the soldiers of the Foreign Legion.

There are over a hundred characters, or, better still, apparitions, in *The Screens*. And the action is the action of a crowd. The plot is refracted in a series of episodes that have as their theme the poverty of the Arabs, the brutality (and the fear) of the settlers and the soldiers, and the violence of the rebels. In scene after scene, each recites his part in a language both lyrical and trivial, in the unbridled use of which Genet surpasses himself. At the same time, in order to emphasize the purely ceremonial purpose of so extreme a verbal lyricism, each scene takes place before a paper screen on which the characters themselves, when they enter the stage, draw, with bold, childlike strokes, the setting of the action: the road, the prison, the cemetery, the orange grove where Sir Harold swaggers, the brothel, and, finally, the beyond, all white.

A succession of lyrical-descriptive scenes that make up the action is projected against this fragile background. From the beginning (poor Said's marriage to the ugly Leila, which is probably the most humanely poetic invention of Genet the dramatist) to the end (the encounter of all those truculent apparitions in the final truth of death, which enables them to live for a moment away from the ravages of time before they are obliterated forever), *The Screens* develops like a phantasmagoria on the theme of revolt, oscillating between the sinister and the burlesque. Theatrically speaking, the seventeen scenes of which the work consists are united by an impetuous and seething lyricism more than by an idea comparable to the one animating *The Balcony* or *The Blacks*.

"If his suffering is too great let him turn to the word," says Genet through one of his characters. An excessive faith in the effectiveness of the word unsupported by the logic of a clearly developed plot is Jean Genet's limitation as a dramatist. But this does not prevent him from being the most original and most purely theatrical playwright alive.

Tempo Presente, November 1966
(Trans. Alastair Hamilton)

15

Simone Weil's
Iliad

Simone Weil has met the fate that nowadays befalls almost every new phenomenon and expression of the human mind. She is accepted by those who, for one reason or another, were already prepared to accept her (and they sing her praises), while others admire her at a distance; she has been endorsed wholesale or rejected outright; but she has been understood and studied very little. Yet she was an extraordinary being, this woman who strove all alone, alone until the very end, to rediscover and to live to its extreme consequences a reality that we have totally lost today, the reality of the spiritual absolute. What she deserves more than anything is serious consideration. Her inflexible courage requires that her work be approached with the same intransigence that inspired her life.

The posthumous collection of her essays, articles, notes, and fragments edited by Albert Camus for Gallimard has a great moral and cultural advantage over the volumes produced by various Catholic scholars, both laymen and priests. It presents her writings (all the manuscripts in her family's possession) just as they are, without any moralistic or "spiritual" motive. That is to say, it is the only edition of her works that enables us to examine her fairly and respectfully. The fifth volume, *La Source grecque*, has just been published.* It is particularly important because it brings together in one volume her essays and

* Paris: Gallimard, 1953. —Ed.

fragmentary writings on Greek subjects. Not only was Simone Weil completely immersed in Greek culture (Greece and the Greeks, poets and philosophers, were her overriding passion), but it was her love of Hellenism that inspired her religious and mystical fervor and at the same time made it impossible for her to accept Catholicism, however Christian and Catholic she might claim to be.

This volume contains one of Simone Weil's most beautiful and most profound works, her essay on the *Iliad*. "*L'Iliade ou le poème de la force*" was written in 1939–40 for the *Nouvelle Revue Française*, but it appeared, instead, under the pseudonym of Emile Novis, in the *Cahiers du Sud*, in January 1941. That is when I first read it. I was a refugee in Marseilles, living under the oppression of Hitler's victory in France, that nauseating and terrible event which then looked as if it might be the final triumph of the "faceless men" over the last fragile hopes of the West. At the time I did not know who Emile Novis was. The author was certainly neither an academic nor a *littérateur*, but someone who had suffered in spirit and had purged through intellect the sense of defeat that had been hanging over Europe for at least four years. That this person would and could express himself through a new reading of the *Iliad* was a sign that "humane letters" could still yield vigorous thought. In 1945, I had a hand in getting the essay published in America (in *politics*, the magazine edited by Dwight Macdonald) and was happy to see how profoundly it could affect a readership of New York radicals, people not especially concerned with ancient Greece and, to all appearances, interested exclusively in ideological controversy.

The real hero, the real subject, the center of the *Iliad* is force. . . . For those dreamers who considered that force, thanks to progress, would soon be a thing of the past the *Iliad* could appear as an historical document; for others, whose powers of recognition are more acute and who perceive force, today as yesterday, at the very center of human history, the *Iliad* is the purest and the loveliest of mirrors. To define force: it is that x that turns anybody who is subjected to it into a *thing*. Exercised to the limit, it turns man into a thing in the most literal sense: it makes a corpse out of him. . . . The force that kills is a summary, gross form of force. How much more varied in its processes, how much more surprising in its effects is the other force, the one which does not kill, that is, the one which does not kill just yet. . . . From its first property (the ability to turn a human being into a thing by the simple method of killing him) flows another, quite prodigious too in its own way, the ability to turn a human being into a thing while he is still alive. He is alive; he has a soul; and yet he is a thing. An extraordinary entity this—a *thing* that has a soul. And as for the soul, what an extraordinary house it finds itself in. Who can say what it costs it, moment by moment, to accommodate itself to this residence, how much writhing and bending are required of it?

This is the theme of the essay on the *Iliad*, and we can hardly help finding it totally relevant to a world in which, today still more than in 1940, everything is a test of strength and fear of the force that "does not kill just yet." The passages of the poem that Simone Weil quotes are so apt, they are rendered with such simplicity of style and make one ponder every word so deeply, that the reader is almost convinced, as he reads the essay, that the *Iliad* is a threnody on the theme of force, misfortune, and death, a sort of *Bhagavad Gita*. Afterward, of course, we remember Helen, Ulysses, the laughter of the gods, and the substance and variety of the poem. But this in no way detracts from the importance of the study proposed to us.

The study of force is necessarily the study of human destiny, of what it is in the world (in every object and in every phenomenon of this world) that defies man's desires, will, and audacity. Manifestations of force in the world of nature may seem mysterious, incomprehensible, or blind, yet man, like Pascal's *roseau pensant*, can maintain his pride intact. But when force manifests itself in the very heart of man, between one man and another, in passion, injustice, or war, then force becomes one with the enigma of the universe: destiny, "the hand of God," or Providence. It seems to deny human freedom at the very moment when it is the most blatant and recalcitrant manifestation of this same freedom. For not only does force turn the defeated into a "thing." The victor, too, in his fury, becomes its victim or its instrument. What a philosopher said about nature can also be said of force: "We can control it only by obeying it." But the problem is that nobody can tell where this obedience may lead. In dealing with nature, it is possible not to exceed the limits of the known; the laws of force are equally certain, but they are as inscrutable as they are certain. It is just as certain that every act entails all its possible consequences as it is impossible to know what the consequences of that act are before they have actually come about. It is folly for the victor to press his victory too far, but it is also folly for him to stop before he has won. He is the sole judge of the limit beyond which he cannot go, and, when all is said and done, his final decision depends on his view of the nature of things animate and inanimate together, that is, the nature of the universe. In other words, the very things he does will show the kind of universe he is gambling on, the sort of world he believes in. It is from this vision of the universe that the sense of limit comes (if it comes at all), a sense that is regulated by a "virtue" of which there is no science. From this vision, too, comes the distinction between what is good and what is bad. But, as in the Platonic myth of lots, "everyone is responsible for his own choice: the deity is not involved."

If the *Iliad* appeared remarkably evocative to Simone Weil in 1939–40, it is because, profoundly distressed by the spectacle of force triumphant over all the hopes of civilization and reason, she found in Homer something we find in no poem, novel, or modern philosophical theory. She found the world of force "contemplated," a world in which the misfortune of the defeated hero and the Nemesis attending the victorious hero are bound together as aspects of the same simple and implacable destiny; the world seen "without any comforting fiction, without any consoling prospect of immortality, without the insipid halo of glory or patriotism." A "geometrical" destiny. "This retribution, which has a geometrical rigor, which operates automatically to penalize the abuse of force, was the main subject of Greek thought. . . . Wherever Hellenism has penetrated we find the idea of it familiar. . . . The West, however, has lost it and no longer even has any word to express it in any of its languages: the conceptions of limit, measure, equilibrium, which ought to determine the conduct of life, are restricted to a servile function in the vocabulary of technics. We are only geometricians of matter; the Greeks were first of all geometricians in their apprenticeship to virtue." Hence the concluding lines of the essay: "Nothing the peoples of Europe have produced is worth the first known poem that appeared among them. Perhaps they will yet rediscover the epic genius when they learn that there is no refuge from fate, learn not to admire force, not to hate the enemy nor to scorn the unfortunate. How soon this will happen is another question."

What is important about the passages I have just

quoted is not the umpteenth observation, correct and sincere though it is, that the Greeks had a sense that measure was dictated to man by the very nature of things and that we lack that sense. What is important is the sentence "We are only geometricians of matter." Our modern minds, precise and penetrating though they be in dealing with the physical world, expert though they be at manipulating the forces of nature, seem helpless when confronted with the human world, incapable of measuring, understanding, or "contemplating" force when force appears in man and between men.

To speculate about this is to speculate about the form that modern men give to the universe. It is to ask what is the basis of their sense of the possible and of the impossible, what they believe in, and what credo, if any, they have in common. This is an existential question. And an inevitable one. But any attempt at a theoretical answer leaves the question untouched. The obvious answer is that the modern world strikes men as having no form, that men's sense of good and bad is altogether uncertain, and that they hold no belief in common, as is amply demonstrated by their collective life. If this answer were not negative, of course, the question would not arise in the first place.

Yet it does arise, and Simone Weil was perfectly right to consider it the only question of any importance. It is a question that involves and concerns us all; it is a "common" question in the deepest sense of the word, common to all men; and any answer that can be applied only to the individual, be it theoretical or ascetic (or a combination of the two, as in the case of Simone Weil), cannot serve as anything other than a more or less convincing exemplum. Modern man does not know how to contemplate or "geometrize" force. He can only bewail it or make it part of an ideology, in other words, try to put force to theoretically "good" uses. To "geometrize" force, to contemplate it, modern man would have to know where, in this world, the human and intelligible end and where the divine begins. He would have to have a sense of sacred limit—a religion that does not betray what he knows about the world. But the fact is that there is no such religion. Moreover, those very Greeks who were dearest to Simone Weil tell us that these subjects had best be left unmentioned.

Determined to discover the elements of a "geometry of virtue," at whatever cost to herself, Simone Weil set out on her own, and inevitably she reached absolute spiritual solitude. But it is hard to remain alone without losing one's lucidity.

It is in the last pages of the essay on the *Iliad* that the outlines of her Christianity are first alluded to, with a discretion that this bold woman was to violate ever more resolutely. A strange form of Christianity it was. One the one hand, she believes that the Gospels are the ultimate expression of Greek civilization and that the Christian message has been betrayed to the extent to which it departed from the Hellenic spirit and submitted to the abominable influence of Judaism and Rome. On the other hand (in the essays "Zeus and Prometheus" and "God in Plato"), she interprets the Hellenic tradition according to an unchecked spiritualism and sees it as a prefiguration of Christianity. Thus, Prometheus becomes no more or less than the precursor of Christ. It is an odd form of Hellenism that leads one to betray Greece in order not to betray the Greek aspect of Christianity. But, in any case, for Simone Weil the human truth of the Gospel was betrayed even by the first Christians. They committed the sacrilege of considering the death of Christ a blessing, when even the Man-God himself could not but tremble before his suffering and death. "The man who does not wear the armor of the lie cannot experience force without being touched by it to the very soul," Simone Weil indignantly exclaims. Even the faith that transfigures can be a lie if it forgets the smallest portion of humanity. We can agree. But what sort of Christianity is this?

It is neither Christianity nor Hellenism. It is Simone Weil's solitary heresy, which begins in the feverish anguish created by the evil of the world and ends in an unrelenting pursuit of spiritual purity, a pursuit not of life but of disincarnation. It is something like the final sacrament of the Catharists, in which, once the body had been destroyed by starvation, the soul of the "pure" man was reunited with the Eternal Spirit.

Il Mondo, May 30, 1953
(Trans. Alastair Hamilton)

SPECULATION

16

Letter to
Andrea Caffi

Villa Magrini
Coletta (Livorno)
September 19, 1951

My dear André,*

If I have not written to you until today it is not out of
laziness or forgetfulness, but because, after our fre-
quent and somewhat inconclusive conversations, I felt
I owed it to myself (and to you) to try to set forth,
with what little order I can muster, the few reasons
why I do not share your views on "revolution," "nihilism," and the duty of the "good citizen." The reasons
are not merely polemical.

Before I begin, I should like to apologize for my
long silence, which you might have taken for lack of
friendship. I trust (1) that the summer heat did not
affect you too much, (2) that Monsieur S. did not keep
you waiting, and (3) that the parcel I sent you from
New York has finally reached you.

As for me, I must admit that the sun of my native
land has been very satisfying.

In broaching the subject about which I should
like to converse with you, I should immediately point

* Andrea Caffi (1887–1955) was an Italian writer born in Russia.
He took part in the 1905 revolution in the ranks of the Mensheviks.
A volume of his writings, *A Critique of Violence*, with an introduction by Chiaromonte, was published in New York by Bobbs-Merrill
in 1970. —Ed.

out that when I say "your opinion" I refer to those views you dwelled on recently. I do not mean this or that view (with which I might even agree) on the present state of society, social justice, etc., so much as the general position you seemed to hold with a certain tenacity during the conversations we had lately and which, through my fault, were all too frequently interrupted. As far as I can define it, this position seemed to me to consist of a combination of three elements: (1) philanthropy, that is to say, the insistence on the necessity of siding with those people whom the present organization (or disorganization) of society keeps in a state of social inferiority or economic oppression; (2) a relativism, which claims to be absolute (and which seems rather fitful to me), respecting the *order* of ideas, that is, of propositions that we should consider true or false in the course of a discussion; (3) a dogmatism that, if not absolute, is at least fairly insistent about our moral duty to accept certain notions about the class struggle or private property, under pain of being classified with outcasts and monsters.

What distresses me most about this triple combination is the moralism—or, rather, the substitution of the moral duty to take a particular side for the intellectual duty to accept only notions that are unequivocal. The confusion of the "moral" with the "intellectual" seems to me especially mortifying. Sartre's maxim "Man is responsible for the whole of humanity" strikes me as being the formula *par excellence* of modern sophistry and false morality. It is evident that if we cease to regard a thought as such and look on it, instead, as a potential act, every single thought can be transformed into a "crime against humanity." Any idea can be invalidated if one considers all the *possible* reasons supporting it, just as any act can be made to appear criminal if one projects all the *possible* consequences deriving from it. But that procedure has no meaning—or, rather, it is the metaphysics of Vyshinsky.* At this point, moreover, the remedy is easy. All we need to do is to protect an idea, be it true or false, with the hard shell of a system and to provide an alibi for our acts by placing ourselves symbolically on the "right side" (for example, that of the "oppressed" and of the "sense of history").

I am not saying (far from it) that you are guilty of such excesses. I simply mean that this sort of conclusion is inherent in a certain mentality which seems to me inappropriate: it appertains to Church and state, not to free men. The whole Marxist critique of human attitudes is rooted in such a mentality, and this is one of the reasons I reject it so radically. Finally, what I demand is the right to regard as false —or, rather, as equivocal—such notions as that of the class struggle, without being accused of being a tool of capitalism. I can say more: I regard it as unfair to try to force me into the dilemma of either proclaiming that I endorse the *total* abolition of social oppression and all its causes or viewing myself as guilty of acts of oppression—and, more generally, of social evils—for which I am not responsible and which I am far from sustaining or countenancing in my conscience and in my behavior. The idea of an "unconscious" or "objective" responsibility seems to me to be utterly unenlightened and to lead nowhere but to abusive criticism. Let me add that Ivan Karamazov's exclamation that the mere fact of hearing a child cry would be sufficiently outrageous to induce him to return his entrance ticket to Heaven has always struck me as both histrionic and incomprehensible—for I cannot

* Andrey Yanuaryevich Vyshinsky (1883–1954), the chief state prosecutor in the Moscow show trials of 1934 to 1938.   —Ed.

imagine it to have any such possible effect. The "materialist" and "critical" revolutionary might go still further; for if I say that the idea of a world without children crying seems to me tantamount to a world without any children at all, he is capable of replying that my vocation is that of child executioner. The truth is, far from longing for Heaven, I simply want to see things as they are (and not as they are interpreted by me).

Not long ago I came across the following quotation from Marx: "The 'popular' economist thinks he is making a great discovery when he dismisses the explanation of the 'inner bond' by confidently saying that *in appearance* things are different. It is as though he were proud of bowing before appearances and of *regarding them as the final explanation*." I shall not trouble to defend the "popular" economist, who, as far as I know, could easily be wrong (or right). What disturbs me is the contemptuous contrast of the *"final explanation"* and *"appearances."* I do not see this as the calm assertion of the scientist who *accounts for* "appearances" by stating the truth that he has discovered and that he upholds against popular opinions or current ideas. I see it as quite the contrary: as the statement of the dogmatic thinker who has opposed the ("apparent") reality of "appearances" with the "superior" truth of the system he has constructed. Moreover, when we talk about social reality and not about nature, the distinction between "appearances" and "reality" (not to mention the claim to possess the "final explanation") seems to me very dubious. To start with, the illusions men have about their "real" situation have no less "reality" (practical consequences) than their "final explanations," for in society we are faced with men's *real* errors no less than with their true opinions. Myths, dreams, religions, superstitions, fear, cowardice, vices, and weaknesses have no less reality or importance than any "final explanation," or even than any obvious common-sense truth. It is only by excluding all awareness of psychological reality that the individual and *individuals* can be made to fit into a type or a class. The ideal statesman can decide to encourage reasonable inclinations and impose measures demanded by common sense. But the man convinced of being in possession of the "final explanation" will, in the long run, be exclusively concerned with eliminating the "appearances" that contradict him.

It is "apparent," for example, that the worker (or any other economically handicapped individual) is naturally inclined to demand the improvement of his condition. But it is also "apparent" that that does not always lead him to subscribe to the notion of the "mission of the proletariat." This is to say that the "final explanation" of the workers' condition by the struggle between capitalism and proletariat is, in many cases, contrary to appearances. In order to prefer the "final explanation" to "appearances," we must rely on authority and not on knowledge.

If we were asked to account for the fact that the majority of the workers in France and Italy today belong to Stalinist organizations, we could choose between two "final explanations." The first explanation would be that the support of these organizations by the workers is genuine, real, and motivated by the interests and struggle of their class (which would mean that these same workers accept and support the most oppressive party and regime of modern times and, purely out of social resentment, pay little heed to the proletariat's mission to fight for freedom). The second explanation would be that their support is only apparent and artificial, that it is the result of a momentary mistake, which will be dispelled once the workers become aware of their true interests. Now, it does, indeed, seem that "appearances"—if we really can credit them—contradict both explanations, or, to be more exact, do not confirm either of them.

For "appearances" bring to mind the political tactics by which the Communist parties gained control of the workers' organizations and the fact (which does not need to be explained by "final" causes) that these same parties do what they do for purely political motives (at least, to the extent that the "superior" political interests they serve allow them to do so), in order to retain the power they have thus acquired. On the other hand, the fact that American trade unions today have agreed to act within the existing organization of the state proves absolutely nothing with regard to the American workers' partiality for Standard Oil and the ideology of the National Association of Manufacturers. Nor does it prove that the workers of Detroit and Pittsburgh are Marxists without realizing it. It is an "appearance," a fact, not the manifestation of a hidden idea, and we can understand it only by examining it in relation to other "appearances." Beyond that, there are simply mental attitudes. There is the proletarian individual and there are proletarians, but the proletarian "class" is an abstraction. It is not a notion on which we can base valid arguments.

I feel that there are two orders of ideas that prevent us from seeing a social fact as it is. In the first order, it is contended that what will be (or *must* be, more or less necessarily) is a seed contained in what is, and all we have to do to discover it is to go beyond appearances. The analogy between social life and plant life seems false to me. When we talk of human life, what will be (or must be) always entails the essential modification, if men want it to be. And this makes the image of the germ totally misleading. In reality, however we formulate it, what will be always signifies what *must* be—a moral imperative that goes way beyond all previous reality. From what is to what must be there is always a sudden leap, due to a transition from the domain of facts to the domain of the ideal (which we can also call "imaginary" or "unreal," if we like). What characterizes the human world is the impossibility of finding in it facts unaccompanied by an ideal image or an ideal image unsustained by facts. But this does not mean that we can derive the one from the others or, still less, reduce the one to the others. Between the two domains there is not only human liberty but also the contingency of the facts—their ambiguity, their "polyvalence," and their individuality, in other words their specific character. The attitude in question fails to take this into account. But it also seems to me to have another disadvantage: it debases and obscures our faculty of awareness and encourages a spirit not of revolt but of inertia. For it is obvious that if there are social laws analogous to natural ones we must come to terms with them, obey them, and adapt ourselves to them. And, indeed, what Marxist and Saint-Simonian socialism requires is a "rational" adaptation* of man to industrial society, far more than the transformation of the entire structure.

The second order of ideas that strikes me as being a source of confusion, not to say of mental paralysis, leads to the widespread habit among our contemporaries of judging every problem concerning social reality in terms of history. "Judging" is perhaps too strong a word, for what we are actually faced with is a suspension of judgment about the future. Political regimes, attempts at action, present situations, social upheavals—there is nothing, not even the individual's thoughts and feelings (cf. Freud), which is not ap-

* An "adjustment"—the great principle of our times.   —Au.

praised in terms of an ulterior development that is more or less imaginary. In fact, this is a form of skepticism, but a very special form of skepticism, for it is counterbalanced by the obstinate belief that the final answer to every question will be provided by the "facts" themselves; by history. So it becomes easy to cut short any argument or even to discredit any objection by calling it "metaphysical" or an "intellectual" subtlety. This mystical appeal to *facts* beyond the limits of ordered discussion and "appearances" seems to me to be at the root of modern fanaticism, whether Communist or Fascist, pragmatic or "realist." A certain "historical" mentality (not a historian's mentality) endows it with invaluable support, for it is by "temporalizing" every phenomenon and every argument that it is possible to maintain that what "seems" bad today will prove good tomorrow—or that a certain thought that seems to be correct "in reality" expresses only a momentary situation (or a particular interest).

The fanaticism I am talking about does not always assume a virulent form. It also has a gentle, nostalgic form, which consists in regarding the delays imposed by historical circumstances on the achievement of a goal deemed desirable or necessary as temporary refutations, which do not affect the essential part of the thesis—as deviations, after which history will resume its normal course. What we have then is the paradox of a faith based on the "event" over which the "event" has no control. To my mind this proves that a faith which started off by being secular and rational has been transformed into a religious faith and transported into the sphere of the Unchangeable and the Timeless, to which it should, by definition, be totally alien. It would, of course, be wrong to say that this logical error damages faith. On the contrary, faith can perfectly well be strengthened by it and established once and for all. For the unreal is undoubtedly a dimension of consciousness and of human existence, and it has an effectiveness of its own.

Believing, as I do, that such attitudes of mind are wrong, I am prepared to propose that we adopt as a principle the notion that "truth cannot be the daughter of time" and, consequently, that we make it a rule to exclude the "temporal" element from every judgment about what is true and what is false, what is good and what is bad, what is just and what is unjust, what is useful and what is useless. We should, in short, consider only the phenomena, the facts and the individuals as they "appear" in the present and never as products of a "process" that prevents us from knowing what they are or what we should think of them, compelled as we are to judge them in function of the past and suspended toward the future or located in a present that is basically suspect, since it is transient.

I suggest that we could adopt such an attitude without any fear of forgetting the ephemeral, temporal, and eminently relative nature of each of our acts. That our being is temporal is a basic fact. That we are the characters of a history is equally certain. But in the "historicist" mentality history becomes what America is for the savages of Pascarella or prose for the *bourgeois gentilhomme*.

I do not scorn history as a discipline and as knowledge of the past. On the contrary, I respect it all the more because I am ignorant about it. Which allows me to say without seeming insolent that history as a *science* (and a love of the past which continues in the present) is *useless*—and this ought to be its glory. It serves no purpose except to astonish us and make us aware of our smallness—it does this more directly than astronomy and other sciences, but in the same way. History, in short, is a sort of *theoria*. However, as a basis for our thoughts and our "existential" activities, historical knowledge seems to me to be of secondary importance and altogether inoperative. For I believe that no present judgment, no living attitude, no real action, is motivated by "historical" reasons. Historical reasons put in an appearance only after the event. They appear to the historian, in whose eyes the present enjoys no privilege whatsoever (and, indeed, it is impossible to write the history of the present; it is dubious by definition).

These considerations do not appear to me to be irrelevant to the question of the "public weal" and justice in society.

It seems to me there are various ways of caring about the "public weal." To start with, there is the "public weal" of the citizen who, without bothering about "final explanations," finds that a certain injustice or form of oppression can and must be removed and who acts, with others, to eliminate it. I do not see how we can reproach such an individual for not having gone far enough, for not having fought for the radical abolition of all forms of injustice or (and this comes to the same thing) of their first cause. All we can ask of him is to act truly (and effectively), within the bounds of possibility, to bring about the change he desires.

On the other hand, it is obvious that the intellectual position of such a man is not very strong, especially if he tries to bring about a change in a tyrannical regime without challenging the political system itself. For the principle of tyranny is that only what is considered good by the authorities in power can be regarded as legitimate, the authorities remaining the sole arbiters of what is "good," in other words, what is useful.

But even in a nontyrannical state the same good citizen can easily be convicted of lack of perspicacity if he avoids (or fails) to take into account the full extent of social evils and to attack their "causes." Yet at that point the critic should also realize that we are leaving the realm of "sound empiricism" and what is "practical"—that is, what is possible in the more or less near future—in order to enter the domain of theories, of attitudes, and, finally, of intellectual speculation (if not pure imagination). However intellectually satisfying it may be, the attitude that stresses the necessity of attacking "final" causes in the struggle for justice has a corollary that makes us pause. We can produce real and sweeping changes, certainly, but we cannot be sure that the ultimate result will satisfy anything outside mere theory and abstract reasoning. It is the theory (or the plan, say, to abolish private property) that is at stake, not the *real* happiness of the multitudes *in whose name* we are acting. The more ambitious the plan, the more true this is. For if I give the man who can afford to buy only bread the possibility of buying cheese, I can be reasonably sure that he will be able to satisfy his appetite slightly better. But if I give the same man the abolition of capitalism or the Socialist state, I no longer know what he will have.

I am prepared to admit that hunger and the yearning for justice (or the resentment of injustice and privilege) are strong enough and legitimate enough passions to warrant harsh action and that they can turn into an impersonal will, which is necessarily insensitive to individual cases (for in actual fact this will to justice is a will of the state, and it ought really to be a pursuit of law). All I am saying is that such a will has only a *conceptual* connection (and not a concrete and empirically demonstrable one) with the human reality from which it claims to originate and by way of which it justifies itself. It can hardly be otherwise.

We might as well say that this will is *Utopian*, directed to an idea existing exclusively in the minds of those who invented it and who make it the object of an active faith.

I have nothing against Utopias. On the contrary, I am convinced that in this "nowhere" land lies the very source of human liberty, creativity, and spontaneity. This seems to me to be proved, too, by the fact that the more or less murderous priests and fanatics who gain a hold in this domain acquire a strength by which they can keep in check for a long time "historical" factors, individual interests, common sense, and reason itself; that is, every criterion of just limit applicable within the established confines of human existence such as it is. Human existence, as we know, is uncertain, relative, transient; and it loses all its rights in the unlimited horizon of "historical perspectives" and "total" demands.

Throughout this long discourse, what I have been trying to arrive at is the question of "limit." Not so much in the sense of "knowing where to stop"; the ideologist consumed by the lust for power can only stop at the very end, and it is foolish to want to teach him a lesson. The "pure" ideologist, on the other hand, can *never* stop, for he expects from the future the fulfillment of an Idea; or, at least, all he can see in the present state of things is the *negation* (the absence) of his Idea, and he therefore tries more or less hopefully to *destroy* this *negation*. No, I am referring to "limit" in the radical sense of the word. I mean the awareness of the *sacred* boundary (the adjective is not exaggerated) that separates ideas from facts.

I am all in favor of Utopias—but Utopias that say what they are: ideal *forms* and *models*.

No "reality" would be more monstrous or grotesque than the practical realization of Plato's Republic. His philosopher-governors would turn into priests swollen with hypocrisy, and his guardians would be ruthless automata. But the Republic is thought out in such a way that this kind of "realization" is inconceivable. The Republic is simply a *model* whose natural purpose is to inspire thoughts, not direct actions. The "passage to action" is entirely absent from such a construction, and if we ask "What real forces, what material means can we use to realize this Ideal State?" the only possible answer is "the human soul," or, in the words of Socrates, "the philosopher-kings and the king-philosophers," which amounts to the same thing. And yet there is no more majestic a monument to the human longing for justice and a city pervaded by reason. But it remains a "statue of words" and not a "plan of action" or a "blueprint" to be carried out by the social machine. In *The Republic* a certain order of ideas obeys its own laws of necessity and gives itself a completed *form* perfectly (or almost perfectly) free from any other concern. To ask it to translate itself into action would be exactly the same thing as asking a statue to move. This seems to me to be the case with every authentic idea, even ideas about society.

(I don't know whether the modern passion for the *fact* and for "historical" action developed at the time when the famous anecdote was told about Michelangelo losing his temper with his statue of Moses because it wouldn't speak and striking it with a hammer. Be that as it may, I feel that the legend is indicative. It expresses the baroque dissatisfaction with form, the idea that form is not enough and that it needs action, force, energy, movement. It is a passion that, as Malraux pointed out, ends with the cinema, with the "dynamic" realism of phantoms flitting across the screen.)

I am not saying that what I call the "pragmatic" Utopia has no historical justification. Far from it. But I am denying that it can satisfy the mind when the mind pauses and reflects upon the notions suggested to it, instead of allowing itself to be carried away by the romanticism of good intentions and the no less romantic idea of an "ideal" transfiguration of reality. And the most contradictory notion of all is that of an idea which is "realized." It contradicts both the experience we have of the nature of reality and the experience we have of the essence peculiar to every "ideal" construction.

It seems to me that common sense is closer to the Platonic Utopian than to the revolutionary, nihilistic, activistic Utopian. I don't know whether or not common sense is a good guide in philosophy, but when it comes to matters concerning collective life I tend to think it has unquestionable rights. In any case, I believe that the image of the "good citizen" is perfectly compatible with the attitude of the man who knows that the social reality surrounding him is very far from being "what it could be if men . . . understood," and who longs for a state of things very different from the present but refuses to believe (and couldn't believe even if he wanted to) that the problem could be solved by siding with a particular group or class. The sophism of the pragmatist would prompt the reply that if we do not side with the proletariat or the democrats or some other ideological category we do nothing at all. But this is not necessarily true. The "good citizen" I have in mind could perfectly well have fought in the Resistance out of a horror of Nazism, he could perfectly well have voted Socialist or even Communist (why not?) after the Liberation without letting himself be recruited under the banner of a "cause." He might not have attached any further significance to his act than that of paying his dues, in all good faith, to the contemporary political situation, confused as it may be. For no man can remain completely outside it, being, after all, one among many others and not a privileged being destined never to make a mistake. But the duties of the "good citizen" end there. He has the right to expect that no further demands be made on him. He has a Utopia in his mind, and he has a longing for a reasonable and just society, but he knows that he can best express these two desires in his behavior toward his neighbors and in his words, that is, in his efforts to communicate to his fellow men his views on human existence, justice, honesty, and the like. For, still in accordance with the dictates of common sense, the "good citizen" believes in the reality of human consciousness. He believes, too, that real transformations have to do with what men believe about reality, not with a mythical objective reality. "Reality," he believes, always remains the same; it is this sublunary world which nothing in our experience shows us to be transformable, but which everything shows to be simply changing. This world is given to us in its entirety and forever—with its *limits*. Our *will* can change very little, since we know very little about the roots of social change. It is even doubtful that important social changes, the few periods of "progress" or of "happiness" we may experience, have been brought about by a conscious and deliberate effort of the will, and it is absolutely certain that they have not been produced by the political will of a party or a class.

Of course, men deserve to be trusted. We should not deny a priori the possibility of their ever managing to create the Happy City. But it remains a pure possibility, an idea that is not self-contradictory and therefore cannot be rejected (unless we indulge in "realistic" comparisons with experience). It is because he has no preconceived contempt for men, nor any love for "humanity" in general, that the imaginary, but by no means implausible, "good citizen" does not consider men according to sociological classifications; he has no programatic love for the "proletariat" or hatred for the "bourgeoisie," but he expects each man to reveal in direct experience what we ought to think of him. We can add that if he is born in a dark and violent period of wars of religion or of ideology, he does not feel that the respect we owe to "the witnesses who die for their opinions" also demands that we share their beliefs. He is partial enough to "appearances," alert enough to the complexity and diversity of facts, to think we should believe only in what appears to be true. In other words, he would prefer people to think he has a hard heart and a "metaphysical" mind, rather than pretending that he believes in something he does not believe in simply out of fear of some ideological Jehovah.

I had made note of a number of other points I wanted to talk to you about, but I am afraid I have bored you enough.

I hope you won't consider my excogitations arguments *ad hominem;* that would be completely contrary to my intentions. I have long felt that I owed you a little more than some hasty observations to explain my occasional criticisms. And since I had the time and the inclination, I did what I could, in the hope, of course, of provoking a reply, which I know will be both precious and instructive to me—if it comes.

I will probably be back in Paris about October 7 or 8. I hope you keep well until then and that the cold wave I read about in the papers has not troubled you.

I embrace you as affectionately as ever
Your
Nicola

(Trans. from the French by Alastair Hamilton)

17

Modern Tyranny

As a consequence of the renewed repression of intellectual life in the Soviet Union and the recent disturbances in Czechoslovakia and Poland, this argument has been put forward in private conversation and in newspaper articles: The protest of intellectuals and students in Eastern Europe is based on merely partial demands—greater freedom of expression, a less intransigent political regime, a more efficient economic policy—demands that have become obsolete here in the West. The *system,* in other words the socialist regime, is not challenged, whereas here the New Left totally rejects the *system,* that is, neocapitalism, or the consumer society. So the revolt brewing in the West is more *advanced* than the basically romantic and nineteenth-century rebellion breaking out in Eastern Europe.

The argument deserves to be examined closely. Apart from its intrinsic merit, which must be appraised by itself, it is a good indication of a certain left-wing mentality in Europe and elsewhere today; it shows the extent of the intellectual's awareness of liberty and of the bases of collective life; and, finally, it enables us to raise the problem of modern tyranny, to distinguish its specific forms and analyze the justifications given for it. The problem is relevant not only to Eastern Europe; it is perhaps still more relevant to the West, where tyranny hides behind various names, including that of democracy.

We should note in the first place that the argument in question contains not so much an insidious as an obscure (and therefore all the more symptomatic) desire to overlook the real significance of the rebellion of the Eastern European intellectuals. Admittedly, this rebellion revolves on the question of freedom, simple freedom: freedom from oppression. But for the intellectuals and students in Russia, Czechoslovakia, and Poland "freedom" does not mean just freedom of speech, freedom of the press, and freedom of assembly (which would be a great deal, if not everything). These intellectuals' demand for freedom has a further meaning: it means the repudiation and denunciation of Stalinist terror and its methods, and therefore the demand for formal legality, which will regulate effectively the relationship between the citizen and authority. It entails (though not always explicitly) a total challenge to the fundamental nature of a regime that rejects any juridical (in other words, objective and stable) limit to its power.

Moreover, the demand for freedom in Eastern Europe is an explicit appeal for a "socialist democracy"—that is, the destruction of the one-party system, which remains the foundation of the regimes in question, not to say the basis of the states themselves and the primary obstacle to any serious attempt at reform. Nobody, except for the Western intellectuals, can fail to appreciate the capital significance of a demand involving a really new and "total" phenomenon—the revival of the question of formal freedom, of freedom, pure and simple, which people had thought the so-called "concrete freedoms" could be a substitute for. So we see that when hard facts are involved "abstract" freedom and "concrete" freedom are either differentiated by a mere play on words or there is no difference between them.

Ultimately, therefore, the demands made in Eastern Europe are not "obsolete" requests for the privileges of intellectuals as a class or for secondary and partial reforms. They are, rather, a basic political protest, but a protest that can be fully expressed only in the secrecy of small groups and that remains partly veiled by nationalistic motives. What is important is that the demand persists, in spite of repeated repression, enormous difficulties, and suffocating limitations imposed by objective circumstances.

Observing the situation from a distance, we must admit that, to us Western Europeans, the condemnation of writers for writing what they think and feel, the dismissal of professors for crimes of opinion, the methods of ideological intimidation, and the arbitrary use of police power—the means by which the brakes are applied in Eastern Europe—are an eerie reminder of the repressive methods typical of the absolute monarchies of the nineteenth century, from the Czars to the Hapsburgs, from the Hapsburgs to the Bourbons. We feel that these methods are doubly antiquated because they are borrowed from the arsenal of defunct police states and because they cannot possibly be effective in the long run, having lost the character of systematic terror they had in the not too distant past and being used to repress rather than crush. They give the impression of being forms of resistance and temporizing in the face of a social situation that swells and seethes more threateningly each day and will end by bursting its banks.

The situation in Eastern Europe, therefore, appears to have a typically nineteenth-century pattern. It calls to mind Tocqueville's remark (already quoted in the same context by Gustaw Herling): "There is nothing worse than a bad government trying to correct itself." This means that, until the day of the decisive crisis, such a government will always be tempted to use force against the increasing momentum of demands that it has fomented itself by wavering constantly between concession and repression. In the end, we feel, it will have to give way. Unfortunately, this is not so certain as we might have concluded from examples taken from the last century, which may not be relevant to our time or may be relevant only up to a point. Yet it remains true that when we ask for "freedom" we are asking for everything. The "confrontation" is total; it is not concerned with the privileges of a class or a corporation, but with the very form of collective life.

But, because the issue is freedom, the freedom that the Western intellectual thinks he owns as he might own a piece of furniture, he finds the protest movements and the changes taking place in Eastern Europe only too familiar, passé, not really significant. Hence the widespread feeling that, although the libertarian ferment shaking these countries deserves our sympathy, it does not really concern us. After all, what is involved is the achievement of a social good that we already enjoy and that has become worn out and cheapened by use. What we need is something else: a stronger medicine, perhaps. Or drugs. Or systematic violence.

At this point, one wonders whether such a method of arguing does not conceal a "comedy of intellectual errors." The societies that have been deprived of freedom with unprecedented severity have simply realized that freedom is the indispensable premise for collective life, whatever political shape it assumes. By rediscovering this, they are challenging not only the value of the socialist regime but the very conception of socialism as it has been fixed in most people's minds by the decisive victory of Marxism-Leninism; they are challenging the idea that socialism is nothing more than a state-controlled economy un-avoidably linked to a rigidly centralized political sys-tem, which grows more oppressive the more it claims to be striving for the fulfillment of a universal end: the unlimited reign of freedom.

On the other hand, in societies that enjoy a more or less well-ordered freedom, intellectuals make the more rigid forms of socialization and centralized power an ideal to oppose to the so-called "consumer society" as a remedy for the "alienation" of contempo-rary man. In reality, this is a somewhat negative, not to say nihilistic, ideal, since, to begin with, it does not even entail serious acceptance of the type of regime they profess to admire.

The question raised by this "comedy of errors" is whether the real crisis of Western society does not reside in the fact that the intellectual class wants to guide us to a new order without knowing what genu-ine freedom is, what socialism can be, or even what the word "society" means. In other words, there may be something else behind our facile rejection of "con-sumer society," the advantages of which we are loath to give up. (And once we have accepted the premises of industrial society, there seems to be no alternative to "consumerism.") This "something else" may be a lack of faith in politics, and not just in politics but in the value of life and human endeavor. In its apparent absurdity and its lack of other than material aims, the "consumer society" expresses and symbolizes the dis-trust that has driven many intellectuals and young people to a sort of gratuitous rebellion, bereft of true reasons as well as true aims.

The validity of socialism in Eastern Europe has been challenged by events; and doubts about social-ism are accompanied by a strong revival of the demand for political freedom. Here in the West, on the other hand, we have an "obsolete" freedom accompanied by the somewhat crude idealization of such exotic forms of government as Maoism.

What do such a phenomenon and such an intellectual misunderstanding mean? In the first place, they mean that we in the West no longer know and no longer want to know what freedom is and are more or less of the opinion that political freedom (together with moral freedom and the dignity of man in itself and of itself) is a sort of commodity. It is one of many commodities that our highly advanced society lavishes on us, and we use it because it is there, as we might use a car or a washing machine. But even if it were not there, no great harm would be done. Indeed, as far as the vast majority are concerned, less harm would be done than if the car and the washing machine were to disappear. Provided, of course, that the intellectuals— and, in particular, writers and artists—continued to enjoy the privilege of writing, publishing, and producing whatever they pleased.

For the crux of the matter is that it is the intellectuals—particularly the literati, but also many representatives of higher and medium culture—who claim that the more or less violent revolt spreading through the West is politically more advanced than the reformism of Eastern Europe. Nor is this all. It is also the intellectuals who flock today to all the extremisms, whether they are political, literary, or artistic. The sad and grotesque reason for this is a terror of missing the boat (or the airplane) of the future and of not heading the tumult of the young. The more violent the tumult, the more promising they consider it, just as, in the field of letters and the arts, the more incoherent the words, the more tortuous the forms and disordered the ideas, the "newer" they are.

Yet it would be wrong to say that most intellectuals in the West today make common cause with the rebels. Most of them are, in fact, on the side of established and recognized interests, whether the authority of the state or of the most active political parties and groups. What they really want is to be acknowledged as the purveyors of ideas to these authorities and movements. They want to hold the posts of those men who were once called "the councilors of the prince." And it matters little whether the prince is installed in power or is simply regarded as the likely successor of the reigning prince. Indeed, the latter position is considered far more prestigious than the other, and it is far more fashionable to hold it.

The only condition the Western intellectual does not seem to consider attractive today is that of independence. Independence involves isolation; isolation means to be outside history, flotsam washed ashore by the great tides of events, and consequently to be, by definition, in the wrong, "in outer darkness," to echo the words of Saint Matthew.

In other words, we are faced today with the following paradox: ever since the seventeenth century (at least), the European intellectual has represented the spirit of criticism and the demand for freedom. He has sometimes done so even at the price of martyrdom. But today intellectuals as a class find themselves playing the part of theoreticians (or, worse still, eulogists) of accomplished facts. It is even more symptomatic that these accomplished facts are not only of a political order but also literary, artistic, ideological, and, more generally, social. In short, since he wants to be part of the avant-garde, the contemporary European intellectual finds himself functioning as the fulcrum of conformity, as the manipulator of ready-made ideas, hostile to the mission as spokesman of doubt and heresy that was once his pride. He has consequently become the best and most useful instrument of modern tyranny, whatever name such a tyranny may choose to adopt.

This paradox is worth analyzing. In order to examine it more effectively, it would be best to return to the situation of the intellectuals in Eastern Europe, that is, to the situation of those who, having experienced one of the essential forms of modern tyranny in its full severity, now reject it, either explicitly or implicitly. They are aware of its full weight of oppression and of the difficulties of the real situation and are, in practice, "reformists" and not "rebels," even when they radically reject the prevailing ideology.

In 1961, Petru Dumitriu, a Rumanian intellectual who had fled to the West, discussed the revisionist movement in Eastern Europe. "As revisionism has revealed," he wrote, "the progressives in the East want to introduce into the operation of the socialist state open and legal conflicts of opinion and interests. They want to introduce the unforeseeable element of the will—in a word, human nature."

This is a lucid and straightforward expression of the vital contradiction (the living contradiction, not the sterilely logical or, worse still, "dialectical" one) that besets those whom Dumitriu calls the "progressives in the East."

On the one hand, since they want to "introduce into the operation of the socialist state" certain modifications and not to "challenge it totally," as we say here, the revisionists do look like reformists. But, on the other, to say that the modifications concern the introduction of "open and legal conflicts of opinion and interests" obviously implies the rejection of the centralizing and authoritarian state to which the socialist ideal has been reduced in practice in Eastern Europe and to which it is still reduced in the theory and programs of many Western countries.

If, in the last analysis, what is at stake is introducing into the operation of the socialist state not just "the unforeseeable element of the will" but, pure and simple, "human nature," the vital contradiction just mentioned appears in all its virulence. For this means the acknowledgment that such a state excludes nothing less than "human nature" and that, logically and necessarily, what is needed in the long run is not reform but radical change. This change will not be called "revolution," simply because the word has become so equivocal and implies two facts that contradict its declared purpose. The first is organized and centrally directed violence aimed at the conquest of power by a minority that is either well trained or is already established in important centers of the government apparatus. The second is the simplistic notion, shown to be wrong by harsh experience, that such an accomplished fact can in itself bring about a radical change for the better.

One can therefore conclude that when Polish, Czech, and Russian students and intellectuals ask for freedom of expression and democratic legality and at the same time proclaim themselves socialists, but without questioning the regime as such, they are doing one of two things. Either they are performing a realistic act of mental reservation, with a view to challenging the regime on the basis of the principle that the regime itself lays claim to, or—since their requests cannot be granted without endangering the very foundations of the regime—they will obtain only minimal concessions, accompanied each time by a more or less severe increase in political and police control. This is the contradiction and the relative weakness of these intellectuals' position. But not to recognize the intractability of the situation in which they find themselves and which they continue to combat tenaciously would be both foolish and ungenerous. The fact is that theirs is a real political struggle, accompanied by a real challenge to received ideas. Moreover, to those truly "committed" intellectuals the "revolutionism" of their colleagues in the West seems utterly frivolous.

For their part, the intellectuals in the West either overlook or do not even see the capital importance of the resurgence of the demand for freedom in a situation in which it should theoretically no longer be necessary, because of its replacement by "concrete freedoms." At the same time, they want to overthrow the so-called capitalist (or neocapitalist) system, or (as in the case of the "progressives" and the disciples of absolute efficiency and technological advance) they call for the introduction of social mechanisms maneuvered from above and devised by specialists. In both cases, we can repeat the words of the Gospel: "Who have eyes, and see not: and ears, and hear not." We could add that they have brains to understand and do not understand.

The ailment from which Western civilization is obviously suffering is not the excess of consumption (which is the consequence of a certain attitude to life and to the purpose of life, not a first cause) but a lack of freedom, due to the state of advanced regimentation and mechanization of collective existence. As far as this is concerned, it is of secondary importance whether the economy remains "capitalist." And it is on precisely this point—the necessarily authoritarian mechanization of collective existence—that East and West meet in the self-same crisis and could meet in the same movement of reform and liberation. The division between capitalist and noncapitalist countries makes little or no sense today; the real question lies elsewhere. Besides, the meaning of the term "capitalist" is far from clear. What is clear is that it no longer means what it meant for Marx and that it is applied to countries where plutocracy, technocratic state control, democracy, and corporativism (the power of "classes" and "orders" organized to defend and impose individual interests) coexist more or less at random. To say this is not to say that we live in a substantially just, ordered, and free society. If anything, the opposite is true: our presumably democratic society is eroded by grave injustices and evils. It is besieged by tyrannies all the more serious in that they are not obvious and are accepted by the majority as inevitable if not actually desirable.

As regards not only the democratic regimes but modern society in general, we should never forget Tocqueville's lesson: the establishment of the egalitarian principle in America meant that in the future all attempts to introduce even an authoritarian system would have to appeal to the principle of equality, simply because there was no other principle that could have any validity. Applying Tocqueville's idea to contemporary society, Raymond Aron wrote, "All democratic societies are hypocritical and cannot be anything else. Nowadays it is only in the name of democracy that an authoritarian regime can be established, since all modern regimes are based on the principle of equality. Thus the only way to establish an absolute power is to claim to be freeing men."

Anyone can see what a wide margin of ambiguity this leaves, not only to political phraseology but also to all political action today. We can see how ingenuous it is (to put it mildly) to think we are saying something noteworthy about politics when we appeal to the ideals of democracy, social justice, or even liberty. Yet we can also see how absolutely necessary it is, in these circumstances, to be intransigent in maintaining the claims of freedom, without qualifications, against any regime that may be vaunted or proposed. So we can go on from Tocqueville and Aron, and observe that the contemporary egalitarian regime, even in its purely ideal form, necessarily entails a substantial measure of uncontrolled and uncontrollable authority. Since it has to serve the collectivity as a whole and to balance its forces, tensions, and conflicting needs, it has to base itself on a complex system of authoritarian measures that guarantee the functioning of both production and political power. We need only think of the extremely high technical standard reached by industry—which is now inseparable from science—and of the equally high level of technicality required today by the fundamental problems of domestic and foreign policy to realize what constraints are placed on the freedom of individuals and groups. And we begin to see how the political problem has changed since the days before the First World War, the Russian Revolution, and what is known as the Second Industrial Revolution, when the issue seemed to reduce itself to the introduction of justice into the system of liberty or the adaptation of the system of liberty to that of economic equality.

If it is true that the egalitarianism peculiar to modern industrial society entails a more or less substantial measure of uncontrolled and uncontrollable authority, it is also obvious that authoritarian measures inevitably generate not only oppression and injustice but also inequality. Now, whether we speak the language of Marxism or that of libertarianism, what is the source of inequality if not the prevailing of the authority of fact and force over the ordinary, ultimately irrepressible, needs of human nature?

We can ask that the "system" become effective either by way of a state-planned economy, imposed through rigorous centralization of political power, or (and the difference is only superficial) by way of the "technological revolution," which has already started and which many people regard as the most radical and truly progressive remedy for the evils of contemporary society. But to ask for this is to ask for the present system with all its defects, only to end up in one form or another of tyrannical collectivism.

"In human affairs," wrote Petru Dumitriu in the article mentioned earlier, "social effectiveness and technical efficiency take different paths." The observation is sound, and it is worth considering his remarks (published in *Critique* in May 1963) on the technocratic "futurism" of both "capitalist" and "socialist" thinking.

Dumitriu observes that the political idea characteristic of our time is that man must adapt himself to the second phase of the scientific, technological, industrial, and social revolution that started in the Renaissance. Tradition is of no assistance to us here; we must break with tradition, and must use scientific means in order to do so. To apply scientific means rationally involves treating society as uniform matter to be molded and as energy to be regulated. But here the Utopian optimism of the capitalist or socialist technocrats comes up against the fact that "the historical inertia of mental habits and behaviour is infinitely greater than the inertia of matter." The technocrat finds himself up against human nature. "There are certain ways of behaviour," Dumitriu continues, "which are found in varying degrees in all human societies. It is these ways of behaviour that form the indefinable, but none the less real, phenomenon we call *human nature*. . . . The technical mentality tends to use direct forces and propulsions. In politics its weapon is the decree, in the worst case terror, and in the best an appeal to civic consciousness. Utopias tend to overestimate these three means and to underestimate social inertia. . . . [But] the distinction between *classical profit* and *collective profit* will never really be understood by the non-ascetic individual (who cannot, by definition, but be the majority . . .). Collective profit will never be able to stimulate individual effort to the utmost as *selfish* personal profit does. . . . Men can only be forced to work by two motives: personal profit or police terror, and even police terror must be compensated for by a modest degree of economic stimulus." On the other hand, concludes Dumitriu, "it is not through a desire for rationalization nor through the purpose of serving the collectivity that we can reduce administrative inertia, but only by means of such forces as criticism and the play of opposing interests. . . . The technocrat adopts the point of view of the State: this point of view is acceptable to the theoretician but not to the single individual. But single individuals are in the majority."

Single individuals are in the majority, and the majority represents human nature in all its inertia. But, we could object, this is surely the heart of the matter. When we are faced with the complexity of contemporary society, the appeal to human nature is ineffective; it seems rather weak, for what is it but an appeal to the social indolence of the single individual, while the true problem is the efficient and, if possible, the just functioning of the collectivity. And it is the effective functioning of the collectivity that now tends to be the object of the intellectual, just as it is the object of the technocrat and the politician. For the intellectual is interested in the coherence of systems (or, as some say, in the possibility of "totalizing," that is, of excogitating total theoretical solutions), rather than in the single individual. He regards the single individual as incongruous and obstinate on the one hand, and on the other as a being that can be reduced to clearly defined and calculable physical, psychic, and sociological "structures."

Things being the way they are in contemporary society, there would seem to be no answer to such an objection. Yet there is an answer, and the answer is that we must choose. *This* is the issue, not calculations about probability, efficiency, or utility. We must choose the type of life we want, the society we prefer, the meaning we attribute to our presence here on earth. Then, and only then, will the individual appear as the ultimate criterion of social changes and an insurmountable obstacle in the way of authoritarian manipulations. For the paradox of collective life is this: while the majority appears to be indifferent to liberty and content with being the receptacle of food and prefabricated entertainment, the individual in a group—that is, the ensemble of individuals, the same majority that seems passive if regarded from a certain point of view—always opposes his own inertia to whatever system people wish to impose on him. He disconcerts it; indeed, he prevents it from being a "system," and by so doing denies it and refutes it. This is the aspect assumed by liberty when matters are observed from the point of view of the ensemble of individuals.

But there remains the *mass*, that is, the collectivity taken all together and reduced to its lowest common denominator of material and moral requirements. Here, too, we must choose. The mass is the very symbol of social inertia (and at the same time of instability), but it is also an eminently artificial entity, a statistic, a mere agglomeration, not an ensemble of individuals. It is perfectly possible to treat human society as a massive aggregate of interchangeable units—and this is what rulers and experts do everywhere. But it is also possible, not to say inevitable, to see society as an ensemble of individuals. To have an ensemble of individuals, we must have, and *want to have*, units that are not interchangeable but incomparable. In order to have a collectivity, we must have a complex of rules and norms that allow each individual to be and to feel "somebody," to have both rights and duties and to know what they are. Finally, in order to have a community we must have "equal laws." But even before we have equal laws we must have an immediate and "natural" solidarity not explicitly formulated in a body of beliefs and norms. And the coherence of the community must be confirmed by each person's way of being, while each person must contribute to its existence by bringing something new and better to it every day.

For the mass, however, the only things that count are subsistence, a quiet life, and the possibility of escaping from the tedium of everyday servitude: the idiocy of private life and the excitement of public frenzies and violence. But while the mass is an artificial entity, maintained artificially, what is undeniably real is the existence of a minority that believes man contains a nucleus that can never be reduced to mechanical manipulation and brutalization. This is the part that wants to live, that resists, and when all is said and done it is the only part that counts.

Throughout history, of course, this is the part

that most frequently, and almost by its very nature, is defeated. But the regimes based on the masses, on power, on enforced cohesion, are also defeated and crushed. Only conformity triumphs every time: the attitude of those who sniff the wind of success and avoid at all costs and at every moment the danger of failure and misfortune.

In any event, people with a hatred for servitude, enslavement, and the stupidity that accompanies enslavement do exist. Not all of them, or even most of them, are necessarily privileged beings who scorn the vulgar throng. If anything, the opposite is true. They are simply the minority, the restless minority, who prevent the social body from slipping into the lethargy of the Dark Ages. Furthermore, the worst insult we can cast on the individual who is poor and oppressed is to presume that all he wants is work, food, clothes, lodging, and entertainment. This is the indignity inflicted on men by industrial society, or by the capitalist system if one prefers, but also by the concomitant idea that, in order to abolish the evils of capitalism, it is enough to put everyone to work, to give everybody the same ration of commodities decreed necessary from above by technicians, economists, and sociologists, and, more important, by men who hold political power. For it is in political power and the way it is wielded that the core of the problem lies. However, as we well know, the socialists regard political power as a mere consequence of economic power. Therefore it is incomprehensible to them that a state not based on economic privilege, profit, and the private ownership of the means of production can prove in practice more tyrannical and exploitative than a capitalist state.

This misunderstanding on the part of the socialists is a particular aspect of a more general phenomenon set forth with great clarity by Leo Strauss, an American philosopher of German origin. In his book *On Tyranny* there is a detailed analysis of Xenophon's dialogue *Hieron,* as well as a most enlightening discussion with Alexandre Kojève, the left-wing Hegelian philosopher. Leo Strauss maintains that it is impossible to discuss politics reasonably today unless we go back beyond Machiavellianism and opportunistic historicism to the premises of classical thought. In order to demonstrate his thesis, Strauss starts by stating that modern tyranny is characterized by the fact that "when we were faced by it, we did not recognize it."

This means that when we people of today, and especially we intellectuals of today, were face to face with the implacable and absolutely authoritarian application of power, we took what we traditionally would have regarded as the worst of regimes for a new and progressive form of government, or at least for a historically necessary, and therefore basically good, phase in the development of our society. This applies to Bolshevism, Fascism, and National Socialism just as much as it does to the tyrannical aspects of capitalist or democratic regimes.

How could this have come about? In brief, Strauss answers that the situation of culture and contemporary societies is such that intellectuals have become the accomplices of tyranny. They have done so for three reasons: first, because modern tyranny is necessarily based on ideology and science; second, because it therefore seduces intellectuals, who see it as the realization of (or the possibility of realizing) their ideas, and especially the idea of the total rebirth of society, which has seemed desirable and attainable for the first time in the modern era; third, because by its nature modern tyranny needs the collaboration of intellectuals, whether men of letters, scientists, or professional philosophers.

According to Leo Strauss, the difference between modern and ancient tyranny resides in the fact that modern tyranny is dominated, first, by a belief in the conquest of nature by men (collectively disciplined) with the help of science; and, second, by a belief in the popularization of scientific and philosophical knowledge, which produces a new and, one should add, completely unexpected kind of dogmatism and conformity, based on the idea of a continual criticism of reality and on empirical knowledge, not on any "revealed" truth. This dogmatism and conformity receive formidable support from the notion that science is a universal language and a superior manifestation of objective truth. And since the declared object of science is the conquest of nature and the rational regulation of human society, it must be spread and popularized. It imposes itself authoritatively, without, however, assuming an explicitly dogmatic form; the form it adopts is that of empirical certainty. And this, incidentally, is true not only of the natural sciences but also of the so-called "human" sciences.

It may be useful at this point, interrupting for a moment our account of Strauss's ideas, to ask how it comes about that not only the intellectual but also the common man can accept this point of view, or, to be more precise, this explanation of the world. The reason seems to be the seductiveness of a mode of thought whose postulate is that every individual, as such, can henceforth consider himself emancipated from any theology or any superior intellectual order and can be sure that he is equipped with an independent conscience subject to no authority but the desires of his own nature. Naturally, this puts the aforesaid free and autonomous individual directly at the mercy of the "hidden persuaders" and all the mechanisms capable of influencing such desires as well as the decisions resulting from them. This "persuasion" is not just the work of technicians of publicity; for every appeal to the individual, to his egocentric impulses and "received ideas" (whose author he deludes himself into believing he is because it is *he* who has received them), is bound to convince him only too easily. "Received ideas" in this context are also, and above all, the ideals of social progress, humanitarianism, revolution, and the total transformation of the human world with the help of technology and the abandonment of all bonds with tradition.

Therefore, it is also in the name of freedom that the individual can today be made into a slave. And so he is. But what we have here is a special conception of freedom. Tommaso Campanella defined it as "the reduction of every man to natural liberty" and, along with it, the reduction of society to a strict order that supposedly reflected nature, since it reflected wisdom and a perfect knowledge of human nature. This was the ideal that inspired the thinking of Campanella, as well as the general intellectual fervor that appeared in about the sixteenth century and that we call "naturalism."

Today we could still say that we share that ideal. In fact, it still seems to us that, in Rousseau's words, "Man is born free, and everywhere he is in chains." Today, however, the chains appear to be forged by the illusion that we can attain "natural freedom" through the release of the individual from every norm and through his subjection to a collective discipline that will supposedly guarantee each one of us at every moment the greatest amount of "natural liberty" (that is, the satisfaction of our own instincts and immediate desires) compatible with the "concrete situation." This "natural liberty," along with its corollary, artificial servitude, also signifies a disregard of and an obliviousness to that natural and inexorable servitude of man to all that he does not know about himself and about nature—to all that he will never know and cannot, will never be able to, control. And it is to this lack of awareness and disregard of his dependence on a mysterious order that contemporary man owes his enslavement. "Accessible everywhere, nature is everywhere unfathomable," said Thomas H. Huxley.

Let us return to Leo Strauss and his distinction between ancient and modern tyranny, or, rather, between the ancient and modern way of regarding tyranny. Strauss goes on to observe that classical political science was based on an idea of perfection, that is, of "how men *could* live." This is a Utopia in the original sense of the word—a reality that exists nowhere except in the mind. For the ancients, this Utopia was "realizable" and "improbable" at the same time. It was realizable insofar as it did not entail any change in human nature, but only the attainment of a certain perfection and harmony. It was improbable insofar as its realization depended on "fortunate circumstances." In an extreme case, as in the illustrious example given by Plato, the "fortunate circumstances" themselves are regarded as absolutely "ideal"—"that which exists solely in our discussion," says Glaucon at the end of the ninth book of *The Republic*. Yet, contrary to what the pragmatic historian affirms, this in no way detracts from the validity of the conception behind the Utopia, that is, of the ideal of perfection it proposes and explains. For the very possibility of conceiving an ideal type of society is exemplary; it incites us to think and work well.

Strauss goes on to say that Machiavelli dismisses every Utopia except the one of his own opportunistic realism and maintains that the question of "how one should live" has no meaning. All that counts is the real, ordinary, everyday behavior of men, while on the other hand the "circumstances," *il caso,* can be regulated and dominated by the "virtue" of the prince. Machiavelli, therefore, takes for granted the existence of an average, unchangeable human nature (the *homo naturalis* or *homme moyen sensuel,* whichever we prefer) and offers to the politically ambitious the model of a realistic, opportunistic, unscrupulous "virtue" used for the purpose of achieving the only political goal that had any meaning for him—a state as great and strong as possible.

This remains substantially the basis of political science today. But the modern historian, argues Leo Strauss, is not necessarily Machiavellian, even if many of the consequences of his ideas are. He sets out with the hypothesis that what matters is the fact—the event—and that thought comes afterward. This thought is the thought of the "historicist," expert at discerning the true meaning and the true trend of events, in the same way that the nature of the atom was spotted by Rutherford and the great physicists who followed him.

So, says Strauss, thanks to the conquest of nature by science (and this includes human nature, which both modern psychology and sociology claim to be able to define), we are confronted by a tyranny that can become everlasting and universal, in other words, that can impose once for all its *significance*—its mode of progressing—on the societies subject to it. Thus, man's thought can be subordinated to the collectivity on the basis of the idea that every thought is "historical," that is, relative, without a truth of its own, and true only in respect to a specific and changing situation.

Since this is so, the intellectual who wants to teach modern tyrants something they do not know—namely, the "laws" of history and society—must ascetically renounce any indulgence in "ideal" views in order to see only factual reality and "opportunity." Furthermore, in modern tyranny the difference between good and bad is supplanted by "historical necessity." This means that both the prince and his councilors regard themselves as the intellectual proprietors of the meaning of history. And so the road to absolute opportunism is wide open.

"One performs miracles," Strauss observes at this point, "with the use of syntheses. Kojève's or Hegel's synthesis of classical and Biblical morality effects the miracle of producing an amazingly lax morality out of two moralities, both of which made very strict demands on self-restraint. . . . Both doctrines (Hobbes's and Hegel's) construct human society by starting from the untrue assumption that man as man is thinkable as a being that lacks the awareness of sacred restraints or as a being that is guided by nothing but a desire for recognition."

Turning from the moderns to the ancients, Strauss points out that the Greeks rejected as contrary to nature those two ideas that seem to be fundamental to modern political thought: the idea that science can conquer nature and, more than that, the idea that scientific and philosophical knowledge can be spread and popularized. "According to the Greeks," says Strauss, "the diffusion of true knowledge among the unwise would be of no help, as knowledge that was acquired by the wise inevitably would be diffused and weakened, and transformed into opinion, prejudice, or mere belief. . . . The utmost in the direction of universality that one could expect is, then, an absolute rule of unwise men who would control about half of the globe, the other half being ruled by other unwise men."

Yet what is contemptuously called "Utopia" is simply an explicit declaration of what is implicit in every attempt to improve society. Every view that maintains that one thing is better than another (a) implies that there is such a thing as an idea of good, and that there is only one idea of good; (b) is *free*, in other words, does not correspond to any factual necessity but simply to an aspiration of the spirit; (c) leads to a Utopia, or to a reality that exists only in the mind; (d) is by definition "impossible," that is, incompatible with the present situation and the current ideas about good and evil, justice and injustice. The essential conclusion is that the proponent of a Utopia, be he philosopher, intellectual, or mere conscious protester, does not want to rule or to be a councilor of the prince, but simply to convince those who share his condition and his dissatisfaction with the present state of affairs. The goal he sets himself is not the enforced realization of some total plan, but, rather, the most honest personal behavior possible and the most intelligent reform of the present state of affairs. As for the ideal, he will support it in the only way ideals can be supported —by nurturing it with thoughts that are just (and therefore also criticizing it) and with actions in accord with these thoughts.

"The classics," Leo Strauss concludes, "did not dream of a fulfillment of History." Today this idea takes on a singularly liberating significance. By accepting its suggestions, we are freed from the tyrannical moralism that makes each individual into a slave of the inhuman obligation of justifying his own thoughts and actions before a nonexistent but terroristic tribunal of generic Humanity, presided over by that implacable judge of each and every one of us. The name of this judge is History. He is a far more jealous God than the God of the Old Testament, but also a pettier God, for he is incarnated in rulers and their intellectual councilors and flatterers.

Perhaps this is the point at which we should state clearly that modern tyranny (the apparently irresistible trend of contemporary society to be organized in autocratic, albeit impersonal, forms) is not so much the result of social, economic, or political pressures as it is the consequence of the fact that modern man cannot conceive of any other absolute than the political absolute, any duty superior to political commitment, or any means of decisive action other than technically organized violence. In other words, he believes that political faith and action are legitimate substitutes for what was once a religious absolute. In practice, there may be a great difference between the means adopted to "build socialism" and those employed to dispose of an ever greater variety of material goods, but the difference is not crucial, for in both cases the objectives are considered final ends; beyond them is nothing that can serve as a limit.

In the last analysis, politics is regarded simultaneously as the ground on which a new vision of life is formed and as the instrument with which to forge the new civilization this vision entails. But, we are prompted to ask, can a political belief ever satisfy the need for an absolute, which accompanies and plagues man's every desire and every enterprise? And, furthermore, does there, can there ever exist a moment at which this new civilization is "realized"?

Now, if we do not start from the totalitarian postulate that politics is action *on* men forcibly to change their relationships in line with a specific ideological plan, it seems hard to admit that a political creed, based by its very nature on the relative, on chance, and perhaps even on the "virtue" of one or more individuals, can satisfy a need that concerns a relationship as intimate as the one between man and the world; the need for justice in politics can only be the expression and the consequence of such a relationship. And it seems equally hard to accept the idea that a new civilization can arise from political action or, more generally, that the birth of civilization can have a date.

In actual fact, the cycle of political regimes described and discussed by Socrates in the eighth book of *The Republic* remains to this day the image that best expresses and explains the relationship between politics and human nature, on the one hand, and the necessity that regulates political changes, on the other. Besides indicating in the simplest way how, from the corruption of one regime, another is born from seeds already present in the preceding one, Plato shows through Socrates how the succession of political regimes finally depends on an ungovernable demonic element that is the center of the human spirit. And he leads us to understand that the true root of historical necessity lies in the recesses of the human spirit and thus in the ultimate nature of things. From the ultimate law that is the essence of the divine to the depths of the human spirit, there reigns one single arcane rhythm.

From these depths there springs the duty of the free and thinking man to concern himself with the common good and to speak out about the events of the community, and, more important, to abandon the field of political struggle, withdrawing with the few to save the savable, when he sees that there is nothing to be done, that necessity must follow its course, without anyone's being able to oppose it, and that every effort to do so simply accelerates its fulfillment. We may well have reached that point today.

To conclude this discussion of modern tyranny and the part played in it by intellectuals, it might be worth asking ourselves what, actually, the principle of authoritarianism is and what specific form it assumes nowadays.

It seems to me, quite simply, that the authoritarian principle is inherent in the very fact of looking at the community, with regard to political and social problems, only in terms of the totality and considering only the conceptual and mechanical congruence of the parts and the efficient functioning of the whole. In fact, the preoccupation with totality implies that human society is an organism whose laws we know, and by implying this it also implies that we can, indeed, that we must, modify it by means of more or less violent external intervention.

Now, it is obvious that if we set out with this postulate we will never arrive at the autonomous individual, the free, self-assured man who is the bulwark, not a "part"—not a cog or even an organ—of any community that wants to be both civil and orderly.

This postulate will lead us, rather, to the factory, the barracks, and the electronic bureaucracy, with the police around to keep order. But perhaps not. After all, the totalitarian hypothesis is based on an abstraction; whereas the factory, for instance, needs rules that are flexible, demanding genuine utility and efficiency and not the police state's theoretical guarantees that everything will always be regulated in the same way and that "not a leaf will stir unless the leaders want it to."

If, after this summary definition of the principle of modern authoritarianism, I were to say something about the meaning freedom can have today, I would start with an observation that does not concern political freedom directly, but that is nevertheless essential. Man is free not because freedom is an essential attribute of his thought and his consciousness, but because he is unable to prove either that he is determined by nature, history, or divine will, or that he is liberated from natural necessities and the conditions and constrictions of society, is *causa sui*, creator of himself, *faber fortunae suae*. Thus he remains *uncertain* on both counts. This means that he knows every choice he makes is determined in some way or other, but he does not know by what or in what way. In spite of everything, his choice will be a free and new act, an addition to the world and a modification of the present state of affairs—something that not even he, the subject of the action, can foresee.

This freedom, which is part of the unknown but incontestable nature of things, cannot be ceded; it can only be debased. As for more strictly political freedom, the first thing to be said is that the "freedom of the individual" is a fraud if the society in which he lives is not free, that is, if there is no free space for each person, in which he can give proof of his value or simply express his true nature. The existence of this space does not, of course, depend solely on laws or even on what the ancient Athenians described, in a word that is hard to translate, as *isonomia*. Long before it is enforced by laws, freedom is guaranteed by the feeling that has formed in a given society and has become common to all its members: the awareness of a bond between the individual and the world, of a sense of human destiny, of the dignity that belongs to man, which is the most profound and indestructible of facts. No tyranny, no artifice of the intellect, can prevail against it. And it is this fact that, more than any other, the Western intellectuals seem to have forgotten.

Dissent, March–April 1969
(Trans. Alastair Hamilton and Raymond Rosenthal)

18

The Mass Situation and Noble Values

I

The mass man attributes no distinctive value to himself, either for good or for ill. He feels that he is just like everybody else, and he is content to be so. He proclaims the rights of the commonplace and would impose it wherever he could. He recognizes no limits of any kind—material, social, or spiritual—and will never appeal to any authority outside himself. For him, practically nothing is impossible, nothing is dangerous, and on principle no one is superior to anyone else.

This is how Ortega y Gasset defined the moral situation of the mass man in *The Revolt of the Masses,* published in 1930. The Spanish philosopher contrasts mass man (who closely resembles Plato's "tyrannical man") with "noble" man, noble because he makes demands on himself, not because he arrogates rights to himself. What is more important is that, for the "noble" man, "to have an idea means having reasons for that idea: it means believing there is such a thing as reason, that is, a world of intelligible truths." The mass man, on the other hand, is characterized intellectually by the fact that he refuses to give reasons, since he does not care about being right. All that matters to him is that he impose his own opinions.

Having defined mass man as an intellectual and

moral state (a disastrous mixture of confusion, arrogance, and self-satisfaction), Ortega y Gasset contrasts him with the classical ideal of the aristocrat and philosopher: the man who is conscious, reasonable, and free because he is his own master. While Ortega y Gasset's book is inspired by an essentially modern form of anxiety and is rich in highly pertinent observations about the state of Western society after the First World War, it is still within the sphere of the great Platonic world view. This is perfectly natural; to the extent to which the European intellectual regards civilization as an acquired good that the "barbarians" (be they the "masses" or the totalitarian hordes) threaten to destroy, he inevitably finds himself turning to Plato. For Plato is the only philosopher who has provided a strict definition, rather, much more than a definition, a limpid image, of that requirement of the mind we vaguely describe by the term "humanism." The strength of the Platonic ideal stems from the marvelous balance it maintains between Socratic doubt and the absoluteness of ideas in and for themselves, the balance between the infinite uncertainty of opinion and the incontrovertible reality of truth. Plato's "humanism" is just as far from dogma as it is from eclectic indulgence toward the world of appearances. In times of crisis, therefore, the Platonic form of reasoning inevitably appears as the only point from which we can again glimpse, if not truth, at least the light of truth.

Although Ortega y Gasset defines the "revolt of the masses" in moral and intellectual terms, he also treats it as a question of number—the growing number of individuals who want to enjoy the benefits of civilization without paying the price. In so doing, he overlooks the crucial question: the downfall of the political and intellectual elites who were supposedly entrusted with the safekeeping of civilized values. This is the book's weakness. It is not that Ortega y Gasset fails to give a detailed account of the material causes of the phenomenon, but that, having set the problem in intellectual and moral terms, he has not delved deeply enough into the intellectual and moral causes. Nor has he gone into the causes of the causes in order to find some sufficiently simple sufficient cause of the entire phenomenon.

We could retort that plain and simple "numbers" would never have prevailed if the elites themselves had not yielded to quantitative and numerical values (or pseudo values) and to a concept of "reason" whereby having an idea does not necessarily mean to have reasons for it. In short, the error of the elites is to have turned into mass, along with the masses or even before the masses. The "revolt of the masses" cannot mean merely an increasing number of individuals progressively forgetting certain moral exigencies. It must be connected with the degradation of "noble" values under the pressure of a phenomenon, or a complex of phenomena, stronger than the collective habit of individuals to respect a certain body of traditional values. But can a material phenomenon cause moral corruption? If it can, there is no ground for assuming the superiority of spiritual values, reason, and intelligible truths to circumstances. We must admit that everything shares the same uncertainty. If, instead, moral corruption has a moral cause, we must elucidate the nature of the moral phenomenon in question. "Number" might be the most obvious and significant aspect of this phenomenon, but it is not the first cause. It still leaves unexplained the moral situation in which "number" assumes such overriding importance as to become a kind of value, a principle more effective than any other, almost a good in itself.

What is evident is that the mere advent of the masses, as described by the great Spanish thinker, does not mean the end of Plato, Spinoza, or Voltaire; it does imply, however, a radical crisis of the humanist tradition, which, as late as 1914, could still legitimately be considered the basis of the moral life of Europe. Indeed, the problem of the masses is the problem of the real or apparent impotence of the intellectual and the teacher in mass society.

The crisis is clearly outlined in an essay by Hannah Arendt entitled "Tradition and the Modern Age," published in *Partisan Review* early in 1954. "Our tradition of political thought," she writes, "had its definite beginnings in the teachings of Plato and Aristotle. I believe it came to a no less definite end in the theories of Karl Marx. The beginning was made when, in *The Republic*'s allegory of the cave, Plato described the sphere of human affairs—all that belongs to the living together of men in a common world—in terms of darkness, confusion, and deception which those aspiring to true being must turn away from and abandon if they want to discover the clear sky of eternal ideas. The end came with Marx's declaration that philosophy and its truth are located not outside the affairs of men and their common world but precisely in them, and can be 'realized' only in the sphere of living together, which he called 'society,' through the emergence of 'socialized men.'"

The Platonic myth of the cave is the symbol of what the ideal of humanist culture was until our times. Marx's thesis, however, is the fundamental thesis of the age of the masses, and it expresses with particular vigor a concept of the relationship between the intellectual and the masses, a concept that is specifically modern. The Marxists are its most consistent supporters, for they make it a first principle of their ethics. But this tendency to regard the relationship between culture and collective life as a relationship in which the former is subordinated to the latter can also be found, in more or less organic form, among non-Marxists. Indeed, there are few intellectuals who do not share it today, and fewer still who are prepared to embrace the Platonic thesis with all the rigor that entails.

The idea that the philosopher must throw in his lot with his fellow men and help free them from error and evil is not peculiar to Marx. It is found in Plato, too. He believed that the philosopher who was fortunate enough to leave the cave and see the eternal Ideas was obliged to return among his fellow prisoners to share the truths he had learned and to persuade them to turn toward the light. Marx, however, does not say this. What he says is that it is the philosopher's moral duty not to leave the cave except in the company of his fellow men. Thought and truth have meaning only to the extent that they help men free themselves of their chains. According to Marx, the intellectual is obliged to think only this particular type of thought, to think only practical thoughts. Ultimately, what Marx is saying is this: the philosopher is a philosopher only insofar as he thinks (*with* and *for* the masses) thoughts that are potential actions. We all leave the cave together or not at all. A "gratuitous" thought is not simply illusory; it is evil, it is a "betrayal." We must think not truth; we must think the present social situation—the cave, that is. We might almost say that for Marx the cave is the only reality, and it is senseless to ask whether this reality is good or bad. From one point of view, the reality of the cave is the worst possible, for the cave is a place of slavery. Yet it is also an essentially good place, for, despite the chains and the error, all the conditions for total liberation are there.

It is important to note that, thinking the way he does, Marx is convinced that he is not rejecting the humanist tradition but is pointing out the only way of realizing it fully, or, at all events, of preventing it from remaining an insubstantial ideal. Marx makes only one alteration in the humanist ideal, but it is an essential alteration: he denies the intellectual the right to feel free and demands that he consider his condition a state of necessity. Therefore the intellectual must submit his thoughts to the same "material" circumstances that weigh collectively on his fellow men. The Marxist intellectual must accept as a rule of conduct the idea that "nobody is superior." We are all under the yoke of necessity except for those who think they are free from servitude simply because they take no interest in the condition of other men, of the majority, and so stand "objectively" on the side of the masters of the prison.

If Marx has provided the formula for the relationship between the intellectual and the masses in modern times, and if his formula upsets the humanist ideal as we have inherited it from the Greeks (while claiming to achieve it), the reason is that he thought out fully the idea of "necessity." We might almost say that the idea of necessity imposed itself irresistibly on the prophet of socialism.

More important than any criticism or refutation of Marx's "philosophy," more significant than his economic and social theories or his claims to have discovered a complete "science" of the laws of nature, is the fact that a great European intellectual was impelled to think out thoroughly and without illusions the reality of his time, and was led to break on one essential point with the tradition he himself represented, which he wanted to carry to its logical conclusions in order to derive a practical rule of conduct. Another revealing fact is that Marx reached these conclusions in the name of real humanity—in the name of the collectivity and, yes, of the "masses." From one point of view, the Marxist idea of the "integral realization of philosophy" is based on the idea that there can be no individuals until humanity is completely free, but only classes, forces, and numbers—a small number of exploiters and a large number of exploited. Between these two powers there is nothing whatsoever, least of all room for the philosopher to go back and forth between the darkness and the light. But, according to Marx, what distinguishes the masses and characterizes the social situation in which they become the dominant factor is the state of necessity. The intellectual has no right to ignore this situation. In order to be worthy of his mission, he must develop a mass consciousness and must think and act *as if* he were simply one element of the great number. Another way of putting it is that, for Marx, the intellectual is not thinking about anything at all unless he is thinking about the historical situation.

Now, Marx may have interpreted tendentiously or even incorrectly the state of necessity in which the individual finds himself in the age of industrialization and organization: the dependence of every man on his fellow men and of everybody on the objective situation. What he did not do was invent it. Whatever we may think of Marxism as a theory, we must agree that, from a purely cultural point of view, the appearance in the mind of an intellectual of the idea of necessity in such a vigorous form is significant in itself. Hannah Arendt is right to say that by upsetting so completely the classical relationship between thought and action Marx marked the end of a tradition and heralded a crisis that still exists, primarily the crisis of culture and "noble values" in the contemporary world.

In the nineteenth century, to speak of "the masses" in the plural was a way of saying "democracy"—government based on equality, or, rather, on the equivalence of individuals, not on a hierarchy consecrated by tradition. This government was subject to both number and law (practical reason).

In modern society (in which industrialization and the sovereign power of money coexist with the democratic principle), "democracy" and "mass" in the singular become synonymous. Were it not so, we would find ourselves arguing the ancient philosopher's paradox about the impossibility of passing from the plural to the aggregate. Ortega y Gasset may be right in theory when he distinguishes between "hyperdemocracy" as embodied in mass society and democracy in the classical sense. But in practice modern democracy never resembled Rousseau's imaged Republic of Geneva, for the simple reason that it has always comprised "masses" of more than the three thousand inhabitants that the author of the *Social Contract* (along with the ancients) considered the ideal limit for a democratic community.

Besides, modern democracy from its very origin is a rational principle applicable to the whole of humanity, a universal *idea*. So it hardly seems logical to criticize "hyperdemocracy" in the name of democracy. It seems, rather, to be a sudden retreat from the disturbing consequences of a principle that one does not reject. If the principle of democracy is accepted, no society can ever be criticized for an "excess" of democracy, for the excessive extension of equality, but only for what inequality and irrationality still remain. Otherwise we would have to formulate a hierarchical principle for democracy, and this seems to be a contradiction in terms.

However paradoxical it may seem, the ideal of democracy (in the modern sense of the term, which is not Athenian or Genevan or even Jacobin) is unassailable; nobody has yet formulated a principle of government and legislation superior to that of the equivalence of all individuals when the interests of the collectivity are concerned. This is probably the heart of the problem of the "situation of the mass" and the mass's deafness to "noble values," which the intellectuals so decry.

Mechanization, bureaucracy, the increasing complexity of technology, and scientific specialization are typical phenomena of mass society today, yet they seem to vitiate the authority of the individual, as well as the democratic power of the majority, in favor of an anonymous principle of organization and discipline. The most rational collective ideal of the modern era, "hyperdemocratic" socialism, has appeared for some time to be leading inevitably to an authoritarian and hierarchical society.

But these problems do not go beyond the facts of the situation; they are simply ways of formulating the difficulties facing us. To blame the masses for them will not help us to find a remedy or to discover, perhaps, the principle we lack. Nor is it likely that we can solve them by appealing from corrupt to sound democracy. The increasing pressure of mechanical and organizational demands on the individual, and the fact that a "hyperdemocratic" state seems to entail authoritarian methods of government, may be abnormal and scandalous, but these phenomena all stem from an unquestionably egalitarian impulse. Even the most intolerably hierarchical state, the most cumbersome bureaucracy, and the sternest subordination of the individual are no longer justified by appealing to some principle of authority superior to circumstances and individuals (a principle that would necessarily be aristocratic), but by invoking the general interest and, hence, the equality of individuals when collective needs are involved. How successfully and how humanly these needs are actually satisfied is another question. But today the power in whose name we govern (and enjoy privileges) is always the *demos:* the great number, everybody. Or, if we prefer, the Mass. The forms of personal or "collective" despotism are called dictatorships, in other words, exceptional or emergency governments established to face the problems raised by war at home or abroad; that is to say, they are considered temporary at the very moment when they are ruling most violently.

In these circumstances, an appeal to "values" would be practical, or at least convincing, only if it were accompanied by some indication of the political principle that would allow us to restore these values *today.* Otherwise, an appeal to "values" must mean an appeal to our cultural heritage, that is, to "the best" of the Hellenic, humanist, and rationalist tradition. This is the tradition that formed our culture, or, if you will, the school that educated those of us who went to school at all, the *clercs,* the intellectuals, whose function is to appreciate "the best."

But appreciation of the best, "the evaluation of values," is not susceptible to physical measurement. It implies an intellectual choice and hence the problem of the validity of this choice. Cultural life is simply debate. And by its very nature disputation among the *clercs* always remains open.

At this point, the intellectual ought to realize that he has taken a wrong turn. His initial concern was not a historical question (for example, the relationship between Platonic *paideia* and Marxist *praxis*) but the present state of things—the moral and political disorder of contemporary society, the fact that "values" now seem to have "lost their power," just like a ruling class.

To discuss a current state of affairs in historical and cultural terms is tantamount to treating the present as if it were part of the past. It means studying not the present situation (and ourselves with it, as the party in question) so much as the *type* of situation of which the present one is merely the most recent example. It is to consider ourselves, who are actually involved in the situation, "rational" outside observers. If he proceeds along these lines, the intellectual does, indeed, fulfill his function as a specialist of culture, but he loses sight of his condition as one individual among others in the world today. In other words, he overlooks both his own personal experience and what it has in common with the experience of others. Thus, even the real motives of his concern fade away, and concern for man's common fate turns into preoccupation with the decadence of cultural values, that is, with a certain idea of the past. This is not the same thing.

Now, how can we examine a collective situation without some conception of what the individuals who experience it have in common?

Objectively speaking, it is surely legitimate to say that the members of a collectivity share, first and foremost, a complex of external and material conditions. But if we approach the matter from the perspective of moral and intellectual values, it is no less legitimate to say that the members of a given society share, first and foremost, a certain consciousness, a certain relationship to "values," and greater or less facility for perceiving these values and putting them into practice.

If we do not have a reference point of this sort, if we do not ask ourselves what relationship we really have to what we call "good" or "true" (and what things we call, or, rather, do, as if they were "good" and "true"), it will be hard to say whether the "mass situation" is good or bad. It will be difficult to find our way out of the dilemma of welcoming the advent of the masses as the arrival of all men on the stage of history or of decrying it as the cause of the degradation of values, that is, as the cause of *nihilism*.

The search for this reference point, the situation of individual consciousness, must begin in subjective experience. No sociological inquiry can provide it. We must trust to the intuitive certainty that, even if the experience of one man is not the experience of the community, it is nevertheless an essential and meaningful part of it.

II

If it is true that we live in a mass society, we must immediately admit one fact: there are some individuals who are more affected by it than others, but there are not, nor can there be, privileged persons. There cannot be, on the one hand, an anonymous and vulgar mass that lacks idealistic motives and, on the other, a few individuals who succeed in keeping intact their nobility and the cult of high values. The mass and the few are inextricably mixed. At certain times we feel we are *individuals*, endowed with emotions, needs, and spiritual requirements that are not those of the anonymous crowd. And we speak of the mass situation insofar as we experience the confusion between, and the mutual involvement of, the anonymous and the personal. We feel a contrast between our individual natures and a social situation in which necessity, automatism, and collective servitude are especially refractory both to the individual's personal demands and to the "noble" values that (at least occasionally) the individual seeks and by which he sometimes feels himself inspired.

What is a "mass situation"? Simplifying greatly, one can say that it is a social situation in which the experience of collective necessity is very strong. Before developing his famous analysis of the "revolt of the masses," Ortega y Gasset "places" the phenomenon of the "mass" by drawing the reader's attention to what he calls a "visual experience"—"the fact of agglomeration, of plenitude. . . . The cities are full of inhabitants, the houses full of tenants, the hotels full of guests, the cafés full of customers, the parks full of strolling people, the waiting rooms of famous doctors full of patients, the theaters full of spectators, and the beaches full of bathers."

"What previously was, in general, no problem, now begins to be an everyday one, namely to *find room*," he observes. Now, if he had dwelt upon this experience of agglomeration, of the crowd, of *not finding room*, he would perhaps have led us to the heart of the "mass situation."

Even if we treat it in his terms, as extremely simple and commonplace, the experience is not at all purely "visual"; it is also spiritual. It signifies for us the *essential* way in which the individual comes in contact with the life of others—or, rather, of *everybody*. This becomes clear once we recognize it as a fact in the life of the individual consciousness, rather than as an external fact.

Not finding room is an agonizing experience. It means feeling shut out, or at least there is the possibility of being excluded—the others are already there, they occupy all, or almost all, the available space. To find room, an effort is necessary; one is obliged to make room for oneself. The struggle is not a struggle for life in general; at an astoundingly humble level, we must fight to occupy the little space we need, which in some sense belongs to us, since we have the same right to it as others do. But no one guarantees it to us, apparently, since the simple presence of others in a crowd obstructs and prevents it. And it is also clear that others have the same right we do.

This experience does not occur merely on certain intermittent and rare occasions. It is regularly repeated in hundreds of instances, whenever, in fact, we come into contact with collective existence instead of remaining in the circle of private relations between individuals. It is an absolutely typical and fundamental experience, more fundamental than the actual situations in which we undergo it (work, the search for material necessities, relations with the bureaucratic machinery, participation in political life, amusements), since one repeats substantially the same experience in each of these instances.

Nor is it a purely physical fact (and even less is it completely "visual") concerning space and material necessities. It is enough to say that "finding room becomes a problem" to become aware that it implies a spiritual situation, to be precise, a situation of preliminary hostility toward others, those who take up that space and threaten not to let us have even the indispensable minimum of it. This hostility, on the other hand, is immediately contradicted by the evident fact that the others are not there to keep us from being ourselves, but because they are looking for the same thing we are and are equally hindered and impeded by the crowd. This hostility, then, is unreasonable and has no right to show itself. But to recognize this does not eliminate the feeling any more than it calms the anxiety to "find room"; it only represses and muffles the feeling, which continues to lie, intact, at the bottom.

Furthermore, our experience of the crowd is not freely chosen. One is in a crowd on the street, on public conveyances, in a movie, in a stadium, not because one has decided to mix with the crowd, but because one cannot help it. One cannot avoid submitting to the numerous bondages of organization and bureaucracy that collective life imposes; one cannot escape even during leisure.

The situation that derives from this concerns everyone, the most refined intellectual as well as the most humble worker. Not even the economically privileged individual escapes. The way in which he enjoys his advantages depends, in fact, on the way in which others must seek to satisfy their needs.

Actually, it is always possible to avoid to some extent the material bondage imposed by collective life. But one cannot escape the predicament of collective living in its spiritual aspect.

Daily participation in "mass" life can seem occasional and transient—limited to certain moments and therefore analogous to the automatic way in which we obey the needs of the body. (Equating the needs of the body and our relations with our fellows is in itself a rather serious matter!) But, in any event, if instead of looking at these moments from the outside, as unimportant intervals of time, we try to think of them from the inside, as moments of life and of consciousness, these, let us say, passive moments will no longer seem so casual.

Immersed in the crowd, the individual feels he is a unit among many interchangeable units. And this, if you think about it, is the beginning of a dissociation that does not stop there. In his family and the circle of his friends and acquaintances, the individual never feels himself a mere unit. It is all very well to think that, once having left the crowd, one regains all one's individuality, whole and differentiated. Meanwhile, one has been aware of an elementary identity with the others that overcomes and wipes out every personal difference as well as every shade of individual thought.

It therefore seems legitimate to inquire whether he who leaves the crowd after feeling himself confused in it is, in truth, the same individual as before; whether he still has the same ideas of himself and of his own ineffable nature; whether, indeed, he has the right to retain such an idea and whether, by being too sure of it, he does not risk forming an idea of himself that is too favorable, too vaporous and idealistic.

This inquiry may seem idle. But when we reason as if the indistinct communication with others, imposed on us by our daily life, in no way injures our individuality or the quality of our "values," our reasoning implies an assumption that is not so simple: that those moments have no importance, are moments effectively indifferent. The trouble is that a sufficient number of unimportant moments and indifferent acts gives us the precise image of the perfect *mass man*— the man whose existence has minimal importance and who passively submits to this fact without even recognizing it.

Even on occasions of little weight (like the examples already given), our experience of the crowd is not limited to the feeling of anonymity. Indeed, to be precise, it is not we who feel anonymous in the crowd; it is the others who are anonymous to us. However, we know that the same thing happens to us in the eyes of others. In reality, no one is anonymous, but we all find ourselves in a situation of anonymity. It is because of this (given the very ordinary necessity that has brought us together) that we can speak of ourselves as all equal, as units that are undifferentiated and interchangeable.

My relations with my neighbor then assume a rather peculiar quality; the person next to me is a stranger and, at the same time, reflects at every point my own condition. Thus reflected by him, my condition is not the "human condition" in general, my "nature" is not the human nature of the novelists and philosophers, but, so to speak, *what is left over of it.* In that situation, I am reduced to the minimum and I know it—just as I know that a panic in the crowd would be enough to crush me.

Thus a rather wretched picture of individual destiny emerges, and one also begins to perceive what is effectively the relation between a mass situation and "noble" values—a relation of externality and suspension.

This appears clearly enough when one realizes that communication between individuals in a crowd is reduced to conventional signs, or, in any event, to a very impoverished language. It is not that I cannot have a conversation with the next man. But since I do not know him; since I have in common with him only a humanity that is both very much reduced and rather general; since in addition, I know that my relation with him is purely occasional and transient, it is evident that there is no room for a genuine exchange of feelings and thoughts between us. One could, indeed, say that, given the situation in which we find ourselves, we can communicate only by remaining external to each other as much as possible, exchanging only the most conventional words. The expression of complex ideas, subtle evaluations, the communication of delicate feelings must evidently be left for other occasions.

Ever since great cities came into existence, we have been familiar with the image of next-door neighbors who meet every day without ever knowing each other, with the singular freedom and the grave solitude involved therein. The meaningless commonplaces people exchange when they meet have already become the subject of irony. We have a picture of human relations reduced to elementary proportions, to the point where their value is negative.

Similar images have been considered comic when opposed to the ideal fullness of authentic human expressions among beings who love each other or who have an ideal in common, a noble interest, a heroic destiny. We have naturally assumed that, while on the one hand there was the common people (the "mass"), which got more and more common, on the other hand there remained, in some circles or privileged classes (the youth, or the people, or the proletariat, or even the elite), the cult of authentic feelings and of "noble" values—a human "nature" more or less intact.

We did not ask ourselves if that were possible, if one could in fact imagine a society in which spiritually privileged individuals (or groups or classes) could exist with others who were subjected to an obscure coarsening without the quality of the one being affected by the material and spiritual way of life of the others.

This sort of thinking was both grossly materialistic and irredeemably idealistic—materialistic because it assumed that relations between individuals in a society could remain purely external, physical, economic, material; idealistic because it assumed the existence (at the center and on the fringes of the common conditions of existence) of a soul, a consciousness, that was impervious to the quality of the relations that could be established between individuals who live together in a determined collective situation.

Given the existence of an elite (or a chosen class) on the fringes of the crowd, what will be the relations between them? What, in other words, will be their common language? At the very least, it will be a mixture of the select and the vulgar. In which case, the spiritual privilege of the elite has already been rather trimmed down. One can, of course, hypothesize a radical withdrawal of the elite from the mass; or assert that, in the last analysis, the only possible relation between the two is violence. But the question of language will not be resolved. How will the elite make itself understood without adapting its language (that is, its values) to the mass?

The example used here, of the situation of the individual in a crowd, may seem frivolous. In fact, it concerns only the most obvious aspect of the "mass situation."

One must, however, keep two things in mind. The first is that the nature of a society consists wholly in the manner of being together that it offers to the individuals who compose it—the way in which they *can* experience that fundamental bond which Aristotle calls *philia*. If mass conditions and mass relationships predominate in the society in which we live, this cannot fail to affect our vision of the world and of human relations; and thereby the effectiveness of "noble" values in collective life.

In the second place, it is evident that the mass situation is not limited to everyday occasional relations of the individual with the crowd. The crowd is neither a prime fact nor an occasional phenomenon;

it is the ultimate form, the most evident and striking form of other facts that are more weighty and serious.

Still, when these general facts are enumerated in the usual way—working conditions, relations between the individual and the state, forms of technical and economic organization—one will still not have a picture of the situation as it takes shape in the individual consciousness.

The collective demands from which the phenomenon of the "mass" is born are all prosaic—so prosaic that they appear indisputable and indisputably rational. It is an elementary rationality, which has the quality both of natural necessity and constriction from above. Thus, to take another simple example, it is natural and inevitable that, in a crowd on a subway, everyone has his share of discomfort. But no one, except perhaps technical specialists, can say whether that is inevitable in an absolute sense or "just"—whether one could not do something better. Indeed, since it is a question of material conditions, the "better" will always seem possible, but also doubtful, since the way of obtaining the "better" remains unclear. In everyday experience, the mass situation appears as an accomplished fact, that is, neither just nor unjust; it is simply there. Its modes depend, of course, on the ability and good will of those in charge. But the law of "necessity" is intrinsic to any form that collective life assumes.

To live in a mass society means automatically to perform acts that are not free; doing what one does not because it is natural, and not even because one considers it positively useful, but because one wishes to avoid the complications and bad results that would come (for oneself *and* for others) from acting differently. For the single individual, this can be more or less painful. That is, the advantages to be derived from yielding to collective demands, instead of resisting them, are relative. What matters to the individual consciousness, however, is that one feels subject to an overwhelming force that comes neither from a moral norm nor from the sum of individual demands, but simply from the fact of collective existence. It is an experience of disorder maintained by laws of iron.

It is natural for the individual in a crowd to count only for what he has externally in common with others. But this is also a grave constriction, because an individual can appear as a simple physical unit only when seen from outside. From *his* point of view, he cannot help feeling that he is a free and mobile center of a network of vital relations that concern not only his fellows, but also the world as a whole and the meaning of his own existence. Now, the conditions of mass society have this in common: the individual's own point of view is regularly repressed and crushed. Along with an inevitable passivity there comes a sense of deprivation and of painful tension. Not having room also means not having room for the spirit.

Such subjugation can be accepted as "natural." But it can never be "just" in the sense in which one says, for example, that among friends it is just that everything be shared equally. The difference is that, in the latter case, even an unequal division could be just, provided that all agreed to it. In the case of the great number, even an arithmetically unexceptionable division is always imposed from outside; it can appear materially equal, but we can never be sure that it is justified.

Except when he recognizes common necessity, the individual who is part of a mass feels that every personal reaction (or attempted reaction) is affective; and affective reactions are out of place there. What is normally required of us is a certain rationality of behavior—a certain *apathy*, at least in the sense of not brusquely opposing one's own demands to those of others. Even when a mass is carried along by "collective feeling," the individual who lets himself be carried along can no longer distinguish his own feelings from those of others, while the passion of all of them feeds on his; he is completely subjected to the occasion. To escape, a violent wrench is required, a decision to separate himself from others, a desire to be *heretical*. Or else he must submit, adapt himself, maneuver, manage things cleverly, and wait for the propitious occasion that will permit everyone to have a little more space, ease, and freedom.

We are together because "we can't help it." This is the prime fact. No one can help it. Everyone knows that others are constrained by the same necessity that has compelled oneself. Here, one could say, is the normative fact of the "mass situation," its justification, and even the foundation of its humanity. Only if we recognize this necessity, this common subjection, do others impress themselves on our consciousness as "fellow men." Otherwise, the relation among individuals in a mass is material, external, and provisional, and the next man appears as a profoundly alien being or even an obstacle and an enemy; if he were removed, our situation would be easier, we would be more comfortable, there would be *more room*.

In a situation like this, we are infinitely far from any fixed principle of truth or consistency; we have a radical sense of precariousness. The individual next to me is nothing to me, and yet he is a man like me; his closeness weighs on me, but so does mine on him. Contact with my fellows is inchoate and transitory, but I never cease being with them. In this way we experience a brutal sense of the ephemeral—material, dreary, overwhelming. *Oi Brotoi.* All is momentary; there is no enduring meaning, either in our acts or in our thoughts. We are mortal.

The condition of the individual in the mass is completely ambiguous and obscure: caused by all and willed by no one; inevitable and "natural," yet unjustifiable and artificial; solitary and social; essentially unstable and dangerous, yet reassuring; loaded with violence and hostility, yet fraternal. What is most obscure and ambiguous is the relation between the individual and his fellow. How does one treat him and speak to him? *Who* is this being, this intimate, this stranger? One can imagine the same enigma facing the first men at the dawn of time.

What relation can there be between such an experience and "noble" demands?

This—to return to the commonplace examples we have purposely chosen—is a little like asking oneself if it is possible to read Kant in a crowded train or to practice Epicurean wisdom in the middle of a mass of striking peasants. Obviously it is not possible, and normally one would not even have such an idea. But why not? All you need is sufficient power of concentration and self-control. However, that is the wrong question. The right question, perhaps, might be this: if, in similar situations, the individual could direct his mind and will in such a high-minded fashion, would he conceivably communicate to his neighbor the fruits of his reflections or persuade him to imitate his conduct? Obviously, we are dealing in absurdities.

Now, if one speaks of the relationship between the mass situation and spiritual and cultural "values," the first point to clear up is that of the language appropriate to the relationship and the meanings it communicates.

When one deals with a worker in a shop or with an individual in a subway crowd, the mass situation is much more neutral and, at the same time, much more rigid than other social occasions. By its very nature, it admits both the Buddhist and the Christian, the humanist and the sectarian, the crudest and the most sensitive person; it is indifferent to distinctions of race, color, or nationality; it is democratic in the extreme. But it is also exclusive, special, and demanding; obviously there is not a Christian way to work a lathe or a humanistic way of riding on a train. Christian, humanistic, or other "values" are reserved for different, more "suitable" occasions.

From the tolerance that is intrinsic to such a situation comes the optimistic attitude toward "modern times." Since the modern situation is presented as a simple state of fact, in itself neutral as to the more complex demands of the individual, one deduces that, whatever its imperfections and present evils, it is always possible to "Christianize" them, let us say, or "humanize" them—to make them evolve toward the "better."

Pessimists, on the other hand, see the opacity and narrowness of the mass as virulent and active negation of complex and "noble" demands; so as far as the uniqueness of the individual and the universality of values are concerned, the situation could hardly seem worse.

The crucial fact, however, escapes both optimists and pessimists. To speak of "values" regarding a concrete situation means to speak of modes of being, not of ideal, pure relations. Now, it is as modes of being that Christian or humanistic "values" are found to be suspended, reduced to suitable proportions (that is, to some form of private cult), and therefore inoperative. Optimism seems groundless. But if one speaks of values in a purely spiritual sense, then certainly no state of fact can contradict them. On the plane of discourse, "values" remain eternally valid, for one can validly talk about them in any situation. It would be absurd to maintain that a given social situation hinders liberty of thought or the possibility, for the individual, of behaving honestly to his fellow man. What a factual condition can hinder is the natural translation of thoughts into acts, or the idea that an individual's noble behavior represents not a private and exceptional fact, but a norm to which all *could* conform.

Now, what the intellectuals' pessimism refers to is the indifference of the masses to discourse about intellectual and moral "values." But the truth of the matter is that the crisis involves something very much deeper.

The individual, in his work, in politics, in the circumstances of social life, may submit to acting in a given way because "he can't help it." In behaving this way, however, he does not deny that it would be better to be able to do what he does with the conviction of doing something good and useful. But he feels forced to postpone the question of good and evil. Naturally, if the necessity to which he submitted seemed to be in absolute contradiction to his firm religious or moral convictions, he would not act as he does; he would be conscious of doing wrong, and his situation would change. But what one does because one cannot do otherwise does not appear as a moral choice, does not openly contradict any "value." Indeed, such an action is characterized by rationality, in the sense in which one considers it rational for the individual to submit to circumstances independent of his will. Thus, it hardly seems reasonable for a worker to oppose the technical demands of the factory on the grounds of conscience; or for a citizen to claim the privilege of individual liberty as against bondage to the collective organization. Such ties do not appear bad in themselves, just as being crushed in a mob does not seem degrading in itself. There is no reason to be opposed to them.

And yet the situation is obscure and troubling.

The question of doing right or wrong, whatever sense it has, is present and disturbing just because it is avoided, or, better, repressed. The ambiguous character of the situation is revealed by the fact that there seems to be no reason at all to oppose it. However, neither does one accept it. There are, instead, many reasons to submit to it. But they are reasons of convenience more than of conscience. Conscience (in the sense of willing assent to what one does) is suspended.

This experience of suspension, of obscurity, of doubt, is the severe test to which the modern situation puts "values"—not only traditional beliefs, but the very idea that it is necessary to believe in something and that the difference between believing in what one does and in *what one is* and not believing in them is a real difference.

For this reason, the mass situation is a morally extreme one. In sum, it is what we mean by nihilism: to live by setting aside the question of whether what one does day by day has any meaning, to know that one sets aside the question, and to recognize, at the same time, that this does not change the course of events.

The course of events, in fact, does not change. But existence is deprived of meaning when it is reduced to a long series of obligatory and indifferent acts. It is stripped of value, not so much with respect to the "values" of culture and of tradition (which can always be in some way maintained and cultivated privately), but in itself. Existence is literally "unbelievable," and an unbelievable existence means an existence that drags on in a state of continual bad faith.

For this to happen, it is not necessary that material, or at any rate "objective," conditions be bad. It is enough for the individual to find himself in an ambiguous situation respecting his own action, to do what he does without conviction—to act without violating any deeply felt belief, but also without clearly observing one.

One can at this point return to what, according to Ortega y Gasset, distinguishes the mentality of the mass man: the fact that "to have an idea does not mean to have reasons for having it."

If one assumes that such a man thinks capriciously; that, good reasons being clear to him, he arbitrarily chooses, *against* them, the idea that suits him; and that, even knowing the place of truth, he "does not care in the least to be in the right," then certainly his will appears as wicked as it is obstinate.

But such an assumption is not legitimate. Such a man, granted that he exists, would be an intellectual sophist, not a mass man.

Even according to Ortega y Gasset's definition, the *mass* man, the "man in the street," *homo communis*, is not someone who refuses to give reasons or does not care about being in the right; he has no reasons to give and, as for being in the right, he *cannot* concern himself with it. He has only the ideas that his situation provides—no more than that. In a situation in which the most obvious reasons are reasons of fact and of necessity, he can receive only conventional, stereotyped ideas. These ideas are not false; rather, they are neither false nor true. The mass man has literally lost true reasons. This is the only fact that explains how, in the modern situation, noble values have, in their turn, "lost power."

In what sense, then, may one say that the intellectual is superior to the man of the masses? In no sense. The intellectual can distinguish himself from the mass only by the greater consciousness he may have of their common situation. And he can show this consciousness in only one way—by speaking the truth without presuming that it has been given to him alone. As a matter of fact, the question is not majority and minority, the mob and the elite. *The mass situation involves everybody.* The necessity of daily relations, which not even the most privileged can avoid, makes us all part of the mass; we are all forced to use the current language, especially those who strongly desire to communicate with their fellows and to address the community as such.

The language of the mass, based as it is on ready-made notions, consists of cut-and-dried formulas in which words have a fixed value, purely indicative and only slightly expressive. The most obvious example is the language of propaganda, advertising, and what are called, not by chance, "media of mass communication." Such a tongue resembles the language of cybernetics, which the experts themselves call a dead language—incapable of transmitting information about *new facts.* The simple mixing of such a conventional language with the more or less authentic language of private life and of significant exchanges between individuals creates a situation without precedent.

So that the situation of the intellectual, or of the Platonic philosopher who, having returned to the cave, seeks to communicate to his fellows the truths he has glimpsed, is paradoxical. Everyday language is ineluctable; no one has created it, but everybody is forced to use it. To the extent to which he preserves some freedom, however, the intellectual cannot accept a situation and the language it involves simply because "he cannot help it." On the other hand, he cannot ignore a state of things and a language to which, since he is only one individual among others, he yields like the others. If he wishes to talk to others, he is obliged to use their language. No matter how refined, sensitive, and aware he may be, he can define his ideas only in relation to the ideas of the mass, even if it is to oppose them. This already sets him in bondage. On the other hand, if he truly seeks lost reasons and truths, if he wishes to communicate meanings and not merely to use formulas, if he feels he is a relatively worthy heir of a tradition, the intellectual must wish to be free. But he knows one thing for certain: he exists and works in a situation in which he himself has only an equivocal and doubtful relation to tradition, to "noble values," to reasons and intelligible truths. This is an extreme situation.

The situation is extreme not so much as regards culture as its *raison d'être*, which is truth lived and participated in. Culture, in fact, is the ground not of truth but of the search for it. Truth appears only in lived experience, in feeling oneself in harmony with the nature of things and the world. And common truth is found and lived in common; it is a vital harmony that no idea or cultural form, no single individual, can ever really express, much less create.

Truth—like man himself—does not merely need to be left at liberty, not to be oppressed; above all, it must be freely sought and desired. Now, to the extent to which the individual's experience of his social existence is an experience of nontruth and of nonfree acts, he does not seek the truth. He wants ready-made ideas, quickly reassuring; he seeks not freedom but the organization of a force capable of assuring the satisfaction of his needs. He becomes aware of truth (and liberty) only when he feels deprived of it, but this awareness is a private one and comes when, face to face with himself, he discovers that reason and meaning are missing from his existence.

So corrupt a situation does not change by virtue of pure ideas, or by violence, but uniquely, "according to the ordinance of Time," through our suffering the common lot in common, seeking to understand it.

And the fact remains that we do not leave the cave in a mass, but only one by one, each helping the other.

Part II published in *Tempo Presente*,
April 1956, and, as "The Individual and the Mass,"
in *Dissent*, Spring 1957
(Trans. Paul Alpers and Alastair Hamilton)

Index

Mao Tse-tung, 59, 61, 63, 213
Marivaux, Pierre de, 48
  La Double Inconstance, 49
  Surprise de l'amour, 48–49
Martelli, Father, 2–9 passim,
  14–18 passim
Marx, Karl, 133, 134, 194, 195,
  198, 211, 218, 239–43
  passim, 246
Massarenti, Giuseppe, 31
Maulnier, Thierry, 48
Meyerhold, Vsevolod, 116–17,
  136
Michelangelo, 204
Mola, Emilio, 23, 24
Molière, 95, 131, 141
  L'Ecole des femmes, 97
Morales, Juan García, 28–29
Moravia, Alberto, 155, 156
  The Empty Canvas (La noia),
  153–59
Mussolini, Benito, 2, 4, 6, 16

Nietzsche, Friedrich, 3
  Birth of Tragedy, 126

Ortega y Gasset, José
  The Revolt of the Masses,
  236–39, 243, 248, 262

Parri, Ferruccio, 10
Pascal, Blaise, 186
Pascarella, Cesare, 200
Pascoli, Giovanni, 82
Patriarca, Vincenzo, 22
Paulhan, Jean, 114–15, 118
Phrynichus
  Capture of Miletus, 127
Pindar, 76, 160
Pinter, Harold, 149
Pirandello, Luigi, 84, 90, 105,
  119, 135, 139, 141, 162,
  173, 174
  and Croce, Benedetto, 80–81,
  82
  De Castris, Leone, on, 90–91

Each in His Own Way (Cia-
  scuno a suo modo), 173
The Late Mattia Pascal, 85
L'umorismo, 80–93 passim
  Puglisi, Filippo, on, 91
Six Characters in Search of
  an Author (Sei personaggi
  in cerca d'autore), 103,
  173
Tonight We Improvise (Sta-
  sera si recita a soggetto),
  173
Piscator, Erwin, 128, 129, 131,
  135, 136, 137, 142, 144,
  146, 150, 151
  The Political Theater, 129–30
Plato, 95, 187, 189, 236, 237,
  239, 240, 246, 263
  The Republic, 203–04, 228,
  233, 239
Prampolini, Camillo, 31
Puglisi, Filippo
  Pirandello e la sua lingua, 91

Racine, Jean Baptiste, 105, 116
Rimbaud, Arthur, 164
Rivière, Jacques, 107–11 passim
Rousseau, Jean Jacques, 227
  Social Contract, 243

Saint-Simon, Comte de, 198
Sartre, Jean-Paul, 53–54, 55,
  193
  Saint Genet, comedien et
  martyr, 167, 168, 174, 175
Schiller, Johann von, 128
Schönberg, Arnold, 123
Shakespeare, William, 78, 85,
  151
  Hamlet, 51, 128
  King Lear, 128, 139
  Macbeth, 54, 97, 102, 119
Shaw, George Bernard, 105,
  135, 139, 144, 151
Socrates, 204, 233